Environmental Spirituality and Wellbeing

Environmental Spirituality and Wellbeing

Integrating Social and Therapeutic Theory and Practice

Edited by
Jeff Leonardi and John Reader

SHEFFIELD UK   BRISTOL CT

Published by Equinox Publishing Ltd.

UK   Office 415, The Workstation, 15 Paternoster Row, Sheffield, South Yorkshire S1 2BX
USA   ISD, 70 Enterprise Drive, Bristol, CT 06010

www.equinoxpub.com

First published 2025

© Jeff Leonardi, John Reader and contributors 2025

All rights reserved. No part of this publication may be reproduced or transmitted in any form or by any means, electronic or mechanical, including photocopying, recording or any information storage or retrieval system, without prior permission in writing from the publishers.

British Library Cataloguing-in-Publication Data

A catalogue record for this book is available from the British Library.

ISBN-13	978 1 80050 583 4	(hardback)
	978 1 80050 584 1	(paperback)
	978 1 80050 585 8	(ePDF)
	978 1 80050 670 1	(ePub)

Library of Congress Cataloging-in-Publication Data

Names: Leonardi, Jeff editor | Reader, John, 1953-2023 editor
Title: Environmental spirituality and wellbeing : integrating social and therapeutic theory and practice / edited by Jeff Leonardi and John Reader.
Description: Bristol, CT : Equinox Publishing Ltd, 2025. | Includes bibliographical references and index. | Summary: "The contributors to this volume agree in a diagnosis of our present human and ecological crisis as more than a physical and political struggle, but also a psychological and perhaps even more importantly a spiritual one"-- Provided by publisher.
Identifiers: LCCN 2025020301 (print) | LCCN 2025020302 (ebook) | ISBN 9781800505834 hardback | ISBN 9781800505841 paperback | ISBN 9781800505858 pdf | ISBN 9781800506701 epub
Subjects: LCSH: Health--Religious aspects--Christianity | Healing--Religious aspects--Christianity | Well-being--Religious aspects--Christianity
Classification: LCC BT732 .E585 2025 (print) | LCC BT732 (ebook) | DDC 261.8/321--dc23/eng/20250821
LC record available at https://lccn.loc.gov/2025020301
LC ebook record available at https://lccn.loc.gov/2025020302

Typeset by Sparks – www.sparkspublishing.com

Contents

Preface	vii
Acknowledgements	viii
Introduction *Jeff Leonardi*	1
Part I: Setting the scene	**15**
1 Knowing and un-knowing: Extending the spectrum of meaning to include what really matters *Jeff Leonardi*	17
2 Connecting with nature and spiritual experience *John Reader*	36
Part II: How spirituality deepens our understanding	**57**
3 Spiritual experiences of interconnectedness *Marianne Rankin*	59
4 Julian of Norwich and spiritual depth: Spiritual experience and relational intimacy *Robert Fruehwirth*	77
5 Beloved on the earth: Buddhist and person-centred perspectives on the ecological crisis *Becky Seale*	97
6 Spiritual experiences and counselling *William West*	115
Part III: Bringing the human being into relationship with the environment	**129**
7 How is the marriage of Heaven and Earth going? Spirituality, health and the environment in Brazil *Marta Helena de Freitas*	131

8 *La Pachamama*'s soul: Understanding eco-spirituality through archetypal intersubjectivity 151
   Hannah Armbrust

9 Wellbeing is the feeling of being 'one with the world and my surroundings': Reflection about the environmental dimension of wellbeing in Brazil 165
   Bettina E. Schmidt

10 Biosynergy and person-centered psychology of ecospiritual well-becoming: Creative Biosynergy of persons, species, societies and ecosystems sanctifies earth's biosphere 184
   Anthony L. Rose

Index 209

Preface

When this book emerged as a proposal I wanted to find someone with whom to share the editing, for all kind of good reasons, practical and relational. John Reader had been a friend and colleague for nearly 40 years and we were in regular contact. John was one of those rare and special people sometimes called a 'scholar-priest': he had been a lifelong Anglican parish priest and equally a much-published academic theologian; he was indeed already one of the authors I had invited to contribute a chapter to the book. When I spoke with him during one of our regular Sunday afternoon Zoom calls, about my wish to share the editing with someone, he immediately offered to help, and we then embarked on the process together. Our proposal to Equinox was accepted in July 2023. He wrote his chapter very quickly and it was the first one I received. The others were beginning to arrive, and I had sent him a first draft of my own chapter, which we discussed again on the afternoon of Sunday 24th September. He was on good form but I did think he seemed a little subdued. The following Wednesday I received a text from his wife Christine to say that he had collapsed and been taken into hospital the previous evening with a 'catastrophic bleed' in his brain. He lost consciousness that evening and died the following Sunday, 2nd October.

The shock and sorrow felt by everyone close to John was enormous. He had retired from full-time parish ministry in the Oxford diocese three years earlier, and they had moved to Honeybourne; he reached the age of 70 in January 2023, and such was his energy and enthusiasm for parish ministry that he had applied for a 'House for Duty' post in Oxford diocese and been appointed and licensed there just three months before he was taken ill. He was 'getting on with life' very fully and already establishing himself in this new ministry.

He is a great loss to all of us, especially his family. John was a great 'connector' of people and there is a very wide network of those who feel his loss keenly. I have continued to work on this book with him very much in my mind and heart, not least when preparing his own chapter for publication. This may well be the last piece of his writing to be be published, and I offer the book very much as a tribute in his memory. Many of its themes were very close to his heart.

Jeff Leonardi
Honorary Research Fellow, Religious Experience Research Centre,
University of Wales Trinity St David, Lampeter.
21 February 2024

Acknowledgements

I should like to thank all the contributors to this volume for the rich and enjoyable conversations we have had during its creation. I know we have all felt that the subject matter *matters* very much to all of us, and that we hope that in some small way what we have written might contribute to the development of what is needed for a more benevolent future to dawn.

I should like to thank the Alister Hardy Trust for all their good work and for the support I have received from them. By name I should like to thank Peter Rawlings for his careful reading of my own chapter and his helpful comments on it. Then, as always, I wish to thank my wife Jean for her patience and unfailing encouragement throughout, and our two daughters Cherry and Rebecca for their care and encouragement also.

Introduction

Jeff Leonardi

A previous collection I co-edited with Professor Bettina Schmidt was devoted to Spirituality and Wellbeing (Schmidt and Leonardi 2020). Wellbeing can be described in purely secular terms, but a spiritual perspective on Wellbeing adds considerable depth and scope, distinguishing it from superficial or momentary happiness. Wellbeing in spiritual terms reaches out beyond the individual towards relationship which can embrace both interpersonal relationships and relationship with the natural world (and beyond, see references to Chapter 9 below). In the present volume and in order to further accommodate the spiritual dimension I offer the term 'Well-becoming', with a focus on the past and the present as they develop into the future, and thus generate an evolutionary perspective. (For this term I am indebted to conversations over the past few years with the author of Chapter 10, Anthony Rose, out of which the term emerged, first by him and then enthusiastically adopted by me also; it can be found in both our chapters here.)

I am an Honorary Research Fellow of the Religious Experience Research Centre based at the University of Wales, Trinity St David. As a student of spiritual experience I am much exercised by the question of the status of such experience: on the one hand it is often seminal and transformative for the life and understanding of the subject, and on the other it can be dismissed as purely subjective, as if this decisively reduces its validity in any wider sense. The issue raised here goes beyond spiritual experience as such, into the human sense of relationship – or not – with our bodies and the environment. Both contemplative spirituality and psychotherapy seek to guide the subject from alienation to integration, from a divided self to a wholeness which includes all the dimensions of human being and awareness. In my own chapter I shall suggest that these insights demand a wider consideration of the value of subjective experience, feelings and intuitions, and that this in turn suggests the need for an expanded paradigm for what counts as truth. Our intellectual parameters need to expand and evolve in order to embrace the subjective/emotional and intuitive/spiritual modes of awareness. Otherwise we are left isolated, with all that matters most, humanly, on one side, and the scientific/

technological perspective divorced from humane values on the other, and threatening to dominate.

Nowhere is this more evident than in the environmental crisis, where human beings enact upon the planet and ourselves the adverse results of a progressive alienation from our physical and spiritual natures, and thereby from our relationship with the natural world. In this volume we look to psychotherapeutic understandings and eco-social interventions into wellbeing and well-becoming to lead us forward from this tragic predicament.

All the chapters in this volume were written independently and so it has been with delight and some excitement that I have discovered how compatible and synergistic so much of the material has turned out to be (as one might hope, but not guarantee). It will be seen that all the contributors agree in a diagnosis of our present human and ecological crisis as more than a physical and political struggle, but also a psychological and, perhaps even more importantly, a spiritual one. If, as I suggest below, spirituality is a matter of the meaning, value and direction of one's individual and corporate life, then it could be said that we have lost our direction and the proper value which can be given to our participation in and with the natural world. In this view we have become alienated from our deepest selves, our own bodies and relatedness. This could be and is a dire diagnosis were it not for the recurrent suggestion and hope, that we can indeed be restored, or perhaps 'fore-stored' to a better and fitting relationship in all these ways. Counselling and psychotherapy, integration and individuation, eco-therapy and healing, can all play a major part in our individual and collective journey towards spiritual, psychological and ecological wholeness.

There are two terms in the main title of this collection, *Environment* and *Spirituality*, and it will be helpful to be clear about what we mean by them from the outset. With *environment* there is a danger that we restrict our attention to an anthropocentric focus on what surrounds human beings and their activities (and what is thereby affected by and for human beings). Tony Rose's *biosynergy* in Chapter 10 applies to the interconnectedness of all life forms without putting humans at the centre or summit. Hannah Armbrust in Chapter 8 defines *ecology* by way of its roots as 'a branch of biology concerned with studying the relationships amongst living beings and their physical environment', again without emphasising the human dimension. In my own chapter I offer the scriptural expression for environment as that 'in which we live and move and have our being' (Acts 17.28) and which can thereby refer to all and everything. For *spirituality* I suggest a simple definition, as that 'which gives meaning value and purpose to our lives'. If this seems close to simply a 'philosophy of life', I suggest an additional quality of 'feeling part of something larger than oneself' (which connects with Sir Alister Hardy's question – see Marianne Rankin's Chapter 3).

For a more complete understanding of the term *spirituality* I offer the definition I have used in my doctoral and post-doctoral research, and to which John Reader referred in his Chapter 2:

1. Spirituality refers to a level or dimension of experiencing, which overlaps with the commonsense and everyday, but which is distinctive, special and seems to connect with a wider or higher level of awareness and being.
2. Spirituality is fundamentally relational.
3. Spiritual experience may include a sense of the presence of, and relationship with, the divine or transcendent.
4. Spiritual experience tends to convey a sense of profound meaning and purpose and connectedness with creation, life and other human beings, and a corresponding sense of responsibility for one's own part in it all.
5. Spiritual experience tends to confirm the value of the subject, and, by extension, all other human beings.
6. In spiritual experience, the senses, feelings, imagination and intuition are all equally important, alongside thought and interpretation.
7. Spiritual experience tends to have the quality of revelation or external event – and this leads to a sense that one participates in a wider and higher scheme of things.
8. Spirituality is informed by the repeated experience of the interconnectedness – and at times synchronicity – of events and relationships.
9. Spirituality is related to sexuality, which is another kind of energy of relationship and connectedness.
10. Spirituality tends to evoke a sense of the supersensible – both positive and negative – and of life beyond death.
11. Spirituality tends to evoke joy.
12. Spiritual experience can, for some, be a negative experience, either in its nature (as in 10) or in terms of other people's response.

If we turn now to the individual chapters, we begin with the two chapters which seek to 'set the scene' for the rest of the book. I have already referred to some of the aims and concerns of my own chapter at the beginning of this Introduction. As a student of spirituality and of counselling psychology I am passionately engaged with the inner worlds of human beings, with subjective experience and the discernment of the integrity and value of such experience. Furthermore I am convinced that the present crisis in our approach to human living on this planet and beyond is caused by the loss of an empathic sense of participation in the world, and can only be remedied by a (re-)discovery of such relationship. The therapeutic relationship in counselling is one of the major routes by which this can be achieved, as many of our contributors suggest also.

John Reader brought to the world two main approaches: one a richly engaged rural parochial ministry, and the other a highly developed understanding and further exploration of contemporary philosophy and theology. Latterly his particular interest was in the impact of the digital on modern society, and that included environmental impact. His contribution to this volume shows both these aspects of his approach, both engaged and reflective.

In his chapter John examines the proposition that current attempts to reconnect with nature have the potential to be stepping-stones to spiritual experience and looks at examples of attempts at reconnection such as forest bathing and Forest Schools, regenerative agriculture and digital apps, but also at some of the more theoretical ideas that are relevant to this. He asks whether secular reconnections can be equated with spiritual experience in the light of ideas about the binary of culture and nature which is then brought into question in the work of such writers as Stengers and Latour.

> Stengers suggests that it is necessary to acknowledge that we are sick through being disconnected with nature and Latour suggests that the language of folds is a means of understanding the reconnections that need to happen. If attention can be focused on nature and lead to such developments then apparently secular attempts to reconnect even though taken out of their original spiritual context can indeed become stepping stones to spiritual experience as defined in the work of Jeff Leonardi, including a sense of the transcendent and the importance of relationships with both the human and the nonhuman.

Reader's chapter is concerned with pointing to two important distinctions. One is the difference between an attraction to nature which is claimed to be spiritual but does not in fact have a clearly spiritual dimension, but may rather be another form of consumerism (and which may therefore be antithetical to the wellbeing of the environment). The other is that being devoted to nature may not actually lead to actual practices which protect and preserve the environment from damage. His illustration of the growth in membership of the RSPB alongside the continuing decline of many bird species illustrates this point very well. (He is not, of course, suggesting that the RSPB itself, or being a member of it, is thereby lacking in merit, only that there is more to halting environmental damage than such membership alone.) He articulates the need, however, for spirituality to go beyond an individual pursuit or experience, and to include the relational dimension of community:

> This could be exactly the danger of a spirituality that attends only to the subjective and individual and fails to recognise the threats to nature or creation in theological terms. They are 'fiddling while Paris burns'. How can we be sure that these attempts to reconnect with nature are not simply a cosy and convenient means of attending to the aesthetic dimension of nature, the beauty of the red of the sunset, when what really requires our attention is the destruction of that which we wish to enjoy but take for granted? In a contemporary spirituality where should our attention be focused?

Many of the chapters in this book suggest that the root of our environmental crisis is our spiritual and psychological alienation or sickness: 'It is not until we accept that we are sick that remedies become essential and then a focus upon nature may lead to that greater depth of spiritual awareness.'

After these two opening chapters we proceed to the second section of the book, about how spirituality deepens our understanding. In Chapter 3 Marianne Rankin, who has been connected to the work of the Alister Hardy Trust and the Religious Experience Research Centre for many years, gives a very good introduction to both of these. In particular she draws upon her doctoral research into the outcomes of spiritual experience, using two thousand accounts from the Archive of the Centre, to explore here the part played by the natural world in spiritual experiences, such as 'experience of the essential interconnectedness of humanity and the natural world' and states that 'this mystical sense of unity seems to lead to a feeling of love and compassion for all living things and often an awareness of an underlying transcendent reality'.

Marianne helpfully roots her account in the founding inspiration of Sir Alister Hardy himself, and his early experiences in nature: 'sometimes (when I was sure no-one was looking!) I would go down on my knees to express this gratitude. At the same time I had become an ardent Darwinian.' In this was his distinctiveness: an equal devotion to the scientific investigation of the physical world and an openness to the spiritual dimension sometimes inspired by nature (and the scientific investigation of religious and spiritual experience): 'he would devote his life to trying to bring about a reconciliation between human spiritual experience and the theory of evolution.'

She regrets the tendency to dismiss such experiences because they do not fit the current scientific paradigm, rather than being scientifically open to investigating all phenomena. She then moves on to her central focus, of the consequences of such experience, again citing Hardy:

> He valued the profound effect of spiritual experience on people, including an awareness of the transcendent, a sense of new purpose in life and closer and better relationships with others. These contribute to wellbeing, a sense of being at home in the natural world and among our fellow creatures.

Another significant outcome of many experiences she found in the archive is a change in attitude to death: 'Accounts describe a lessening of fear brought about through an understanding that death is not the end of consciousness.'

A recurring theme in investigations of the outcomes of spiritual experience is that much depends upon how they are received by significant others and, for example, medical practitioners (if they are shared; many individuals never communicate their experiences for fear of negative judgements). Marianne writes that 'many people explain that they did not receive help from within the church when seeking to understand their experience and descriptions of rejection of RSEs by clergy can be found in the archive. Some correspondents feel that their profound experiences are dismissed, and as a result they often leave religious institutions, many becoming spiritual but not religious.'

Her chapter concludes with a sentiment which recurs throughout this collection, of the need for reconnection:

> The benefits for humanity and the environment from a turn away from self-absorption to an acceptance of interconnectedness are boundless. ....Some of our deepest experiences seem to bring a recognition that we and the whole universe are interlinked and this leads to love and compassion for our fellows and a deep concern for the environment.

In Chapter 4 Robert Fruehwirth draws upon a lifetime's dedication to the teachings of the fourteenth-century mystic and anchorite Julian of Norwich, and makes a profound connection between one of her core insights and that of the Person-centred approach. In the field of the study of religious and spiritual experience Julian provides an extensive and compelling example in her *Revelations of Divine Love*, a very personal account of her visions at a time of great physical peril for her. Their very survival into our own times is quite remarkable, and especially because her mystical theology seems to speak very penetratingly to so many of us now.

Julian reflected in great depth upon these revelations for the rest of her life and the second, longer version of them, written much later, conveys the fruit of her mature understanding of them. Drawing upon a Person-centred understanding of the individual's journey towards self-acceptance, Robert details Julian's journey from the self-rejecting attitudes to herself in the earlier version, to a loving self-acceptance in the later. Part of this development is shown in her ability to be comfortable with aspects of not knowing (cf. Becky Seale in Chapter 5): she learns to rely instead on relational trust in profound unknowing.

> Julian invites us into a state of radical unknowing. The world as it is and faith in a God of all-powerful love make no sense together. There is no understanding, no intelligibility here, and any theorising we do either diminishes God's love or God's power or it minimises the horror of suffering. You might say that Julian invites us into a way of non-sense. This is not a nihilistic nonsense, cracking jokes into the void. It is the nonsense of being held open to the pain of this world exactly as it is, with sustained compassion and love for this world, and with sustained faith that God is at work in everything for well-being.

Robert focuses especially on the statement by Julian that God is at one with *the soul which is at peace with herself,* and from his understanding of the healing journey in Person-centred counselling, recognises that a soul being at peace with herself can be clearly understood to be closely connected to the one who has found real self-acceptance at a deep level. Therefore the spiritual journey and the psychological journey towards wholeness are seen to be alike.

Robert extends this understanding to the relationship with the world we inhabit:

> We might reasonably hope that this kind of spiritual formation would allow people to live less greedily, fearfully, and more free from materialistic compulsions. The aim of life would not be to create an epicurean enclosed garden, a gated community, where suffering and poverty could be externalised, where threats could be so managed that feelings of contentment could more easily arise, where entertainments could be offered with increasing, passive absorption and even the self becomes a project, physical and spiritual, of technological management.

In Chapter 5, Becky Seale presents the personal challenge of the climate crisis as a Zen *koan* and also a kind of 'not knowing' which is not the same as ignorance or avoidance:

> Koan-like, my inquiry at the heart of this chapter has grown from my unanswered and unanswerable questions about the eco-crisis: what can I do to respond to the knowledge that human beings are having such a devastating effect on our beloved Earth? I find myself in a place of not knowing; a moment of stasis and inaction as I struggle with the uncomfortable feeling that I should be doing more.

I suspect that in this statement she expresses how it is for very many of us at this time. She goes on to suggest that our creation of the crisis and seeming paralysis in the face of it raises for her profound questions about human nature, which in turn resonate with some of the less then helpful themes from earlier religious and philosophical answers to the question: What does it say about human nature that we have created this crisis and don't seem concerned enough to do what it takes to solve it? Does that make us fundamentally selfish and uncaring beings?

Instead of yielding to such a condemnatory perspective, she reaches instead towards the resources of the Person-centred approach and of Buddhism. With the former she points to the formative and actualising tendencies of this theory, and to congruence: 'Our disconnection from the natural world therefore may be viewed in terms of our "incongruence" or disconnection from ourselves and our organismic experience' and conversely: 'the ability to cultivate the conditions that enable the development of greater congruence or authenticity may consequently enable the development of greater environmental sensibilities' (which is also one of the main arguments of this volume). From Buddhism she points to the *Buddha nature* in every sentient being, and the path of realisation of this nature and of connection to all: 'It is through this realisation of our connection to all that exists, that human self-centredness can be transformed.'

In Chapter 6 William West addresses the significance of spiritual experience from the perspectives of his own spiritual experiences and that of working in counselling with clients and their explorations in this area. In the counselling context he writes about how the counselling relationship itself can at times amount to a spiritual experience. This is very much my own territory of research, into what I term 'relational spirituality'.

As we have noted in relation to Marianne Rankin's research in Chapter 3, the value of spiritual experience can depend very much on how it is received by significant others, including counsellors and for West, 'it is crucially important that counsellors are aware of their own stance on spirituality, spiritual experiences and religious faith.' In relation to the climate crisis, and in agreement with all the contributors to this volume, West recognises an urgent need for a change in consciousness and culture world-wide, and perhaps especially in the West: 'I do think that the only hope for the future of the human race is a change of consciousness away from individualism, which remains popular in the USA and the West as a whole, to a sense of interconnectedness between people and between people and the planet.'

He sees the psycho-spiritual development of individuals leading towards an enhanced appreciation of and reverence towards the natural world, and again a sense of the connection between all creatures. Again echoing one of the strongest themes which emerge from this collection, he recognises the part that the counselling profession can play in this movement: 'Counsellors and others who assist and support individuals and communities in their soul journeys could have a key part to play if they have the skills to work effectively with clients addressing issues that arise around spirituality and spiritual experiences.'

In Chapter 7, Marta Helena de Freitas presents a powerful argument consistent with so much of what has been written in this collection, suggesting that the spirituality and mythology of some of Brazil's indigenous peoples offer a vital understanding of the need to decentralise the human race on the world stage, and to recognise the mutuality and reciprocity of life forms, at both the physical and also spiritual levels, a relationship encapsulated by the metaphor of *the marriage of Heaven and Earth*. She provides a historical context for the relative denigration of indigenous culture into the present, 'sustained on the false belief of omnipotence and anthropocentric centrality (of human beings)' and 'reductionist, jargon of "scientific neutrality"'. She affirms the health-giving relevance of many of those indigenous beliefs for the present environmental crisis, and discusses also the implications of this for Brazilian people's physical and mental health. At the same time she is concerned to avoid glamorising or idealising those systems of belief and practice.

She illustrates these themes by providing a contemporary account of the relationship between the culture of indigenous people and of health professionals 'based on studies whose results illustrate the confluences and conflicts between indigenous cosmology and medical science' and she discusses 'the challenges and implications of the health policy situation for indigenous people in Brazil, and for the population in general, relating to cultural identity, physical and mental health, and the environment.'

She contrasts the indigenous beliefs in the *intentionality* of all the elements of the environment with the *objectivity* of the scientific-medical model which 'the world becomes "disheartened" and devoid of subjectivity, the more one knows it.' In one of the most potent statements in her chapter she quotes Kopenawa:

> The forest is alive. It can only die if the white people persist in destroying it. If they succeed, the rivers will disappear underground, the soil will crumble, the trees will shrivel up, and the stones will crack in the heat. The dried-up earth will become empty and silent. The *xapiri* spirits [spirits of the Amazon rainforest] who come down from the mountains to play on their mirrors in the forest will escape far away. Their shaman fathers will no longer be able to call them and make them dance to protect us. They will be powerless to repel the epidemic fumes which devour us. They will no longer be able to hold back the evil beings who will turn the forest to chaos. We will die one after the other, the white people as well as us. All the shamans will finally perish. Then, if none of them survive to hold it up, the sky will fall. (Kopenawa, 2010, p. 8)

In Chapter 8, Hannah Armbrust brings a Jungian perspective to the consideration of our relationship with the earth (and universe). She offers a comparable theme to Chapter 7's 'Marriage of Heaven and Earth', that of *Pachamama* – or Mother Earth – for the ancestral people of the Andes. To these ancestral peoples, the Earth was sacred: the great mountains, the rivers, Pachamama and majestic trees; they all had subjectivity and alterity (cf. what Chapter 7 says about *intentionality* above). She argues that our nature is interbeing or intersubjectivity, and introduces the concept of archetypal intersubjectivity as an epistemology that can 'offer new insights into the ethical paths we can choose to restore human relationship with Mother Earth. Archetypal intersubjectivity's epistemological assumption is that the essence of Being is intertwined and dependent on relationships. Those relationships are not restricted to other human beings, or to the environment, and include our relationship with the symbolic.'

She writes of Jung, for whom 'psyche is Nature itself' and that he 'implies that our connection with the environment transcends the physical world.' She rejects the dominant narrative 'that places human beings as "superior" and separated from "nature"'. and instead we need 'a story founded in trust and interbeing, which will offer just and healthy perspectives of life on this planet, might take decades to accomplish. Still, without starting it now, it will not ever be possible.'

Quoting Von Franz, Armbrust suggests that creation myths are '…the deepest and most important of all myths' – they 'are concerned with the ultimate meaning, not only of *our* existence but of the existence of the whole cosmos'. Following Jung she invites us to ask by what is the myth we are living? In relation to *Pachamama,* this supreme being possesses a dual aspect, of nurture and also punishment: 'In other words, by engaging in a predatory relationship with the *Pachamama,* suffering will inevitably come as the natural consequence of our acts.' We need to rescue the sense of wonder and belonging and reignite 'our spiritual connection to the *Pachamama* by reflecting on the concept of interbeing and archetypal intersubjectivity as the baseline of recognizing Earth's rights and starting a new relationship with this planet.'

This work can importantly be seen as the work of psychologists and therapists, and links it closely with the *individuation process*: 'As a psychotherapist, I encourage my clients to learn to unlearn. And what I mean by unlearning is to reject a provisional ego-centered personality, which is one-sided, and aligned with the promises of the Anthropocene (consumerism, exploitation of the environment, accumulation of resources) to answer to summons of the soul (wholeness, spirituality, collaboration).' She is optimistic about 'recovering the emotional energy we once had through our profound and intersubjective relationship with the environment'. (This compares with what is said in Chapter 1 about Barfield's *Final Participation.*)

Four of the contributors to this volume have strong connections with the Religious Experience Centre of the University of Wales, Trinity St David, and of these Bettina Schmidt, the author of Chapter 9, has the strongest, as Director of the Centre. She has a broad perspective on spiritual and religious experience from both the resources of the Centre, and also from her own wide research into these matters in the Brazilian context. Her recent work focuses particularly on the connection between spiritual experience and Wellbeing, and in this chapter she makes further connections between these themes and the relationship with nature and the environment, which is perceived there as a living entity with which (whom) to develop relationships..

She criticises the One Health policy of the World Health Organisation, which overlooks the spiritual dimension of wellbeing. Adopting an expanded concept which does include this vital dimension 'illustrates the interconnectedness that is at the core of the expanding understanding of wellbeing'.

She applies the concept of 'extrovertive' to mystical spiritual experiences to distinguish them 'from other mystical experiences by their orientation towards the natural world' as opposed to other perhaps transcendental or interior mystical experiences. In a section which matches some of John Reader's arguments in Chapter 2, she quotes Beringer on *ecospirituality* approvingly for her definition of 'true ecospirituality' as an extension to ecospirituality used simply as 'connection to nature'. She extends the 'purchase' of the concept to be 'not just about the spiritual sense of interconnectedness but also about the need to integrate ecological harmony and social responsibility'.

She quotes from Rodríguez to argue that wellbeing, far from being purely about achieving individual happiness, requires also 'living well together' as human beings but also with nature, and with spirits, deities, or ancestors: 'In African-derived traditions, this spiritual connection is enabled via a spiritual energy called *axé*… *Axé* is the spiritual force that links all living being with the divine. It is needed to live and exists in every living being, humans, animals, and plants' and 'nature is seen as the cathedral, not made by humans but by the divine.'

In Chapter 1 I argue for the recognition and 'rehabilitation' of a wider spectrum of 'ways of knowing' than simply the scientific-rational-empirical (while retaining a proper place and regard for the latter). I then point to the paradox of presenting such arguments in precisely the latter form, of rational discourse supported by example and evidence, whereas the 'wider' spectrum of ways of knowing could include many more approaches:

> In some ways a more effective statement of these matters might be to weep and laugh, to touch and embrace, to utilise art, music, dance, poetry and film, to sit quietly in nature, to offer images of human oppression and environmental devastation, and conversely of celebration and blessing.

All our contributors bring a real passion to bear on this subject, and often use poetic language, but it is in our final chapter that we find the fullest expression of at least some of these dimensions of communication. In Chapter 10 Tony Rose calls us to respond to a clarion call of passionate concern for the harm we are doing to our planet and all its systems and lifeforms, and offers a heartfelt affirmation of our inter-relatedness with them all, and indeed with the whole universe. This is no small invitation and requires a very full expression of such a vision.

Although Tony presents *Biosynergy* as a complete theory in itself, his chapter is underpinned throughout by reference to the profound experiences of interspecies 'epiphanies' which set him on his journey and continued to lead him further. In that sense he appeals to us all to reflect on our own experiences of empathy for and from the natural world, and adopt them as signposts to where we need to go by way of healing relationships with the rest of creation. Tony also explores his own near-death experience in his youth, and the death of his father and what that enabled in him.

Tony Rose has espoused and promulgated his theory and vision of Biosynergy since the 1970s and at this stage in his life it finds its fullest and widest expression. I know from my many conversations with him that he feels the last few years have engaged him in developing the last and, he now considers, most important dimension of his theory, that of the *spiritual* perspective. Indeed, he believes that it is only by recognising and developing a vision of the fundamental coherence of all that is from a perspective which includes *Spirit* and *Eternity* that we can begin to honour our real context and its implications. I know that he also believes that the religious and spiritual communities have a vital role to play in our engagement with the ecological and spiritual crisis of our times.

Much of this book addresses the past and present context for the ecological crisis, and looks to the future with concern and trepidation, and with a great call to avert catastrophe. In this final chapter of the book Tony Rose is above all *forward-facing* in inviting us to partake of a Person-centred Biosynergistic vision of what is both true and necessary for our healing. In Chapter 8 Hannah Armbrust posed for us the Jungian question of by what myth we live. Tony Rose offers us a redeeming framework by which to evolve into a viable and creative future. In this sense I think of his chapter as a *Hymn to the Future*. His closing words offer an eloquent conclusion – and prayer – for the book and this Introduction:

> May we all flourish in Creative Biosynergy with myriad beloved fellow earthlings as we wander through Earth's sacred Wilderness gathering Revelations in Nature and experiencing the Epiphanies of Eden that inform and enable our all-inclusive, mutually compassionate, ecologically adaptive, biosynergy-driven Quest for Global Well-becoming that enlightens Personal Pathways to Eternal Bliss in the Infinite Loving Universe.

Biographical note

Jeff Leonardi is a person-centred counsellor, supervisor, trainer and spiritual companion, and a retired Anglican priest who was for 17 years Bishop's Adviser for Pastoral Care and Counselling in the Lichfield Diocese of the Church of England. He has been a qualified person-centred counsellor for the past forty years, and has a PhD in the spirituality of person-centred counselling in relation to Christian spirituality, and the implications for Christian ministry and pastoral practice. He is an Honorary Research Fellow of the Religious Experience Research Centre at the University of Wales Trinity St David at Lampeter, undertaking research into relational spirituality.

References

Kopenawa, D. and Albert, B. 2010. *La chute du ciel: paroles d'un chaman yanomami.* Paris: Terre Humain, Plon.

Schmidt, B. and Leonardi, J., eds. 2020. *Spirituality and Well-being: Interdisciplinary Approaches to the Study of Religious Experience and Health.* Sheffield: Equinox.

Part I
Setting the scene

1 Knowing and un-knowing: Extending the spectrum of meaning to include what really matters

Jeff Leonardi

Introduction: Slender threads

In this chapter I am seeking to affirm subjective awareness and ways of knowing, and the profound significance of not-knowing as a respectful response to mystery. In so doing I have been struck again by a recognition that some of the most significant human experiences are not writ large but are subtle, *slender threads* if you like. I have found this to be true in my own life, and also in the study of religious and spiritual experiences more widely. It seems to me that everyone is endowed with a capacity for subtle levels of awareness, but my own experience is that this capacity has developed in me over a lifetime. I remember struggling with a big and difficult decision early in my adult life, and telling someone that the urge to follow what seemed the riskier path had come to me as 'a quiet voice'. Without hesitation she said: 'You must always listen to "the quiet voice"'. I took that riskier path and it has led to the rest of my life in a way I could not have imagined.

Similarly I remember reading an account of the counsel given to someone by a member of a religious order: 'I don't think that sounds like the guidance of the Holy Spirit: in my experience the Holy Spirit always works *deftly*'. Subtle and deft, not loud and blatant. But this very quality is also intriguing and maybe even frustrating. If 'God' wants us to believe in God, why doesn't God write 'I exist' in a recognisable script in the sky? Well, for those 'with the eyes to see' maybe the sky and all creation is a visible testimony to the existence of God. (The Franciscans view the world as the first 'Bible' in just this sense). But this 'evidence' is clearly not compelling, otherwise all would have reason to believe. So this chapter seeks to affirm the tremendous potential value of subjective awareness and 'subtle' ways of knowing – and even 'un-knowing' – whilst acknowledging that such awareness requires a different kind of discernment from empirical evidence of the externally verifiable kind. It seems that religious and spiritual experience resides in a paradoxical ('liminal') space of subtle awareness and promptings, the capacity for which can be developed as we shall see, but cannot be demonstrated or proven directly. For the writer of the Letter to the Hebrews in the Christian New Testament, faith was 'the substance of things not seen' (Hebrews 11.1). This is a delightful expression of the substantial ('substance') and insubstantial or subtle ('not seen'). I would suggest that one of the primary – and pressing – challenges of our time is to expand our epistemology to encompass spiritual awareness and to do so in ways that simultaneously also embrace rational inquiry and questioning.

What follows has three main strands of dimensions, which interconnect. The first is to affirm the value of *subjective awareness* and to argue that we need to find better ways of incorporating such knowledge into the intellectual sphere, not as 'second best' to objective or empirical knowledge, but as equal and equally significant. This in turn requires the development of an appropriate means of discerning the claims for subjective awareness to any wider validity than the purely personal (while still affirming how important the 'purely personal' is).

The second theme, which can be understood as one type of subjective awareness, is that of *spiritual understanding*. Human beings in the various religious and mystical traditions have dedicated lifetimes of study, discipline and application to the exploration and development of spiritual awareness over millennia and we do well to approach this body of knowledge and practice with respect for what it can offer our present and future (as well as discerning what of that store is of its time and place and perhaps now no longer helpful or appropriate). In particular, the experience of *unitive consciousness* affirms our inter-connectedness with the universe and our co-inhabitants, and in so doing leads towards a vital and necessary reform of our exploitative and harmful approach to the planet. I should note that when speaking of spiritual understanding I draw primarily from the tradition I know best, the Christian spiritual tradition, and also from Buddhism. I also recognise and respect the other main spiritual traditions which often connect with these same themes, but with which I am less qualified to engage.

The third theme, *the psychology of integration*, draws from the riches of counselling psychology, and in particular the Jungian and person-centred approaches, to suggest ways in which the healing and integration of the individual can and does heal the 'soul sickness' which divides us between mind and body, self and other, species and planet. The quality of *empathy* is suggested as one of the connecting principles for this healing process. In this way the three strands also extend to *environmental awareness* and the present crisis.

Subjective awareness and ways of knowing

There is a paradox at the heart of the contemporary intellectual culture. It is a paradox which mirrors C.P. Snow's protest at the gulf between the Arts and Sciences (Snow, 1959), but this paradox involves an even greater stand-off between two complementary poles of great stature: that between objective and subjective knowledge. So much of our impressive development as a scientific and technological world owes itself to the rigorous scientific practice of detached, empirical research, so much so that we seem to have tipped over into largely 'worshipping' this approach without ever recognising that we do so at the cost of diminishing and disdaining whole areas of human awareness which are are of equal or even greater significance, such as imagination, creativity, beauty, emotion, intuition, reverence, relationship, empathy, spirituality, awe, mystery, compassion, nurture, hope, serenity, wholeness, and being or becoming. The secular/scientific mindset is such that spiritual and religious experience, which can be some of the greatest influences and motivators in human life, may be viewed as an aberration and even delusion which intelligent human beings will escape from or transcend. (The evidence for the countervailing claim about the significance and value of religious and spiritual experience can be found widely in personal accounts of the impact and outworking of such experience, not least those in the Archive of the Religious Experience Research Centre of the University of Wales Trinity St David, to which I am connected as an Honorary Research Fellow, and which are accessible online, and also in the writings of Sir Alister Hardy, who founded the Centre (Hardy, 1979), and successors such as David Hay (Hay, 1982, 1990); see also Woollacott and Lorimer, 2022.)

It may be salutary at this point to acknowledge a certain paradox about the writing of this piece. I am of course seeking to communicate broadly speaking with an intellectual community, and I am doing so with words, reason and conceptual thinking. But I will be suggesting that there are serious limitations and imbalances about the exercise of a purely rationalistic perspective, and I am doing so by employing the very tools and methods which I am critiquing. In some ways a more effective statement of these matters might be to weep and laugh, to touch and embrace, to utilise art, music, dance, poetry and film, to sit quietly in nature, to offer images of human oppression and environmental devastation, and conversely of celebration and blessing. But in this context suffice to say that I am mindful that I am employing rational discourse to communicate with others similarly about the limitations of an exclusive reliance upon such discourse and associated world views. In affirming the essential value of each of the other ways of knowing it is no part of my intention to denigrate or undervalue the rational faculty, which contributes an enormous amount to our human understanding. Rather it my intention to affirm the contributions made by the other faculties to human awareness and understanding, and to commend a better balance and integration between them all. In so doing I believe it will be possible to begin to construct an epistemology which can embrace subjective experience including spirituality and mystical experience, and thereby recreate the necessary space for the religious dimension of human life, with its profound contribution to health and wellbeing, now affirmed in the context of a rationality which can still critique its dangers and excesses. I believe that this is the fulfilment of human potential expressed by Owen Barfield as the third stage of the evolution of consciousness: *Final Participation*, which is the re-entry into participatory relationship with the world but now also combined with intellectual understanding (Barfield, 1988).

We have a disparity then, I suggest, between a view of primary human concerns such as love, family and relationships, art and culture, nature and the environment, all fed by myriad subjective feelings and responses, and a view that such matters are intellectually of lesser significance than 'hard' scientific analysis based on external observation. The subjective life, being subjective, is thereby viewed as less reliable, almost illusory, in comparison with hard facts. This would be comic if it did not have such tragic, and harmful effects.

Jung and personality types

In modern times Jung was and is one of the most important students of the inner life of the person. In a well known Face to Face interview with C.G. Jung in 1959, John Freeman asked him whether he believed in God. Jung's much-quoted answer was: 'I don't need to believe, I know' (Jung, 1959c). Although Jung felt afterwards that this was a somewhat unsatisfactory response, because it did not clarify what was meant by 'God', and that the primary truth about God was mystery, his reply was in fact consistent with a statement he had made four years earlier in a newspaper interview: 'All that I have learned has led me step by step to an unshakable conviction of the existence of God. I only believe in what I know. And that eliminates believing. Therefore I do not take his existence on belief – I know that he exists' (Sands, 1955, p. 6). He recognised the limitations involved in any claim to 'know' God-who-is-mystery by asserting the limitations of purely intellectual understanding and by implication the possibility of (an)other way of knowing: 'The God-image is the expression of an underlying experience of something which I cannot attain to by intellectual means...' (Jung, 1959a). Many spiritual authorities, and of course especially mystics, have asserted the impossibility of knowing God by the intellect, and have encouraged their followers to practise various alternative ways of knowing through bodily and mental disciplines, fasting, yoga, prayer and meditation etc., and through openness to Grace and revelation. In Jung's case his devotion to psychoanalysis and the study of the unconscious had provided some of the means for this knowing, as well as his engagement with the world religions and a focus on the various symbols employed by them and which can also surface from the unconscious (Jung, 1964).

Jung also developed a typology of human personality which recognised that there are a variety of ways in which we apprehend and process reality, and that different individuals have a different balance of ways of knowing and experiencing reality, of which the intellect is only one, however important (Jung, 1921/1959a). In fact, it can be seen that the discursive intellect is intrinsically unable to experience reality *at first hand*, but only after the event as a form of reflection and deduction. The senses are the primary firsthand means, and it can also be thought that intuition is a 'direct apprehending' akin to what is said about mystical awareness (cf. unitive consciousness below) and what we refer to as 'feeling' (as in 'having a feeling about something') is also a direct apprehension of phenomena. But the senses are not necessarily 'pure' and untrammelled in their application, being also informed by culture and learning, and therefore expectation, and similarly feeling and intuition can be reliable indicators but are not guaranteed to be so: but they 'matter' greatly to the person experiencing them.

The personality types outlined by Jung have been further developed and made known by the work of Katharine Briggs and Isabel Briggs Myers, and thereby popularly known as the 'Myers–Briggs' theory or personality inventory. Whether in its original formulation by Jung, or its further development by Myers and Briggs (Briggs Myers and Myers, 1995), the theory postulates four essential personality types and four modalities by which they are expressed. The personality types are described in terms of how the persons concerned primarily access and process reality: by thought, feeling, sense or intuition respectively. The suggestion is that each person has one of these as a primary mode or disposition, two more in lesser degree, and one as the least developed approach. In addition, such types are modulated by their character as either introvert or extrovert (focusing primarily on experience from 'within' or 'without' the person), and as favouring clear definitions ('judgement') or fluid approaches ('perception'). There are thus 16 primary configurations or types of personality and the inventory enables one to progressively discern which one dominant type or modality characterise the individual.

As with all systematising approaches to human consciousness, there are inevitable limitations to this one, and questions to be asked. In the context of the present paper, it is not my intention to explicate this theory of personality typology so much as to draw attention to the ways of knowing it identifies. Jung posits four such primary modes of processing reality as we have seen: thought, feeling, sense and intuition. In earlier stages of human development, feeling, sense and intuition played a very great part in human activity and culture. Owen Barfield was a fellow member with J.R. Tolkien and C.S. Lewis of the Oxford 'Inklings' and he suggested that consciousness evolves in three distinct stages (Barfield, 1988), of which the first stage is *Original Participation*. As the word suggests, 'participation' refers to the stage in awareness where the individual is very much 'part of' both their human family and community, and of the natural (and supernatural) worlds. This stage has potential advantages in terms of human relationships, and also respect and understanding for the world, and potential disadvantages in terms of inaccurate, mistaken and inhibitory beliefs and a reluctance to test beliefs as to their validity by debate and experiment.

Barfield's terms the second stage *detachment* or *non-participation* and this corresponds to what we generally describe as the 'Age of Reason', and then the 'Enlightenment'. There is a strong implicit sense here that what went before was lacking in rationality or understanding, and that progress occurs when reason is employed and, for want of another term, 'superstition' was discarded. Along with 'primitive' beliefs and superstitions, religion and spirituality also become increasingly marginalised. Scientific and technological development provides a compelling 'proof of the pudding' and human beings move from participative *relationship-with* to *mastery-over* the world.

What is being suggested here is that the Enlightenment elevated reason to the highest place in human endeavour and relegated the other kinds of intelligence to lesser or no places. Emotion, intuition and sensory and sexual awareness all have a highly significant part to play in human consciousness, alongside intellectual processes, and human beings can be viewed, as we have seen, as having a different balance of priority to any and all of these ways of experiencing and knowing. But the ages of reason, science and technology have privileged these particular approaches far beyond their companions, and in that sense have become overbalanced and exaggerated in one dimension and direction, with difficult and dangerous consequences, not just for the environment and our fellow creatures, but for our own human wholeness of being. Mastery suits global capitalism, which in turn generates powerful coalitions of interest and associated media, and these in turn consolidate the direction and momentum of imbalance and harm, externally and internally.

The relative neglect of 'emotional intelligence' can leave us culturally vulnerable to demagogues and political manipulation.

More or less Enlightenment?

One major source of the loss of integration and balance between the various human ways of knowing can be seen to have developed out of the Rationalism epitomised by Descartes' primary statement that consciousness and existence reside in cognition ('Cogito ergo sum': 'I think therefore I am'), and this in turn gives rise to 'Cartesian dualism' and the radical separation of minds and bodies, and in turn the elevation of the mind to the control room and therefore, again, 'mastery' over the body, which is thereby relegated to be the servant, slave or mechanism of physical endeavour. In a sense this corresponds to a tendency in many spiritual traditions to separate not just mind, but also soul and spirit, from the bodily and physical, usually with the presumption that the former are 'higher', 'purer' and more spiritual, and that the latter are the zone of immoral temptation, decay and corruption – and certainly much less reliable (Leonardi, 2020). Historically the former are frequently seen to be the preserve of rational men, and the latter the domain of emotional and sensual women, cf. the Genesis narrative where Eve first yields to the temptation to eat of the fruit of the 'tree of the knowledge of good and evil', and then brings it to Adam (Genesis 3).

In this way, rationality is seen as a/the (masculine) defence against temptation and sin, and emotion and the flesh as the (feminine) danger of deception and entrapment. Eventually Freud will enshrine this philosophical and theological view in a psychological theory where the libido and the unconscious correspond to the latter forces, and the ego and superego to the former. Although Freudian psychoanalysis may in practice provide an extent of moderation between the two tendencies, it is Jung who will offer the greater hope of an integration by affirming that both dispositions have essential contributions to make towards genuine wholeness and integration. Part of how he will do this consists as we have seen in recognising a wider range of ways of knowing than the cognitive, and thereby rescuing human beings from the trap of Cartesian or other dualisms. But he also developed the psychology of *anima* and *animus*, the female and masculine principles, both present in both women and men, and requiring to be raised to consciousness and integration (Jung, 1959b).

Implication for our relationship with the environment

The dangers of detached intellectual dominance and control are powerfully played out in our relationship with the natural world and its creatures. The term 'environment' can suggest a secondary or background role for something, the backdrop as it were to the thing that really matters, which is then the proper focus of our attention. The human race has treated the physical world as a means to an end and as subservient to our human needs for a long time, certainly since the Industrial Revolution. Most of us can now see the misguidedness of treating our host planet and fellow creatures in this way, and the dreadful consequences for us all of doing so. But 'environment' can be defined otherwise, drawing upon a biblical phrase, as that in which 'we live and move and have our being' (Acts 17.28). Here Paul is referring to God, but if we in turn apply it to the environment, it implies a comprehensive and crucial dimension of existence, and perhaps a reciprocal relationship, a relationship of mutuality and indeed respect, between human beings and the world 'in which we live and move and have our being'.

Early human beings, and those cultures which have survived more or less intact from our hunter-gatherer origins, seem to have enjoyed a relationship towards the natural world and its creatures which contained more respect and mutuality (Barfield's *Original Participation*). I do not wish to invoke a sentimental or romantic Arcadian idyll. It is clear that a life which depends on hunting, trapping and killing other creatures cannot be too tender for their wellbeing or feelings, especially when times are hard and survival precarious. But many (most) native cultures are based in a relationship of respect, sometimes worship, sometimes fear, of the natural world. Animals and plants and places may be accorded a totemic significance. It is taken as a given that communication between the human and natural milieux is vital and frequent. From what I have learned about them, the Native Americans of the Great Plains, for example, would never have engaged in a wholesale and wanton slaughter of the buffalo such as occurred during the settlers' occupation of their lands, and this is a fairly typical example of the change in sensibility which developed from pre-industrial to industrial and post-industrial 'civilisation'.

The cost of detachment or non-participation, whereby human beings no longer feel connected with the natural order, is enormous, and there is a loss of a sense of *belonging*. This phase has continued into our present times, and permits all the kind of ruthless treatments of the natural world to which we have referred.

Much of the philosophical tradition of the relationship between Mind and Body is characterised by dualistic thinking. By contrast the spiritual teachings of the world religions develop towards a more inclusive both/and perspective, especially in their mystical spirituality. Franciscan theologian Richard Rohr's works frequently invoke the transition from dualism to inclusive thought as *the* major step in spiritual maturity (e.g. Rohr, 2011, pp.

146–156). He suggests that contemplative practice leads to the transcendence of dualistic or binary thinking patterns, and a recognition that human beings are not separate from, but connected to, all life and indeed the universe. So it is no longer a question of me/them, but 'us'; no longer body/mind/spirit, but whole being; no longer inside versus outside but a continuum. This leads us into a spiritual perspective on the sense of a loss of participation in the natural world.

A spiritual understanding: Healing the wound of knowledge

The Wound of Knowledge is the title of an early major work by Rowan Williams, a history and analysis of Christian Spirituality (Williams, 1979). It take its title from a poem by R.S. Thomas, 'Roger Bacon', in which the poet writes about the disciple Thomas, sometimes referred to as 'Doubting Thomas', when he encountered Christ at the Resurrection, and refers to the spear wound in Christ's side.

'The wound of knowledge' is a marvellously evocative phrase which could be said to describe the primal rift between human beings and the natural world which we have been discussing, and also what is described at the beginning of the Hebrew and Christian Bible, in the section which has become known as 'the Fall of Humanity' (Genesis 2.16/3.1–19). In the earlier verse God expressly forbids the proto-humans Adam and Eve from eating the fruit of the 'tree of the knowledge of good and evil', and in Genesis Chapter 3 we read the account of their disobedience and its consequences: expulsion from the Garden of Eden.

Getting back to the garden (Joni Mitchell, Woodstock)

The human sense of having 'come from' a previous place or state of primal wholeness is widespread, and so also the recognition that our actual state is somehow less than ideal ('strangers and exiles on the earth' according to the New Testament *Letter to the Hebrews* 11.13). In Christian terms this is referred to as 'the Fall' of Adam and Eve, and thereby as representative of the human condition. In the Christian tradition, and especially in the Western tradition, the emphasis in this 'fall' from a state of grace, is on an act of disobedience to God the Creator in the eating of the forbidden fruit, and this carries with it a stern moral judgement: disobedience as sinful. This story can be read as a profound account of the process and consequences of the development of intellectual capabilities (knowledge) and the either/or nature of *binary thinking*, which in one way advances our awareness, but carries with it the danger of separating us from our bodily or organismic awareness. When we say of a person 'S/he is all in their head', or refer disparagingly to 'head knowledge', we seem to be acknowledging that intellect detached from other dimensions of awareness is somehow deficient or limited.

As we have seen, it is the intention of this chapter to explore these questions of 'ways of knowing', and to ask whether we might seek a further and better integration of them in order to fulfil our human potential. As if the 'wound of knowledge' were not severe enough in itself to need remedial attention, we are confronted in our times with what I shall argue is a further dire consequence of this suggested lack of integration or more starkly *alienation* from our true selves, namely the degradation of the environment and the environmental crisis. It will be argued that only by recognising this collective separation from our own organismic awareness and the physical world can we understand the source of the crisis, and find its remedy. One such suggestion for the latter is to be found in the spiritual approach of *unitive consciousness*.

Unitive consciousness

Unitive consciousness is the antithesis of the dualistic rational model. At the extreme of dualism we find persons as isolated 'islands' indeed (cf. John Donne, 'No Man Is an Island'; Paul Simon, 'I Am a Rock'), separate from other persons, other creatures and the world. Within this perspective a further scepticism can bring into question the truth claim to know anything at all, certainly as an objective reality. In a sense there is nothing left to stand on upon which to find reliable objective ground, and the asker themselves becomes a shadowy might-be illusion: 'I think therefore I am, I think!'

In contrast with this 'radical solipsism', the world's mystics and religious teachers suggest, with remarkable coherence of agreement, a 'radical connectedness' or relationality of all things, the awareness of which is impeded only by our attachment to a narrow ego-consciousness. In simple terms this affirms that we are each a part of the whole, connected not separate, and capable of experiencing this to a greater extent by suitable practice and discipline – or it may emerge into awareness as a sudden realisation 'out of the blue'. Sir Alister Hardy referred to it, in his extensive research into religious and spiritual experience (see reference to the Archive in Wales above), as 'the unitive experience' (e.g. Hardy, 1979, p. 28, 78). In a recent collection of spiritual experiences recounted by 'scientists and academics' there are many examples of the unitive experience; one representative example is by Mario Beauregard, a neuroscientist who recounts an experience when he was aged eight of unity with the natural world: 'It felt like the rock, the trees and I were part of a much larger whole, much bigger than my small self' (Woollacott and Lorimer, 2022, p. 198). Then in his early 20s, at a time of acute and prolonged physical and therefore mental distress, he 'reached out' to God for help, and received a potent response such that he felt united with 'the source of the Universe and all life on our planet' (p. 200).

In my own experience, unitive consciousness has been a reality glimpsed at times, for shorter or longer periods, but always temporary, and which nevertheless inform the rest of my existence and remain a constant aspiration. I refer to experiences which seem to be purely spiritual, glimpses of a transcendent reality or being; times when I am brought into intimate relationship with the natural world, 'illuminated by the Spirit' as it were; and relationships with other human beings at times of emotional intensity, intimacy and connectedness, and with transcendent reality.

Walter Stace (Stace, 1960, p. 110) and Walter Pahnke (Pahnke, 1963) refer to the characteristics of 'unitive consciousness' and these are consistent with the kind of classifications and analysis employed by Hardy. They include: a sense of unity, both external and internal: transcendence of time and space; inter-subjectivity (cf. Buber's 'I-Thou' relationship; and Walter Berry: 'the world becomes a communion of subjects more than a collection of objects' (Berry, 2009, p86); a sense of utter validity; sacredness or holiness; peace and joy; inexpressibility; and positive outcomes in the subject's life.

In the history of Christian spirituality, unitive consciousness can refer to union with the divine, e.g. St Teresa of Avila in her work *The Interior Castle* (Teresa of Avila, 2007, p. 119). Jesus prays, in St John's Gospel, that his disciples may be one as he and God are one, with this 'Godness' dwelling in them (John 14.23, 17.20–1). The Eastern Orthodox doctrine of *Theosis* or *Divinisation* affirms that the goal of human development is to realise the divine nature in the person. St Athanasius expressed it well in the saying: 'God became human (in Christ) so that humans might become God'. Contemporary Orthodox theologian Bishop Hilarion Alfeyev expresses it similarly: 'God made us so that we might become partakers of the divine nature... so that we might come to be like him through deification by Grace' (Alfeyev, 2002, p. 191). In Orthodox teaching, such becoming cannot be achieved by purely intellectual effort, but by devotion, experiential engagement with the reality of God through prayer and devotion, and Grace.

A second kind of unitive consciousness declared by Christian teaching is that between believers as *the Body of Christ* (St Paul, 1 Cor.12.27) or as members of *the Communion of Saints*: the fellowship of all believers, living and dead, with Christ as the head. By referring to these inclusions as 'body' and 'communion' they emphasise an experiential reality beyond purely conceptual thought: we are members 'one of another' (v12).

Belonging in the world

Another form of unitive consciousness conveyed by Christian spirituality is in terms of intimate relationship to the natural world and all creation, exemplified for example by St Francis of Assisi in his *Canticle of the Sun* or *Praise of the Creatures*, a hymn of praise to God for Creation, in which he refers to the Sun, Wind and Fire as 'brothers' and Moon, Water and Earth (and indeed Death) as 'sisters' (St Francis of Assisi, 2015). He used such relational language also for animals and other creatures, and in this way proclaimed the divine harmony in all things, and was in this sense a precursor for Tony Rose, one of our contributors, in his theory of *Biosynergy* (See Chapter 10). Teilhard de Chardin, Thomas Berry and Ilia Delio, among others, have also continued the theme of environmental spirituality in the Christian tradition (Teilhard De Chardin, 1965; Berry, 2009; Delio, 2014).

Buddhism also offers a rich environment for the understanding of unitive consciousness. The Buddha's *enlightenment* amounted to a release from and transcendence of the human ego state. When there is no separate self there is only awareness, of the All, interdependent reality.

Unknowing and the apophatic tradition

One of the dangers of philosophical clarity is that it can lose touch with the extent of unknowingness and mystery which is an inevitable counterpoint to any claims to knowledge. The *Apophatic Approach* in theology is the perspective that God is transcendent and unknowable except through particular manifestations which do not and cannot in themselves contain the fulness of God's being (see for example Spearing, 2001). In this approach we find a humility which contrasts greatly with the mastery and control modalities of dualistic thinking referred to previously. In contemplative spirituality we find that holding the 'not knowing' in silence and in nature becomes the context for a deeper and wider awareness and sense of connectedness with all things, and through that to an enhanced desire to improve the well-becoming of all: this can be said to be the heart of Christian teaching, and in Buddhism this is the *Boddhisatva vow*. For the human race it may be the best chance of survival. I am encouraged in this hope in part by my experience of the human development which can occur through counselling and psychotherapy, with individuals and in groups, and to this we now turn in the final section.

The psychology of integration

Psychology can inform our understanding of the nature of the self, and of the relationship between the self-concept and wider awareness. Jung developed the concept of *Individuation*, the process by which an individual progresses towards greater self-awareness by embracing the contents of the individual unconscious and recognition of the *Shadow* or repressed parts of the psyche. Jung makes much use of symbols of integration such as the Mandala, and this in turn speaks of unitive consciousness. Deeper or further than the individual unconscious for Jung resides the *Collective Unconscious*, and here we find a theory that human beings are connected, albeit below conscious awareness, and that this level of consciousness can emerge into awareness in dreams and other non-standard states of consciousness. He found the ubiquity of common symbols and *Archetypes* across the human race to be impressive confirmation of a shared, 'universal' repository of such awareness (Jung, 1959a, p 42).

In the more recent person-centred counselling theory of Carl Rogers we find a new statement of the nature of self and awareness, in the concepts of the *Formative* and *Actualising Tendencies*. Rogers' primary focus was on a theory of the therapeutic relationship, but he presented this theory in the wider context of a theory of life and evolution. The Formative Tendency is stated to be the directional tendency towards increased order and interrelated complexity in all that exists, a *syntropy* in counterbalance to entropy (Rogers, 1980, p 124–6). The *Actualising Tendency* is an integral property of all life forms, a particular manifestation of the Formative Tendency, which consists in a developmental capacity of the organism to grow towards more of what it can become, to manifest its potential in relationship to its environment (Rogers, 1961, p. 351). Like Jung, Rogers recognised that this positive growth tendency can be impeded or thwarted, especially by adverse environmental conditions. In human terms, such adversity might be environmental, as in poverty or disease, or relational in terms of negative aspects of parenting and other close relationships, peer group and the wider culture, to the extent that these impose negative constraints on the individual's healthy development.

The wisdom of the organism

Rogers suggests that a person is much more than their intellect and beliefs, but is rather a complex combination of internal and external dispositions, involving intellect, emotion and a 'gut' or visceral level of awareness, which together amount to the individual *organism*, or *organismic self*. The focal point in awareness of this self is the internal *locus of evaluation*, the person's access to the wisdom of their organism at whatever point they have reached in their development (Rogers, 1951, pp. 149–50). Such awareness may not be comprehensively reliable for a variety of reasons, but it is nevertheless the best wisdom available to the person at that point, subject to further development. One of the main sources of mistaken judgements by the person derive from the developmental adverse conditions to which we have referred, by which the person's integrity of valuing has become impaired to a greater or lesser extent by the intrusion or *introjection* of values and beliefs derived from external authorities (significant others) and which are at variance with the individual's internal integrity or organismic valuing (Rogers, 1951). The process of becoming a person (cf. Jung's *Individuation*) through therapy and other relationships and the life process, involves sifting and separating the inauthentic sources of value from the authentic, and growing towards a greater integrity of being, termed *Congruence*, i.e. an accurate matching of the data from the person's internal and external environment with their perception and understanding of it, and in turn their responding to it.

For Rogers, the Self is not a primarily a structure or fixed set of beliefs or response, but essentially a continuous process of awareness and responding, and is itself only a component of the wider organism (Rogers in Evans, 1975, p. 16) (cf. the self in Buddhism). The concept of the experiencing self does not deny the reality of the individual's *self-concept*, which is the structured awareness of the person's history, likes and dislikes, dispositions and relationships etc., but insofar as this is a somewhat fixed conceptual system and may well contain introjections, it is not likely to do justice, either conceptually or experientially, to the person's authentic organismic awareness, if this can be accessed. In a nutshell, in this view, the person is 'who they are becoming' moment by moment, even more than who they have been or even consider themselves to be. Again this resonates with Buddhist thought.

Restoring participation

Carl Rogers' theory of psychotherapy and counselling rests on a triad or trinity of three 'necessary and sufficient *Core Conditions*' of the therapeutic relationship (or six in their full statement, but the three mentioned here are the most commonly used summary): *Empathy*, *Genuiness* and *Unconditional Positive Regard*. In terms of relationship with the natural environment, one of these – empathy – may be considered to be of greater significance. Empathy in human relationships is understood to be the capacity to enter into the emotional life of another person and experience their world *as if* one was that person (but without losing the 'as if' distinction, i.e. this does not amount to *identification*). When communicated appropriately, such empathy may be recognised by the other with relief and positive feeling, such as 'Yes! That's just how it feels/I feel.'

When deep empathy occurs, the empathiser may feel so close to the other person's inner life as to anticipate what they are about to say, even before they become aware of it themselves. This can be like a very real interpersonal communion. Such experience is not, of course, limited to therapists and therapy. Many human beings are naturally empathic, and intimate relationships can also foster this kind of closeness of feeling. But empathy extends beyond interpersonal relationships. We have earlier referred to *unitive consciousness*, one of whose major dimensions is the sense of being connected to others, including other creatures and the natural world. Many dog-owners experience a sense that their dogs recognise how they feel, and respond to them accordingly, and vice versa, and many people, gazing into the eyes of another creature, can feel a sense of the presence of a consciousness like our own – as well as at other times one which is extremely different. Rupert Sheldrake has written about the evidence for animal and plant consciousness (Sheldrake, 2003), and Tony Rose, one of the contributors to this volume, has written about encounters with animals – 'epiphanies' – which have had a transformative effect (Rose, 1998/2006, pp. 15–32), and Allan Hamilton similarly with regard to consciousness in horses (Hamilton, 2011).

Many of the accounts of spiritual experience in nature contain this sense of *empathic connection* and lead to a desire to care for nature and our fellow creatures. In this sense we are describing the opposite and contrasting pole of attitude from that of detachment and manipulation without regard for the being of the other. If we turn the direction of travel the other way, we might suggest that developing empathy training in the education system, together with opportunities for direct and intimate encounters with the natural world and its creatures (of which there are burgeoning numbers of retreats and workshops under the general heading of 'eco-therapy'), would make less likely a destructive attitude, and more likely an attitude of care and respect towards them.

The goal of development

This line of thought in relation to the development of empathy is one part of a wider potential agenda with regard to the integration of human 'ways of knowing' to include more regard for the emotional, physical and intuitive/spiritual faculties. At the very point where our behaviour as a species seems to exemplify the most destructive capacity for ruthlessly despoiling our planet, we could also be in sight of better ways of being and becoming, ones which offer tremendous benefits and riches of greater awareness and connectedness, but also of respectful and caring stewardship of our world and its creatures. The crisis is also an opportunity and an occasion for growing into what we have it in us to become. An important dimension of what is being suggested here is that it is not the case that human beings need to learn something new, previously unknown or strange to us, but rather that we need to regain that sense of connection which is the deepest truth of our being, and do so with all the faculties available to us.

A wider epistemology?

The human intellectual endeavour seems presently trapped between the two poles of, on the one hand, an empiricism and rationalism which denies, devalues and excludes the inner and subjective dimension of awareness, and on the other a postmodernism which undermines the truth claims of any discourse such as religion and spirituality as being no more than 'merely' personal and subjective: a rock and a hard place indeed! I recognise that postmodernism has been superseded by other modernisms and directions which others are better equipped than I to evaluate. But my central aim is to ask whether there might be a better version of an epistemology which can respect empirical truth and avoid claims to any absolute truth while yet embracing and affirming the subjective dimension of human experience, and indeed suggesting ways to evaluate its validity and discriminate between its different claims to truth telling?

We have so many accounts, down through the ages and into present times, of the religious and spiritual experience of very many individuals, and some of these have developed into traditions, schools and religious faiths. There has usually been a healthy caution within these movements, about accepting each and every claim by an individual to have had a divine or other revelation. Such claims are sifted carefully as to their credibility, and with good reason. The discernment process usually involves checking as to whether a given account is consistent with what has been previously understood by way of sacred texts, teaching and tradition, and is credible in terms of content and meaning. (It is still possible that an individual can bring a claim to a new revelation which is a challenge to traditional understandings. The discernment process in such instances may be longer, more complex and potentially contentious: the debates in the Christian churches about the ordination of women, and sexuality, are recent examples. But as long as open debate is permitted progress can be made, and what was once considered unorthodox and unacceptable may become accepted.)

I would suggest that this kind of model of a process of discernment of the truth claims by individuals to a personal and often interior revelation can be seen to offer a reasonable approach to a wider exploration of the truth claims of subjective experience. In a way it compares well with the scientific approach, which also requires extensive testing and review of truth claims against established theories and practice, and in the case of paradigm shift may be comparably contentious.

A further perspective on subjective truth claims can be provided by those who spend their professional lives listening and responding to individual's expression of their concerns in counselling and therapy. There was an earlier reference to the wider person-centred statement of *Core Conditions* amounting to six. In this fuller statement these include the condition for therapy that the client or person receiving therapy is in a state of *incongruence* while the counsellor is in a state of congruence, that is the client is struggling with a disparity between their conscious and deeper selves – which is the focus of therapy – while the counsellor is accurately self-aware in the relationship. In my experience the disciplined development of professional and personal congruence and awareness over a lifetime enhances one's discernment with regard to one's own and others' shared experience. It is that combination of a capacity for deep empathy together with congruent self-awareness which makes it so.

Carl Rogers wrote that when an individual is most personal they are simultaneously likely to be speaking universally (Rogers, 1961, p. 26). I have frequently been present in multi-lingual groups where an individual may be sharing something deeply personal with feeling in a language only shared by a minority of the group, and yet is somehow understood – and empathised with – by everyone. At such times the group relationship has transcended barriers of language and separation. These are some of the experiences which I believe should be researched further.

Conclusion

The aim of this chapter has been to argue for embracing the subjective dimension of human awareness, especially as regards the spiritual dimension, both for its own sake and for the perspective it can bring to the environmental crisis and our sense of interconnectedness with each other and the natural world. It has been suggested that our extent of alienation from the world and each other, whereby we prefer the mastery and exploitative approach to that of nurture and respect, corresponds to an extent of alienation from our own selves as physical and spiritual beings. This leads to the inference that one vital step in our restoration of proper relationship with the natural world can be encouraged by a psychotherapeutic approach to learning to listen to ourselves, others and the world with deep empathy and indeed love, and to bring our corresponding congruence to the table of intellectual engagement. If I am right, this presents a better chance that we will engage with a profound psycho-spiritual process of development which will lead us (back and also forward) as worthy participants of the well-becoming universe.

Biographical note

Jeff Leonardi is a person-centred counsellor, supervisor, trainer and spiritual companion, and a retired Anglican priest who was for 17 years Bishop's Adviser for Pastoral Care and Counselling in the Lichfield Diocese of the Church of England. He has been a qualified person-centred counsellor for the past forty years, and has a PhD in the spirituality of person-centred counselling in relation to Christian spirituality, and the implications for Christian ministry and pastoral practice. He is an Honorary Research Fellow of the Religious Experience Research Centre at the University of Wales Trinity St David at Lampeter, undertaking research into relational spirituality.

Bibliography

Alfeyev, Bishop Hilarion. 2002. *The Mystery of Faith*. London: Darton, Longman and Todd.
Barfield, O. 1988. *Saving the Appearances: A Study in Idolatry*. Barfield Press UK, 3rd edition, 2011.
Berry, T. 2009. *The Sacred Universe*. Columbia: Columbia University Press.
Briggs Myers, I. and Myers, P.B. 1995 [1980]. *Gifts Differing: Understanding Personality Type*. Mountain View, CA: Davies-Black Publishing.
Delio, I., ed. 2014. *From Teilhard to Omega: Co-creating an Unfinished Universe*. New York: Orbis Books.
Evans, R.I. 1975. *Carl Rogers: The Man and His Ideas*. New York: Dutton.
Hamilton, A.J. 2008. *The Scalpel and the Soul: Encounter with Surgery, the Supernatural, and the Healing Power of Hope*. New York: Jeremy P.Tarcher/Putnam.
Hamilton, A.J. 2011. *Zen Mind Zen Horse*. North Adams: Storey.
Hardy, A. 1979. *The Spiritual Nature of Man*. Oxford: Clarendon Press.
Hay, D. 1982. *Exploring Inner Space: Is God Still Possible in the Twentieth Century?* Oxford: Mowbray.
Hay, D. 1990. *Religious Experience Today: Studying the Facts*. Oxford: Mowbray.
Jung, C.G. 1921. *Psychological Types*. (London: Routledge, 1971)
Jung, C.G. 1959a. *Collected Works* vol. 9.I, 'The Concept of the Collective Unconscious' [1936]. Abingdon: Routledge.
Jung, C.G. 1959b. Vol.8 *The Structure and Dynamics of the Psyche*.

Jung, C.G. 1959c. *The Face to Face Interview in C.G. Jung Speaking: Interviews and Encounters*. Princeton: Bollingen Paperbacks [1977], pp. 424–439.
Jung, C.G. 1959d. *Letter to Valentine Brooke in C.G. Jung Letters, Volume 2, 1951–1961*, edited by Gerhard Adler. London: Routledge and Kegan Paul, pp. 520–523.
Jung, C.G. 1964. *Man and His Symbols*. New York: Doubleday.
Leonardi, J. 2010. *The Human Being Fully Alive: Writings in Celebration of Brian Thorne*. Ross-on-Wye: PCCS Books.
Leonardi, J. 2020. The Christian Understanding of the Body. In: Schmidt, B. and Leonardi, J., eds., *Spirituality and Well-being*. Sheffield: Equinox.
McGilchrist, I. 2009. *The Master and His Emissary: The Divided Brain and the Making of the Western World*. Newhaven and London: Yale.
Pahnke, W.N. 1963. *Drugs and Mysticism: An Analysis of the Relationship between Psychedelic Drugs and the Mystical Consciousness*. PhD Thesis, Harvard University.
Rogers, C.R. 1951. *Client-Centred Therapy*. Boston: Houghton Mifflin.
Rogers, C.R. 1961. *On Becoming a Person: A Therapist's View of Psychotherapy*. Boston Houghton Mifflin; 1974, London: Constable.
Rogers, C.R. 1980. *A Way of Being*. New York: Houghton Mifflin.
Rohr, R. 2011. *Falling Upward: A Spirituality for the Two Halves of Life*. San Francisco: Wiley.
Rohr, R. 2013. *Immortal Diamond: The Search for Our True Self*. London: SPCK.
Rose, A.L. 1998/2006. On Tortoises, Monkeys, and Men. In: Solisti, K., Tobias, M., eds. *Kinship with the Animals*: Updated edition. San Francisco: Council Oak Books.
Sands, F. 1955. Men, Women and God: An Interview with Frederick Sands – Part 5: I Believe in God (Daily Mail). In: Heisig, J.W. 1979. *Imago Dei: A Study of C.G. Jung's Psychology of Religion*. London: Associated University Presses, p. 90.
Sheldrake, R., 2003. *The Sense of Being Stared At: And Other Aspects of the Extended Mind*. London: Random House.
Snow, C.P. 1959. *The Two Cultures and the Scientific Revolution*. Oxford: OUP.
Spearing, A., trans. 2001. *The Cloud of Unknowing and Other Works*. Harmondsworth: Penguin.
St Francis of Assisi. 2015. *The Little Flowers of St Francis of Assisi*. Victoria: Leopold Press.
Stace W.T., 1960. *Mysticism and Philosophy*. Philadelphia, PA: J.B. Lippincott.
Teilhard de Chardin, P. 1965. *Hymn of the Universe*. London: Collins.
Teresa of Avila, trans. Fr Benedict Zimmerman 2007. *The Interior Castle*. New York: Cosimo.
Williams, R. 1979. *The Wound of Knowledge*. London: Darton,Longman & Todd.
Woollacott, M. and Lorimer, D. 2022. *Spiritual Awakenings: Scientists and Academics Describe Their Experiences*. Tucson: AAPS Press.

2 Connecting with nature and spiritual experience

John Reader

Introduction

This chapter will examine the proposition that current attempts to reconnect with nature have the potential to be stepping stones to spiritual experience. In order to do so it will look at examples of attempts at reconnection but also at some of the more theoretical ideas that are relevant to this. I take as the spur to the project an unlikely quote from the film 'Casablanca'. In an exchange between Ilsa and Rick she asks if he remembers their time together in Paris at the moment when the German troops were entering the city. His response is: 'The Germans wore grey; you wore blue.' Innocent enough, but making it clear that his attention at that moment was less upon the military invasion and its consequences and more upon Ilsa, their relationship and what she was wearing. I will suggest that the key to the proposition lies in the focus of attention in any particular instance, and that both the practical examples and theoretical arguments substantiate this idea.

Two disclaimers are required before we begin the examination in detail. The first is that many of the examples emerge from what are now non-religious sources, even though they might stem from older spiritual traditions. One must beware of appearing to colonise these by claiming them for religion when that is not their explicit intention. The question of how to interpret and understand such practices is addressed later in the chapter. The other thing that needs to be pointed out is that even when such practices are followed it doesn't necessarily lead to appropriate or adequate practical responses in terms of environmental action. One must be careful to separate the spiritual from the environmental in the sense that the first must not be evaluated by judging whether or not there are direct and quantifiable practical outcomes. If those occur then that is all the better, but that is not the ultimate objective from a religious point of view, that being the relationship with God, or the divine.

To give an example of this possible disconnection one only needs to look at the work of the Royal Society for the Protection of Birds (RSPB); its levels of support over against its overall impact. January each year is the occasion for the Big Garden Birdwatch in the UK, which takes place over a weekend and invites anyone to make a note of the species they can spot, record them and then report the numbers to the RSPB. As 2023 begins, the fear is that this will see a 'Silent Spring' (echoing Rachel Carson's famous book of the 1960s) as not just the UK but the world generally is being devastated by avian flu, with the full impact yet to become clear. Despite the supposed interest in birds and the numbers who are now members of the RSPB, the state of the nation in terms of birdlife continues to decline at a disturbing rate. According to Macdonald, the RSPB has undergone an explosion in numbers (2019, p. 238). In 1972 it had 100,000 members but eight years later this had tripled. In 1997 the membership had passed the 1 million mark and the organisation was playing an increasing role both purchasing sites and lobbying government. With over 200 nature reserves across the country it is now the largest nature charity in Europe. Yet despite its successes reintroducing certain species: 'Britain has experienced the worst bird declines, faces the most prospects of bird extinction, and suffers the most degraded landscapes and smallest natural areas on the continent' (p. 238). The explanations for this and proposed remedies lie beyond the scope of this chapter, but the figures illustrate that numerical support but does not easily translate into appropriate environmental action. One must not assume then that, even with a spiritual dimension to back this up, it would lead to the turnaround in action required to address even this one set of issues. Spiritual experience – and I now use that phrase advisedly rather than 'environmental spirituality' as I want it to embrace fully all dimensions of creation not simply the animate nonhuman – is not in itself the solution to the major problems we face as societies and as a species. It may contribute, but that is not the focus of this exercise. We begin by looking at another recent example of reconnecting with nature.

Forest bathing

One impact of the pandemic and especially as a response to the various lockdowns appears to have been a renewed interest in accessing the great outdoors. An example of this is 'forest bathing'. In an article posted on the Heart of England Forest website on 30 July 2020 advice was offered about the benefits of forest bathing, of which the crucial claim was that being in nature makes us feel better. At one level this is a marketing ploy for the Heart of England Forest, but one assumes there is validity in the claim judging from general experience. At what stage, though, and under what circumstances might this become a spiritual experience? The origins of the practice have a spiritual root, but does this mean that current attempts to reproduce this in a very different context can make the same claim? Having walked round part of the Forest with one of the older members of staff who had worked across this area for many years and heard his sceptical comments about the latest middle-class fad, compared with his twice daily practice of walking the same stretch of land over many years and noting the variations from day to day and sometimes hour to hour, one wonders how deep forest bathing really goes and whether it will outlive the lockdowns?

From an environmental perspective one could question the practice as being solely focused on human wellbeing and apparently not giving attention to the environment in its own right. One could, however, from the opposite perspective, question whether the concern for human spirituality is likely to be determined by environmental concerns once the focus becomes 'the natural world'? What needs to be explored is the relationship between the human and the nonhuman of 'nature'. What exactly do we understand by 'nature' and, indeed, what do we mean by 'spirituality'. This chapter will aim to deepen our understanding of this relationship.

Spirituality

I take my guidance on what is meant by spirituality from the following definitions offered by Jeff Leonardi as my fellow co-editor of this book. First, spirituality refers to a level or dimension of experiencing, which overlaps with the common sense and the everyday, but which is distinctive, special and seems to connect with a wider or higher level of awareness and being. Second, spirituality is fundamentally relational. This may include a sense of the presence of, and relationship with, the divine or transcendent. Then spiritual experience tends to convey a sense of profound meaning and purpose and connectedness with creation, life and other human beings, and a corresponding sense of responsibility for one's own part in it all. Spiritual experience tends to confirm the value of the subject, and, by extension, all other human beings. Finally, in spiritual experience, the senses, feelings, imagination and intuition are all equally important, alongside thought and interpretation (definitions taken from Leonardi, 2008, p. 22 and Schmidt and Leonardi, 2020, p. 2). Beginning from these criteria we then need to examine how nature is currently understood in order to reveal the tensions and limitations of a straightforward equation of the interest in reconnecting with nature with spiritual experience.

Slowing down

Another perspective on this can be found in the work of the philosopher of science, Isabelle Stengers (2018, pp. 80–82). She suggests that slowness, like speed, has a meaning which links researchers to all those who know that the imperatives of flexibility and competitiveness condemn them to destruction.

The stakes inherent in such destruction may evoke the period of enclosures, when peasant communities were not only robbed of vital resources but also what held them together. With the commons privatised, what was destroyed was practical know-how, along with collective ways of acting, thinking, feeling and living. In other words, an attitude which more closely represents a different relationship with the natural world has been lost as a result of these developments. She argues that if capitalism today seems to be getting on very well with modern States it is because both are rooted in this kind of destruction. The democratic individual, the one who says 'It's my right', is the one who takes great pride in an 'autonomy' which, in fact, hands back to the State the responsibility for thinking through the consequences. Stengers is talking about the ways in which scientists avoid engaging in the 'big questions', the ethical consequences of their research, on the basis that this is for others to undertake. However, it could also link to the idea of disinhibition, which is the attitude which discourages critical reflection on the implications of one's actions. If it can be done then it is fine to do it, irrespective of the consequences: that will be someone else's problem to sort out. So both environmental and digital spheres are allowed to develop without due thought of constraints or limits. This is a wider cultural problem. A strange liberty it is not to have to think further than one's own immediate interests. As for capitalism, it is running free in a world exposed to its redefinitions, all of which intensify our dependency on modes of production that presuppose and entail, as with the enclosures, a form of 'progress' that destroys all possibility of collective intelligence.

To speak of destruction is to speak of a resistance that can only exist alongside what American activists call 'reclaiming' – recuperating, healing, becoming capable once again of linking with what we have been separated from. This links to the religious ideas of reimagining, reconnecting, religion as binding together or the opposite of negligence or re-enchanting. This 'recuperation' process begins with the jolting realisation that we are well and truly sick, and have been for a long time, so that we no longer recognise what we are lacking, and think of our sickness, and whatever sustains it as 'normal'. What Stengers has tried to do, in the particular case of scientific research and evaluation, is to start thinking about what is lacking, about the way this lack makes us sick. We may well be critical and lucid, but we are crucially incapable of resisting what is destroying us.

According to Stengers knowing that one is sick creates a sense of the possible. It is a matter of unlearning an attitude of more or less cynical (realist) resignation, and becoming sensitive again to what we perhaps know, but only as in a dream. It is here that the word 'slow', as used in the slow movements, is potentially important. Speed demands and creates an insensitivity to everything that might slow things down: the frictions, the rubbing, the hesitations that make us feel we are not alone in the world. Slowing down means becoming capable of learning again, becoming acquainted with things again, reweaving the bounds of interdependency. It means thinking and imagining, and in the process creating relationships with others that are not those of capture. It means, therefore, creating among us and with others the kind of relation that works for sick people, people who need each other in order to learn – with others, from others, thanks to others – what a life worth living demands, and the knowledges that are worth cultivating.

Stengers therefore helpfully identifies themes central to our concern. The disconnection with nature that has developed over time and particularly the recent role of science in that process is a major one. This includes the influence of digital technology as used to mediate our relationship with nature. Then she highlights the suggestion that until or unless we can recognise the sickness that stems from this approach we are unlikely to seek the reconnections which might lead to a different attitude and instead focus our attention on the damage we are doing to nature. Essential to this is an awareness that humans are always already fully entangled with the natural world rather than seeing ourselves as distinct and exercising external control. Slowing down, paying attention to, and simply being in the presence of, in ways that sound similar to forms of meditation might then be stepping stones to a deeper level of awareness.

Regenerative agriculture or agroecology

Another potential example of reconnecting with nature but this time on a more commercial level is that of regenerative agriculture. Writing on his experience as an RSPB warden in a Lake District project Lee Schofield (2022) reports that this is an approach where farmers and conservationists are in apparent agreement. With soil health as its primary goal, this is now gaining traction amongst farmers in the area. What rewilding is to conservation, regenerative agriculture is to farming. At the heart of this is the concept of rest – a link perhaps to Stenger's proposal of slowing down? – hence a break from grazing can repair damaged soils and deliver benefits both to the environment and to farm businesses. Interspersing grazing with rest appears to be even better for soils than simply rest alone. Grazing is after all a natural process and can benefit other living organisms such as fungi, insects, plants and also other animals. This will take slightly different forms according to the actual landscape and local ecology. It is also much more in line with what were traditional farming practices, which would move livestock around on a fairly regular basis rather than risking overgrazing particular locations and would also happen where there were smaller fields rather than the massive ones created by removing hedgerows.

Regenerative Agriculture describes farming and grazing practices that, among other benefits, reverse climate change by rebuilding soil organic matter and restoring degraded soil biodiversity – resulting in both carbon drawdown and improving the water cycle. Specifically it is a holistic land management practice that leverages the power of photosynthesis in plants to close the carbon cycle, and build soil health, crop resilience and nutrient density. Regenerative agriculture improves soil health, primarily through the practices that increase soil organic matter. This not only aids in increasing soil biota diversity and health, but increases biodiversity both above and below the soil surface, while increasing both water holding capacity and sequestering carbon at greater depths, thus drawing down climate-damaging levels of atmospheric CO_2, and improving soil structure to reverse civilisation-threatening human-caused soil loss. Research continues to reveal the damaging effects to soil from tillage, applications of agricultural chemicals and salt-based fertilisers, and carbon mining. Regenerative Agriculture reverses this paradigm to build for the future. Regenerative Agricultural Practices are: practices that (i) contribute to generating/building soils and soil fertility and health; (ii) increase water percolation, water retention, and clean and safe water runoff; (iii) increase biodiversity and ecosystem health and resiliency; and (iv) invert the carbon emissions of our current agriculture to one of remarkably significant carbon sequestration, thereby cleansing the atmosphere of legacy levels of CO_2.

A farmer in North Dakota who is now pursuing this approach argues that this requires focusing and working for change on 'common ground for the common good' (*Farmers Weekly*, 16 September 2022). In other words, this is of benefit to the wider community as well as to the individual farm and, of course, the land itself. The barriers which may prevent others switching to this means of production are peer pressure; an education gap, and then the thin profit margins associated with it. Each of these can be overcome by changing the attitude to the natural world and working in greater harmony with the land and its natural rhythms and cycles. In that sense this represents an attempt to reconnect with nature.

Forest schools

Anyone of my generation who encounters the concept of a Forest School might ask how the practice differs from what we might have been brought up with at primary school as Nature Walks. Is it simply a matter of spending time outdoors – in the countryside if one is lucky enough to be so located – and paying attention to and learning about the natural world? The current movement, however, is more complicated than that.

It began in Sweden in the 1950s and is now gaining popularity as a means of enhancing various aspects of child development. The documentation available refers to developing such skills as concentration, coordination and indeed intellectual attainment. It is seen as adding to self-esteem, wellbeing and emotional intelligence as well as providing skills such as building fires and more general countryside requirements. There are links to other areas of the curriculum such as maths and English as the whole experience can be used as the basis for what is argued to be a holistic approach to child development. All of this is highly commendable from an educational perspective but it does raise other interesting questions. For instance: is this a means of establishing what is a purely instrumental approach to nature (or the nonhuman)? Is it a means to an end rather than viewing the natural world as having an intrinsic value? If this is the case, how does it link to other projects which would aim to go beyond this and to build an understanding of a much deeper relationship to the nonhuman and indeed to God? What does such an approach say about our contemporary culture and the removal of humans from their wider environment which has to be reversed or challenged by such means? Are we now so detached from the natural world that this process of re-engagement becomes vital for an understanding of ourselves?

Once one begins to examine the project in proper detail there are so many other issues in play: those of buildings, land ownership, finance, parental choice, government educational policy, legal requirements, let alone the questions of child development and the more obviously environmental ones as above. What Latour, whose work we examine in a later section, highlights is the need to reassemble all the different components of what appears to be a straightforward project in order to make decisions, in addition to establishing some ethical evaluation of the whole. This is characteristic of any serious matter of concern and requires of those involved close attention to detail and an understanding of the complexities entailed. Once again, we might question whether and in what circumstances this practice might lead to a spiritual experience.

Mediating nature through digital technology

A more recent development associated with reconnecting with nature is the use of digital devices to assist in this task. For this reason I would argue that a spirituality of the environment which fully encapsulates the various constituents of the environment should also address a new area which could be termed a spirituality of the digital. In due course I will draw upon the work of Latour in order to begin this process and to raise questions of the relationship between the human and the nonhuman which now take account of the nonhuman as artificial or human-produced. A few examples must suffice to illustrate and support this claim.

BBC's 'Countryfile' has produced a list of the ways in which digital devices are being deployed to engage with the natural world. One obvious area is that of the identification of species. Armed with the appropriate app, one is in a better position to recognise what one encounters as there is instant access to the relevant data. In the old days one might have carried a book and notebook to record sightings, but now these can be replaced by an app which tells you what you need to know and enables you to record a sighting. A further application is that of maps. Instead of carrying a paper copy around, it can all be accessed on one's smartphone, either by Google Maps or a dedicated website devised for the purpose. Environmental organisations as well as tourist guides now operate in this way. Gaming is apparently another means of connecting us with nature through the digital, with even games such as Pokémon Go encouraging people to get out into the countryside to discover its delights and assets.

Virtual reality is now also more readily available, whether one is talking about the Metaverse or some other equivalent. Rather than simply the two-dimensional experience of the TV screen, one can have a fully immersive one instead by entering the space as one's avatar. This in itself raises important theological and philosophical issues that I have addressed elsewhere (Reader, 2023), those relating to the problematic claims of a full presence associated with such devices. Then there are Nature Networks available, in which one can participate online as part of a virtual community, and also the possibility of writing and reading the blogs that can be produced. Last but not least are the digital cameras, which now make for more effective and even possibly less intrusive access to observe wildlife in closer detail. One is aware that there are Nature Finder apps; apps for bug counting and also apps for identifying birds and birdsongs. One can assume that people will increasingly engage with nature through these devices simply because they are available and effective. An underlying question, though, is what happens to the relationship between humans and the natural world when it is mediated through the digital. Is it the same as the direct contact which was the norm previously, and what is gained and what is lost in the process? How might this influence or shape the spirituality of the environment? These questions need to be addressed.

Nature/body dualisms

One possible way of beginning to address these questions is to articulate the dualisms that might underpin an approach to nature mediated through the digital which itself assumes a distinction between nature and one's own embodied existence. This relates to the binary or dualism of physis (nature) and techne (the technological or human-created) which is central to the issue to a spirituality of both environment and the digital. When direct contact or engagement is no longer the norm, does this not make the efforts to reconnect more problematic? One can see below some of the possible dimensions of this the dualism between self and the body.

When either or both nature and one's body are treated as external or inert one encounters the following approaches.

Nature/body	Response
Enemy/threat	to be defeated.
Obstacle	to be overcome.
Partner	to work with.
Home	space to retreat and be safe.
Beauty	to be admired or viewed.
Playground	to be enjoyed.
Resource	to be exploited.
Entangled	to cooperate with.
Mystery	to be explored.
Environment	to be protected.
Creation	to be respected
Other	to be feared.
Female	to be controlled
Subjective	to be analysed, measured and directed accordingly.
Mechanism	to be manipulated.

This leads us to question the term 'nature' as possibly representing this dualistic approach.

Questioning 'nature'

According to the ecofeminist Elvey (2023), when applied to 'nature', homogenisation and stereotyping entail a denial of the complexity of nature, of the difference within nature and of human continuity with nature. In this regard the word 'nature' is problematic in itself, as a generalising term which masks differences between the many constituents of Earth and cosmos, species, kinds, ecosystems, galaxies and so on. Because a system of mastery fails to account for the multiple more-than-human others on which the master depends, it will collapse, since it neglects and/or denies the things which sustain the 'master'. This leads to a suspicion of any spirituality which rests upon a framework of a nature-body or matter-spirit dualism. Hence the binaries of nature and body, and indeed physis and techne need to be brought into question. Elvey agrees with Plumwood, who writes of ' achieving more earth-friendly and counter-hegemonic forms of spirituality' that honour 'the material and ecological bases of life'. Such a spirituality will be 'counter-centric in affirming continuity and kinship for earth others as well as their subjecthood, opacity and agency. It will be dialogical, communicative, open to the play of more-than-human forces and attentive to the ancestral voices of place and of earth' (pp. 89–90).

As will be described in the following section, in Latour's terms, how does one describe and negotiate the human-nonhuman relationships which are at the heart of this? What is, or should be, the relationship between nature and culture, physis and techne?

To refer to an anti-Christian source, Jeremy Lent's *The Web of Meaning* (2021), an ontological dualism goes back to Plato with his division between an eternal, divine dimension, and a changeable, polluted, worldly one. This was adopted by Christianity and recast by Descartes who substituted mind for soul. 'Dualism rejects the existence of animate consciousness, upholding human identity as residing solely in conceptual consciousness, sees an inherent distinction between the material and the spiritual, and perceives a fundamental separation between humanity and nature, which is viewed as a mere mechanical resource for exploitation' (p. 389). He proposes instead an integrative intelligence, weaving together the conceptual and the animate, permitting humans to access the deep wisdom of the natural world for the benefit of human and nonhuman flourishing. This is an attractive proposition, but can Christianity in fact establish common ground with such an approach?

Reconnecting with nature – or not

In *The Science Delusion* (2013) Rupert Sheldrake sets out the argument that science risks developing into 'scientism' based on certain uncritically accepted assumptions which he then proceeds to critique in turn. One of these is that 'nature' is essentially mechanical and thus all matter (including the human) lacks inner life and subjectivity (p. 7). Whether or not one agrees with this diagnosis it is certainly the case that one impact of the Enlightenment has been to separate the worlds of technology, science and reason (techne) from that of nature (physis). Romanticism reacted against this and rejected the mechanical metaphors being used and replaced them instead with the imagery of nature as organic and alive. As a result there is a sort of split personality or what the philosopher Whitehead called the bifurcation of nature (1920, pp. 29–31) As Sheldrake says:

> The living world is celebrated in poems and songs and in works of art. Nature is most strongly identified with the countryside, as opposed to cities, and especially by unspoilt wilderness. Many urban people dream of moving to the country or having a weekend home in rural surroundings. On Friday evenings, cities of the Western world are clogged with traffic as millions of people try to get back to nature in a car. (p. 39).

Sheldrake wrote this before the pandemic, since when his comments become even more apposite and the trends towards moving out of cities and into the country have become more prevalent. Working from home or operating hybrid with less commuting and travelling are now features of this new world, alongside a new movement which one might call attempting to reconnect with nature. Is this still, however, another symptom of Whitehead's bifurcation and the split personality rather than a genuine move to restore an earlier relationship between physis and techne, between the world of 'nature' and that of the largely mechanical and rationally determined worlds of commerce and science? Is it anything other than a nostalgic romanticism which has no impact upon the rest of life? Is there another way of understanding how humans relate to and operate in both of these worlds that leads to a genuine restoration or perhaps new form of relationship?

One means of doing this is to examine more closely what is understood by techne, and for that I turn to *The Marvelous Clouds* by John Durham Peters

(2015). He suggests that the notion that technology is inhuman has a long lineage (p. 88). Since the ancient Greeks and Hebrews there has been a view that technics marks the expulsion from the presence of gods. When paradise was lost, people had to live by their wits, tools and tactics. There is a danger in subsequent discourse that when one talks about technology, the role of humans in the processes of development and application is underplayed.

> The denunciation of 'technological determinism' in the name of popular agency, however, not only underestimates the power of devices but also overestimates the power of people...... The claim that technologies should be subject to humans portrays our wills as immaterial and disembedded, as if we were not already networked creatures, and if matter were blank nothingness. (pp. 88–89)

It suggests that our actions and intentions are transparent to ourselves when invariably they are not, and fails to acknowledge that our bodies are technical systems as strange and mysterious as any of the technical devices we use. The nature of our agency as human beings is a question we should answer rather than a fact we should assume. In other words, things can be alive and people can be machines, so however we choose to represent these worlds as distinct and separate, they are always already messily interconnected and entangled. As Peters says, the challenge is to rethink technology as constitutive of the human being without providing Silicon Valley with one more marketing argument (p. 90).

Latour and the nonhuman

The philosopher who has done most to take this argument forward is Bruno Latour, best known for his work on the environment in recent years and up to his death, but also concerned with how better to interpret and describe the relationship between physis and techne, and the detail of the attachments between them.

As Latour has shown throughout his work in Science Studies, it is the intricate and intimate detail of these attachments that is the reality of how science, politics and other areas of human life become interwoven and connected (Latour, 2007). Science, technology and what we call nature are more closely related than ever before and yet there is still this paradoxical attempt to tear them apart as if this constituted some form of progress. A further consequence of this that is also damaging to efforts to incorporate the pre-autonomous and ethical dimensions into political debate on environmental issues is that humans and nonhumans are treated as if they must be pulled apart and kept in separate worlds. By pre-autonomous I mean that which occurs at a subjective or pre-reflective level even before one is consciously aware of what is happening – the moment of eye contact which begins a relationship for instance. This category of human thinking and experience is to be separated from other categories such as the rational and post-autonomous (Reader, 2005).

What needs to be recognised, by contrast, is that the complexity, confusion and entanglement which invariably occurs as a consequence of the unforeseen effects of human activity, is precisely what is to be expected and requires constant monitoring and response. It is the interventions, the wanting things to be different and the caring for all that is happening, that have to be taken up into the political debates and turned into action. As Latour says, however, we seem to lack the appropriate emotions and attitudes which would allow this to flourish. We lack the mental, moral, aesthetic and emotional resources to follow through on the attachments. At this point in the argument he turns to an unexpected source for a model of how to counter this.

Latour examines the strange connections between mastery, technology and theology. Drawing on the Frankenstein myth he concludes that the sin involved in the story was not that of the creation of this strange creature, but when the Creator abandoned the creature to itself. So it is this failure to follow through, to keep faith with our creations and attachments, which needs to be brought into question. It is not technology itself, but the absence of love for the technology we have created, as if we had decided that we were unable to follow through with the education of our own children. To imagine that emancipation from or distancing from creation is an accurate reflection of what the Christian God is about is surely a gross misrepresentation, as this is a God who gets folded into, implicated with and incarnated into His Creation. If this is mastery, then it is very different from an understanding which presents a detached form of autonomy or power. Latour concludes that what we should be working towards is a politics of things in which humans are entangled, involved, implicated and indeed incarnated. In language that he uses elsewhere, this requires an assembling and reassembling of the human and the nonhuman which takes into account all the different dimensions of human subjectivity, the pre-autonomous, the autonomous and the transformational.

The whole way of setting up the relationship between agent and structure is misconceived. What is wrong with the term 'actor' is not that it is limited to humans all too often but that it always designates a source of initiative or starting point, the extremity of a vector oriented towards some other end. Instead, one actant making another do something is not to be equated with causing or determining but is the mediating of a relationship. The more attachments or mediations any particular actant has, the better. Emancipation does not therefore mean being made free from bonds, but rather being 'well-attached'. In language that I have used, it is about being blurred, entangled, bundled up and interconnected. Rather than being distanced and detached, one needs to be in proximity to and a companion to all those other components that go to make up a particular gathering or matter of concern.

What this new approach offers to the debate about creating a credible public discourse for the articulation of ethical concerns and moral values so essential if there is to be a politics of life in the current climate, is the insight that instead of detaching or removing from the public square those apparently pre-autonomous dimensions of what it is to be human, they need to be more firmly connected and included in the debates. Without explicit recognition of how these impact upon and relate to what we describe as 'autonomous human action', we are operating with an inadequate and inaccurate understanding of human subjectivity. But this is never the end of the process, only a more promising beginning. Once the myriad of connections is acknowledged and permitted into the circulating references and which form the process of truth formulation, it can be seen that fidelity, conviction, commitment and openness to the novel and unexpected can be catalysts for change. By reassembling the human in this way and allowing for the entanglements that go to make up matters of concern, one can challenge the mantra that 'there is no alternative' and argue that life is indeed open to new possibilities and imaginings.

In a later publication, *An Inquiry Into Modes of Existence*, Latour (2013, Chapter 8) expands his ideas on this and refers to possibilities for a spirituality of technology.

> If the very term ECOLOGIZE is to become an alternative to MODERNIZE we shall need to establish quite different transactions with technological beings...the beings are waiting for the spirit of technique to raise them up. (p. 231)

What Latour provides us with is an alternative way of understanding the relationship between physis and techne, between nature and the entangled subjectivity of humans as always already part of nature.

Dangers or things to be watched and guarded against by taking spiritual practices out of their original religious context

As we have already seen with some of the practices which are an attempt to reconnect with nature, there is a tendency to take them out of their original religious context and so this raises the central question of how and when these might contribute to or be part of a spirituality of the environment. Before I address that directly it is important to identify some of the dangers that might develop from this process. It is also important to note that the same dangers can be true of such practices retained in their religious setting, so this is not a straightforward denial of or critique of the process.

An obvious limitation would be the diminishing or reducing the depth of relationship with the divine. If this is neither an explicit nor implicit objective, then it leaves the question of whether, under any circumstances, a spirituality of the environment could evolve from the practice. I will suggest, however, that this is still possible. Then there is the problem of entering dangerous territory, for instance through meditation without a guide or religious framework with which to support one when deeper feelings emerge. Such a religious framework would involve prayer, for instance, and other resources from faith traditions. Something that is increasingly familiar in the current culture is the use of mindfulness and other similar techniques being employed as a diversion from addressing deeper issues within organisations. Again this could relate to the danger of not being part of a community of fellow travellers in a tradition such as sangha in Buddhism. In that case what is being encountered are commercial interests dominating the process, probably as part of a Human Resources approach. A further tendency is that of syncretism; the pick and mix mélange of different traditions related to uncritically. It is also the case that talk of resilience is being used as a ploy to switch responsibility onto the individual when the real responsibility should be with the collective. As we have already learnt from Elvey, the idea of a hierarchy of spiritual responses or states is to be challenged and probably rejected. Then, of course, there is often the risk of worshipping nature itself rather than God, so a form of pantheism. This is not, however, to be confused with panentheism.

Recognising the dangers of all the above, we now move on to identify ways in which attempts to reconnect with nature might become stepping stones to spiritual experience and the beginnings of a spirituality of the environment, or even of technology.

Folding and the focus of attention

Since one of the ways in which the problem of relating physis to techne is described is Whitehead's 'bifurcation of nature', it is worth looking in more detail at how he attempts to approach this, but as in the interpretation of Stengers (2011). This will enable us to see how the question of focus of attention creates open possibilities for current attempts to reconnect with nature. At one point Whitehead refers to the dualism between body and nature, saying that sometimes we treat the body as purely a part of outer nature, but that at others we think of it as 'mine' and with a different sense of engagement and ownership. This has implications for the spiritual: 'if an event must be said to be spiritual, it is not in the sense that the spirit must be opposed to the body, but in the sense in which the event is opposed to any confusion between the bodily life that passes and what is there once again as an object' (Stengers, 2011, p. 80). These two different senses coexist and are different modalities of experience which, when it comes to nature, are cultivated in divergent and specialised ways. On the one hand there is objective nature, split into objects about which we ask ourselves abstract questions, but, on the other 'spiritual' nature, multiple passages in unison. He takes as an example of the spiritual the expression of another's face, as this is the way that another enters our field of experience in a way that resists any type of objectification. We attend to that person and they become the focus of our gaze and attention but not as an object to be analysed or quantified.

What about nature itself then? The suggestion is that it is neither knowable, definable nor unknowable (Stengers, 2011, p. 106), but rather a 'mute reality' onto which we project human linguistic or social categories. The binary alternative which shapes so much philosophical discussion is fatal for common sense. 'Nature is that about which relevant knowledge may be produced. If we pay due attention to it, we can learn, discern relations, and multiply entities and ratios' (p. 106). So once again, paying attention is central to this relationship and can yield a diversity of responses. This is a pragmatic approach to nature, which acknowledges the validity of both what we see as a scientific response but also what might count as spiritual as they are different modalities and ways of being human. As Stengers goes on to say: '…the concept of nature must be such that nature provides a "foothold" for knowledge, but it must not legitimize any particular form of knowledge, it must not duplicate, by any kind of justification, the empirical fact of the eventual success of certain ways of paying attention' (p. 107). This must always allow for 'more to be discovered' but without predetermining what that might be or attempting to explain it. This feels like a good way of describing how attempts to reconnect with nature that don't have a supposedly spiritual approach could yet yield exactly that.

There is a famous quote from Whitehead which supports this view: 'when you understand all about the sun and all about the atmosphere and all about the rotation of the earth, you may still miss the radiance of the sunset' (Stengers, 2011, p. 140, from Whitehead, 1967). In other words, paying full attention to the phenomenon will yield deeper insights and experiences and it is not that one is more valid than the other, but that a range of different engagements is always possible and one should not rule out any in advance as there is always more to be discovered. As with Rick and Ilsa, what one sees depends upon the focus of one's attention but allowing for the possibility that these limits will be challenged as one pays deeper attention.

Latour, as we have seen, talks about technology as folds upon folds with its implications, complications and entanglements. As I want to address the possibility of a spirituality of technology alongside and in conjunction with a spirituality of the environment, I will suggest that the language of folds provides further resources for understanding how reconnecting with nature can be a stepping stone to such spiritualities. One thing that is clear in this approach is that human agency is to be understood as always already implicated and involved with the nonhuman, that being both the natural and also what might be termed the artificial of the digital. They function as different and often shifting assemblages of activity where the human responds to the nonhuman in creative and unexpected ways. Other possibilities remain open as Whitehead seems keen to point out.

The theologian who also uses the language of folds is Catherine Keller (2015) as she draws upon the work of both Whitehead and the philosopher Deleuze (pp. 168–195). 'It all comes down to folds. Wave folding upon particle, breath into body, hand into hand, melody into ear, seed into dirt, earth into human, violence into trauma, carbon into atmosphere, climate into climatology' (p. 168). The language is inevitably deeply expressive and poetical, but the point is clear enough. This is an ontology or way of understanding existence that refuses strict hierarchies or categorisations but instead opens up different possibilities that may or may not relate to each other directly, but are yet still part of that same reality. 'The fold signifies for Deleuze what we have been calling a nonseparable difference, a relation of difference; the differential relation is not a resemblance or a similarity, not a slide toward sameness' (p. 177). Yet there is a requirement for folding of the one in the other, and, as Latour says, this prevents technology, for instance, being simply a pile or list of one thing on top of another. Humans folded into the digital technologies for which we are responsible and yet which shape us at the same time. We are enfolded and yet capable of unfolding to examine and understand more closely, and then refolded as we move on in conjunction but now in new and creative ways. This refolding might also be the case in our reconnecting with nature, and as our relationship with nature is mediated by and through the digital. This is a dynamic process never fully in the control of an external human agency but only ever as always entangled with those others who go to make up our world. In the midst of this process, who can say that God is not to be encountered or cannot be present whatever the human intentions might be? One cannot say, however, that there is a clear equivalence between the human search, even when it deems itself to be spirituality, and the presence of the divine. The apophatic is that which escapes our perception and remains beyond, somewhere in the folds, and perhaps to be glimpsed only momentarily if at all. It is in the process and the searching and the attending to what emerges that spirituality evolves. This is the case both for our relationship with nature and indeed technology.

The focus of our attention

What remains then is to return to some more folds to see how reconnecting continues to be played out.

Rick and Ilsa offer us an example of the danger of attending only to the most immediate and personal, so wrapped up in their own romance that they are effectively oblivious to what is going on outside them in Paris and beyond. This could be exactly the danger of a spirituality that attends only to the subjective and individual and fails to recognise the threats to nature or creation in theological terms. They are 'fiddling while Paris burns'. How can we be sure that these attempts to reconnect with nature are not simply a cosy and convenient means of attending to the aesthetic dimension of nature, the beauty of the red of the sunset, when what really requires our attention is the destruction of that which we wish to enjoy but take for granted? In a contemporary spirituality where should our attention be focused?

There is no doubt that climate change has become the most high-profile environmental issue in the mind of the general public and one could suggest that it has become a contemporary form of apocalyptic. It is as if we are now thinking that time itself is starting to run out – or, at least, the time when human life on earth has run its course and what remains of the planet will not be suitable for human survival. Other issues such as the loss of biodiversity get less attention but are equally important.

According to the Stockholm Resilience Centre there are nine planetary boundaries, those being: ozone depletion; biodiversity loss and extinction; chemical pollution; climate change; ocean acidification; freshwater consumption; land system change; depletion of phosphorus and nitrogen; and atmospheric aerosols. In other words, there is far more to the problems than simply climate change and biodiversity loss, even though these receive the most public attention. It was reported in May 2022 that six of these nine boundaries have already been crossed and that the others are under threat. This is a measure of the scale of the environmental dangers we now face.

Northcott (2013) suggests some spiritual practices that should now become central to any spirituality of the environment, and these will be costly and require sacrifice as one might expect of any spiritual practices worthy of the name.

In order to mitigate climate change he argues that it is the central duty of moral and political communities to train their members in new ritual practices of daily living (p. 263). These include such things as using less energy (this was written before the energy crisis of 2022); living more lightly on the earth by eating less meat; consuming less stuff generally; and driving and flying less. He offers the examples of the Transition Towns movement and Eco Congregations which encouraged local community-based practices such as using less energy, local food growing and a low-carbon lifestyle. 'And as I argue elsewhere, the ecclesiastical rituals of pilgrimage, sanctuary and eucharist play a distinctive and shaping role in sustaining such everyday rituals among Christians' (p. 263).

More recently the A Rocha initiative of Eco Church has built up momentum, with many individual churches, benefices and even Dioceses in the Church of England signing up and earning their bronze awards and above. The target of achieving Net Zero Carbon by 2030 is another means of getting churches to take the issues seriously and to engage in practical changes in terms of energy use. Whether one interprets these as simply practical responses or sees them as being grounded in theological and spiritual principles, these are all examples of reconnecting with nature at some level, although there is a danger of reducing these activities to a tick box exercise which might help people feel more virtuous without having a wider impact. Northcott raises the issue of the need for governmental and collective action as the purely local and individual will not be enough. But which then takes priority: the spiritual in its own right or the spiritual as a means to the end of tackling the environmental challenges? Is there not also a danger of limiting spirituality to concerns with nature seen as environment when it is all aspects of creation which should ideally be the focus?

Without trying to offer definitive answers to those questions, there is another which underpins this chapter and is still unresolved, which is: under what circumstances or conditions can current attempts to reconnect with nature become stepping stones to a spirituality of the environment or the basis for spiritual experience as defined? Are such practices no more than an engaging with an idealised or romanticised version of nature available only to a select few with the time to spare and resources to hand? Two related factors could guard against this. The first is awareness of what is known as shifting baseline syndrome (SBS), which makes it clear that nature as encountered now is different from and indeed reveals a deterioration of what was the case a generation ago and even further back. So much has already been lost or destroyed, as Stengers and others remind us. That being the case, once this is recognised the response may well be one of anguish, remorse, bereavement or trauma, not to mention guilt, as we as humans acknowledge the depth of our responsibility for this destruction and the need to take positive action in the present. Perhaps this becomes the tipping point or moment of epiphany when encountering nature moves into or towards an awareness of some form of transcendence? The experience opens up other levels of being in which we participate, however poorly. There is always more to be discovered as Whitehead said, and this more can be the relationship with the divine as experienced in and through nature, but not to be equated with it. Then that reconnecting may go beyond the immediate and individual. It is not until we accept that we are sick that remedies become essential and then a focus upon nature may lead to that greater depth of spiritual awareness.

Biographical note

John Reader (1953–2023) had degrees from Oxford (MA), Manchester (MPhil) and a PhD from the University of Wales, Bangor. He was Senior Research Fellow of the William Temple Foundation. He had published six solo books and co-edited or with chapters in a further 16. Recent publications included *A Philosophy of Christian Materialism* (co-written with Baker and James), *Theology and New Materialism* (Palgrave Radical Theologies series) and *Postdigital Theologies: Technology, Belief and Practice* (co-edited with Savin-Baden). ORCID ID: http://orcid.org/0000-0003-3851-8801

Bibliography

Elvey, A. 2023. *Reading with Earth*. London: T&T Clark.
Keller, C. 2015. *Cloud of the Impossible: Negative Theology and Planetary Entanglement*. New York: Columbia University Press.
Latour, B. 2007. *Reassembling the Social*. Oxford: Oxford University Press.
Latour, B. 2013. *An Inquiry Into Modes of Existence*. Cambridge, MA: Harvard University Press.

Lent, J. 2021. *The Web of Meaning*. London: Profile Books.
Leonardi, J. 2008. *Partners or Adversaries: A Study of Christian and Person-centred Approaches to Spirituality, and the Implications for Christian Ministry and Pastoral Practice*. PhD Thesis, University of East Anglia.
Macdonald, B. 2019. *Rebirding: Restoring Britain's Wildlife*. London: Pelagic Publishing.
Northcott, M. 2013. *A Political Theology of Climate Change*. Grand Rapids, MI: Eerdmans Publishing Co.
Peters, J.D. 2015. *The Marvelous Clouds*. Chicago, IL: University of Chicago Press.
Latour, B. 2005. *Blurred Encounters*. Vale of Glamorgan: Aureus Publishing.
Latour, B. 2005. *Reassembling the Social*. Oxford: Oxford University Press.
Latour, B. 2023. The Postdigital and Human Agency. In: Reader, J. and Saven-Baden, M., eds. *Postdigital Theologies: Technology, Belief and Practice*. Cham: Springer Nature.
Schmidt, B. and Leonardi, J., eds. 2020. *Spirituality and Wellbeing: Interdisciplinary Approaches to the Study of Religious Experience and Health*. Sheffield: Equinox.
Schofield, L. 2022. *Wild Fell*. London: Penguin Random House.
Sheldrake, R. 2013. *The Science Delusion*. London: Hodder and Stoughton.
Stengers, I. 2011. *Thinking with Whitehead*. Cambridge, MA: Harvard University Press.
Stengers, I. 2018. *Another Science is Possible: A Manifesto for a Slow Science*. Cambridge: Polity Press.
Whitehead, A.N. 1920. *The Concept of Nature*. Cambridge: Cambridge University Press.
Whitehead, A.N. 1967. *Science and the Modern World*. New York: Free Press.

Part II
How spirituality deepens our understanding

3 Spiritual experiences of interconnectedness

Marianne Rankin

Introduction

In this chapter I will explore the kind of spiritual experiences which lead people to an understanding of the world as intrinsically interconnected and consider how this affects their wellbeing. These experiences come from a database of self-selected personal accounts, initially sent to Sir Alister Hardy in the late 1960s and early 1970s, when he established the Religious Experience Research Unit at the University of Oxford. Today the collected correspondence, added to over the ensuing years, forms the archive of the renamed Alister Hardy Religious Experience Research Centre (RERC) held at the University of Wales Trinity Saint David in Lampeter, which is available online.

Despite a lifelong interest in spirituality, Hardy first established his reputation in mainstream science, as a marine biologist, holding professorships in Hull, Aberdeen and eventually becoming Linacre Professor of Zoology at Oxford. Only on his retirement was he able to devote himself to the study of religious experience, when he began to gather ordinary people's accounts of their religious and spiritual experiences (RSEs). After a meagre response from within the religious press, he placed notices in the secular newspapers, the *Guardian*, *Times*, *Observer* and *Daily Mail*. People responded to what is now known as 'The Hardy Question': 'Have you ever been aware of, or influenced by a presence or power, whether you call it God or not, which is different from your everyday self?'

This open question, usually illustrated by an example or article to explain what he was looking for, led to the receipt of thousands of letters. These described profound experiences which the writers had found transformative, but which in many cases, they had not fully understood. Frequently the correspondents admitted that this was the first time they had shared their experience.

It was Hardy's respected academic standing which encouraged people to share their deepest experiences with him, knowing that he would take them seriously. There was, and often still is, a reluctance to admit to such experiences, as they are personal, precious and often deeply meaningful. Experiencers are wary of an unsympathetic response or plain scepticism. A national survey in 1986 recorded that 40% of those who claimed to have had a spiritual experience, had never told anyone about it (Hay, 1990, p. 58). Correspondents with no religious background frequently find such events puzzling or fearsome, leading them on occasion to doubt their sanity, whereas religious people are sometimes surprised at the lack of content related to their particular tradition. Some people feel a confirmation of their previously held beliefs, some embark on a spiritual search, whereas others turn away from religion altogether. It does not seem possible to trigger such events, although spiritual or religious practice certainly seems to open people up to recognising them. Some experiences are sudden and dramatic, whereas others involve a more gradual change of perspective. But once accepted as significant, the apparent message is not easily ignored.

There remains a taboo around such experiences, variously named as RSEs, religious, mystical, spiritual, enlightening, transcendent, exceptional human experiences (EHEs), peak, intense, paranormal, anomalous, or more specifically as out-of-body (OBEs), end-of-life (ELEs), near-death experiences (NDEs) or after-death communications (ADCs). The reluctance to accept these experiences as valid is often because they 'are deemed to contravene fundamental principles that have been repeatedly demonstrated in other areas of science' (Roe, 2020, p. 46). These are the prevailing materialist worldviews, particularly among the scientific community. However, there are signs that things are changing.

Science and spirituality

There are many different types of experience in the RERC archive – of light, love, guidance, of making sense of life, lifting of depression and also experiences around death. However, of all the various descriptors, that of mystical experience comes closest to the theme of this chapter, an experience of the essential interconnectedness of humanity and the natural world. As quantum science increasingly demonstrates this fundamental unity, the gulf between mysticism and science seems to be narrowing. Mystical experiences, whether theistic or monistic, give an awareness of unity and interconnectedness (Happold, 1990, pp. 46–47; Franks Davis, 1999, pp. 58–63). They may be considered as 'an intense experience of the unity of all things or a state of achieving unity with the divine' (Rankin, 2008, p. 16) and there are various strands and scholarly definitions of mysticism (Astley, 2020, pp. 37–40).

Especially apposite here is nature mysticism, 'a joyful, sometimes ecstatic, self-transcending and illuminative awareness of and relationship with the physical universe and biological life' (Astley, 2020, p. 49).

Lawrence LeShan links the worldviews of mystics and theoretical physicists, showing their similarities by juxtaposing quotations relating to their perceptions of reality, as both indicate that sensory data offer only a limited picture of reality (LeShan, 2003, pp. 265–291). This links mysticism to the view of the physical world as interconnected on a subatomic level, which is evident in quantum entanglement (Polkinghorne, 2005, pp. 53–54) and the 'butterfly effect' where 'a butterfly stirring the air with its wings in the African jungle today could have consequences for the storms over London in three or four weeks' time' (p. 55).

John Polkinghorne, a former professor of mathematical physics, who was later ordained, considers our scientific explorations to be insights into the rational order with which God has endowed the universe, and he maintains that we need both science and religion in our quest for understanding. Another ordained scientist, Arthur Peacock, explains that, 'The individual systems of the world are increasingly demonstrated by the sciences to be interconnected and interdependent in multiple ways' (Peacocke, 2001, p. 54).

This quantum understanding of unity and interconnectedness is beginning to confirm scientifically what the mystics have said for millennia, that we and all phenomena are one. It is a holistic view, which can lead to our own wellbeing and altruism towards others as we recognise that as human beings, we are all intrinsically interlinked. The theologian and philosopher of religion John Hick refers to 'the transforming awareness of the interconnectedness of all things in a living universe' (Hick, 1999, p. 114). David Hay links this new science and spirituality:

> The idea of an objective world out there that we observe coldly and scientifically from some Archimedean point is no longer tenable. The cosmos is one, indivisible whole. …to take this deep ecological worldview is to enter the spiritual dimension. (Hay, 2006, p. 249)

In my own research into the consequences of spiritual experiences in the RERC archive, instead of including William James's four marks of mystical experience – ineffability, noetic quality, transiency and passivity (James, 2002, p. 295) – or the seven characteristics of mystical states as expounded by F. C. Happold (Happold, 1990, pp. 45–50), which were found to be extremely rare, I substituted 'awareness of unity and interconnectedness'. This was in fact inspired by Happold's fifth mark of mysticism, '*consciousness of the Oneness of everything*. All creaturely existence is experienced as a unity, as All in

One and One in All' (Happold, 1990, p. 46; his italics and upper case). This is often experienced as a result of a mystical experience, but is also found more widely in the RERC archive, leading to a recognition of our interdependence and involvement with the lives of others.

For my recent research into the fruits of spiritual experience, I read two thousand accounts of spiritual experience: the first thousand in the RERC archive and the most recent thousand. This was to enable a comparison between the early and later accounts, particularly in terms of religious background. I found that each experience was unique, embedded in the life story of the individual. The effects were also different in each case. So I explored whether there was any underlying similarity in how people responded to these elusive occurrences. I found that in many cases, the experiences took place in solitude, and in nature, leading to a profound resonance with the natural world, an awareness of being part of a greater whole, and a feeling of involvement with other creatures. This mystical sense of unity seems to lead to a feeling of love and compassion for all living things and often an awareness of an underlying transcendent reality.

Experiences of interconnectedness

In my quantitative research I found 21% in the first thousand accounts and 15% in the later thousand as reflecting a sense of interconnectedness. Few correspondents mentioned any special training, apart from yoga, and it was evident that these were almost all spontaneous experiences. Hardy and David Hay, who became RERC Director in 1985, also investigated such experiences. Hardy found 5.9% reflecting a 'feeling of unity with surroundings and/or with other people' and Hay and Heald found 5% 'experiencing that all things are "One"' (Hay, 1994, p. 7).

Hardy himself had experiences of nature mysticism in his youth, which inspired his later research. Despite his life-long interest in spirituality, he kept these to himself until in his eighties he admitted that in studying the natural world as a boy:

> I came to feel the experience of God through the beauty and joys of nature. …I would sometimes feel a presence which seemed partly outside myself and curiously partly within myself. My God was never 'an old gentleman' out there, but nevertheless was like a person I could talk to and in a loving prayer could thank him for the glories of nature that he let me experience. …sometimes (when I was sure no-one was

looking!) I would go down on my knees to express this gratitude. At the same time I had become an ardent Darwinian. (Hardy, 1985, p. 2).

This quotation is taken from the speech Hardy prepared for his acceptance of the Templeton Prize for progress in religion, which unfortunately illness prevented him from delivering in person. Instead, the speech was read for him and later published as an Occasional Paper. The prize was important to him, as it was the fulfilment of a youthful vow, made as he left the University of Oxford to serve in the war in 1914, that if he survived, he would devote his life to trying to bring about a reconciliation between human spiritual experience and the theory of evolution. Thus in his speech he immediately follows the description of his mystical experiences with a reference to Darwin. His studies of the written records of people's spiritual experiences were 'to use the methods of science to make a systematic natural history study of human experience' (Hardy, 1985, p. 1).

For Hardy, spirituality was what made life worth living, including a sense of beauty and adventure, music and art, all of which contribute to human thriving. Hardy felt a deep sense of reverence in nature, and he also experienced the numinous in quiet chapels and empty churches rather than through formal worship. He valued the profound effect of spiritual experience on people, including an awareness of the transcendent, a sense of new purpose in life and closer and better relationships with others. These contribute to wellbeing, a sense of being at home in the natural world and among our fellow creatures.

The extracts from the account below describe a life-changing experience which leads to a sense of interconnectedness. It is a lengthy account, but one which clearly highlights the consequences in the life of the correspondent. It is an early response to one of Hardy's appeals. Accounts taken from the RERC Archive are anonymous, retain the original spelling and the number of the account is given in brackets at the end. For clarity, I have paragraphed the text.

23rd. March, 1970. The Director, Religious Experience Research Unit, Manchester College, Oxford OX1 3TD. Dear Sir, I reply to your invitation in the Observer to send details of such personal experience. Age: now 47, Sex: Male, Nat: English; …the 'experience' followed a long period of inner unrest during which nothing seemed worthwhile,… A time arrived when I was left much to myself in a rural setting, and here my unrest became more marked.

There was no positive religious inclination and I had no personal belief whatever; I had, however, recently read a life of Tolstoy, who led

> me to Ghandi {Gandhi}, and, directly or otherwise, I had read something of St. Francis, and the local vicar had presented me with a copy of a Kempis' 'Imitations' in return for some favour, which I thought nice but did not read. Of these I remember being deeply affected by some ideas of St. Francis – simplicity, feeling for nature, etc.
>
> A particular moment came when, overwhelmed by what seemed the utter futility of things, I utterly broke down and, in blind desperation (sitting alone by the margin of some field) spoke into space something like, 'Oh, God! You come and see to my life, I can't run it alone.' I did not, of course, expect any kind of response. Following this I sat quietly, feeling exhausted, for some minutes. I was then aware of a curious 'light' which seemed to grow up within me, and which became stronger and more defined as the minutes passed. I cannot now say how long it took to develop, but the 'ecstasy' lasted over roughly three weeks. The main sensation was of being loved, a flood of sweetness of great strength, without any element of sentimentality or anything but itself. The description is quite inadequate.

This account begins with the correspondent's description of a sense of dissatisfaction and unrest, which is frequently found preceding a reappraisal of life. Although without any religious faith, he had been exploring spiritual ideas, but without success. His distress intensified, until he found himself alone in the countryside and completely at the end of his tether. He admitted to being unable to cope. A desperate appeal to a God he didn't believe in seemed to trigger an experience of inner light. This is not unusual, as the experience of 'handing over' is frequently found to lead to a spiritual experience. As in this case, many people do not believe that there will be any result from this, but they have simply run out of alternatives.

This is followed by a description of his sense of interconnectedness,

> I also felt a unification of myself with the external world: I did not lose my own identity, yet all things and I somehow entered into each other, all things seemed to 'speak' to me. I have since read descriptions of this, particularly in F.C. Happold's 'Mysticism'. Something was communicated to me, not in words or images, but in another form of knowing. Towards the end of the period I was aware that the 'light' was being withdrawn.

Here the experience of light is described as an ecstasy which lasted about three weeks, and brought a sense of being loved. The experience seemed to happen to him, he was not in control but was in the hands of a greater power, reminiscent of James' passivity as a mark of mystical experience. It was also an illumination which he later recognised in the writings of Happold. The noetic aspect of the experience was also described, a different way of knowing, again reminiscent of James. This led to him being open to what he might have considered a mere coincidence before, through finding in a previously unread book, a message apposite to him at that moment.

> An odd happening towards the end of this time must be mentioned. Still astounded and bemused, I found myself saying aloud 'What does it all mean?' I then seemed to hear for the first time a voice, which said, 'Take up and read!' I was standing indoors, and by my hand was the a Kempis. Unable to resist, I opened it, pointedly closing my eyes beforehand in order to prevent myself 'searching', and read, 'Son, neither is it an illusion if (at times?) thou art suddenly rapt into an ecstasy'. In retrospect I have discounted this (manipulation of physical objects) yet there is not another passage in the book, or any other that I know of, of equal significance to me at that time. It does not, in any case, invalidate the experience.

After the whole experience, he was left transformed, a new person with a connection to everything around him. He felt a sense of wellbeing – not just within himself, but including everyone else. This is a clear example of a sense of interconnectedness leading to a new understanding of the individual and of his relation to the world. The change is fundamental and lasting.

> Although the freshness of the vision has faded, it is clear that my life is quite different as a result. Only positive things are of any significance to me, negative thoughts and actions (whether 'true' or not) give pain, whether relating to myself or not. This is somehow bound up with the unification of myself with the world, 'I' am a different 'I', partly again overlaid with selfish desires, yet with 'self' still extended in some way to include external things, in whose well-being or otherwise I actually participate.

He then describes the profound, permanent effects of the experience,

> ... The real point is that this is not a matter of adopting a set of intellectual precepts, but of becoming simply a different person in essential nature, of being 'born again', as if a deep well had opened within the depths of the self, and within this depth and in the external world a 'something' is encountered with which a personal relationship is

established, and this is based not upon thought, although the intellect is satisfied, but upon emotion or love, as a child reacts to a parent.

He then links the experience to God, as there seems to be no other way of describing what has happened, apart from the use of religious language. However, he stresses the difference between this overwhelming experience and church services.

> I identify this experience with 'God'; this is inevitable, as a mere fact of language. I have never, before or since, gone willingly to church; it seems irrelevant. ... I still experience a correspondence between myself and natural things, particularly trees and fruit. This 'something' does, against all reason (e.g. tormenting thoughts on decay, undeserved suffering and the ultimate extinction of life etc) yield an absolute knowledge of the value of life; not as a belief requiring 'faith', but as a simple fact of experience. ... [000793]

The connection to all living things remains with him and despite life's challenges, he is convinced of its intrinsic value. The experience has made him a completely different person from his self-description at the outset.

Change of perspective

As in the experience above, numerous accounts sent to Hardy as a result of his appeal described a change from depression or lack of purpose to a new sense of wellbeing. Hardy recorded 18.4% of RSEs as being triggered by 'depression, despair' (Hardy, 2006, p. 28). He noted that 18.5% found a sense of purpose or new meaning in life (p. 29) after their experience, which I recorded in about a quarter of the accounts.

The example below illustrates how a recognition that the root of the correspondent's misery, both physical and psychological, was self-pity, led to a transformative experience. Acknowledgement of her own self-centredness led to a deep feeling of contrition and to a new perspective. She was comforted and received help and guidance for the rest of her life. The fruit of the experience was not only a lifting of her own unhappiness but an abrupt and lasting change. That transformation was expressed in love of everyone and everything. From her self-centred misery, she became aware of her connection to others, which lifted her from despair. Once again, enlightenment is sensed as light and the transformation is complete and lasting. She writes:

I think it may be relevant to say that from 1957 to 1966 I was almost all the time very unhappy indeed. I suffered from acute pain in the back, lived in poverty, in a state of sorrow and a good deal of loneliness. I experienced unhappy relationships with relatives and neighbours and suffered from doubt in God or after life and many other troubles. In 1966, I was one day alone in the house when quite suddenly I became aware of my own attitude to life.

I realised that I was wrapped up in deep self-pity, that my thoughts were all for myself and my own sorrows, that I had not thought of others. I thought how others in the world suffered too. I was rather shocked at my selfish attitude and was filled with compassion for others; then, as if without thinking I knelt down in the room and made a vow to God that from then on for the rest of my life I would love and serve mankind.

The following morning when I awoke I had a sudden experience, for into my mind poured knowledge (which knowledge has remained with me ever since). I knew that the love and service of mankind was the will of God for mankind. ... To explain my experience figuratively, it was as if all my life I had been in a darkened room and then I had suddenly walked out of it into the sunlight of day. ...[000002]

This transformation from self-focus to a sense of interconnectedness is studied by David Yaden. He explores self-transcendent experiences (STEs), where:

> the subjective sense of one's self as an isolated entity can temporarily fade into an experience of unity with other people or one's surroundings, involving the dissolution of boundaries between the sense of self and 'other'. (Yaden, Haidt, Hood, Vago, Newberg, 2021, p. 143)

Experiences around death

A profound consequence of many experiences in the archive is a change in attitude to death. Accounts describe a lessening of fear brought about through an understanding that death is not the end of consciousness. I found that it is not only NDEs which led to a belief in the continuation of consciousness, but also many other kinds of experience, including after-death communications (ADCs) and end-of-life experiences (ELEs). Dreams also featured in the accounts, at times giving pertinent messages from the deceased or offering comfort. This understanding links earthly life with the hereafter in another aspect of unity and interconnectedness.

It is above all through scientific studies of NDEs, which explore consciousness as all-embracing, and transcending physical death, that result in a lasting sense that we are part of a greater reality (van Lommel, 2010). This understanding can be of great comfort to the experient, lessening the fear of dying, as well as offering comfort to the bereaved, many of whom report a sense of contact with their deceased loved ones. I recorded 14% in the first thousand and 19% in the final thousand who reported a sense of assurance of survival. In many cases this was unexpected as the experiencer had previously assumed that death marked the end of consciousness. Hardy found 3.6% feeling a 'sense of release from fear of death' (Hardy, 2006, p. 27). A slightly different experience of 'supposed contact with the dead' was recorded by Hardy at 8% and 'awareness of the presence of someone who has died' was included in the survey undertaken by Hay and Heald, with 18% answering in the affirmative (Hay, 1990, p. 83; 1994, p. 7). I did not come across any accounts expressing the opposite, changes to disbelief in life after death.

A reduced fear of death after an NDE was frequently found by Paul Badham and his doctoral researcher Penny Sartori (Badham, 2013; Sartori, 2014). Another frequent outcome of NDEs, also revealed by Sartori's work, is an increase in positive attitudes to life and to others (Sartori, 2014; Sartori & Walsh, 2017). The fact that such experiences appeared in the RERC archive before NDEs were named by Raymond Moody in *Life After Life* 1975, and are found throughout the ages and in different cultures (Shushan, 2016), suggests that they may be innate. Those who recounted such experiences were changed, as they became less materialistic and more spiritual, valued life more deeply and developed a more accepting and empathetic attitude to others.

NDEs can begin with darkness, a tunnel or even demons, but the experience can develop into a positive scenario and then over time and with further reflection, changes are wrought which are ultimately of benefit. In many cases people are convinced that they need a complete transformation of the values they have espoused hitherto and a change of lifestyle in the future (Parti, 2016).

The correspondent below describes a sense of oneness as a lasting fruit of her NDE. She mentions what is found in so many NDEs, that the experience brings a sense of knowing everything (details of which experiencers cannot recall afterwards) – but the gist of this noesis is an understanding of oneness:

> And I was realising that in my true-essence I am this Whole, Clarity, Love, Abundance, Compassion and all that was being conveyed to me. I

am One with it all. So although I have now forgotten most of the details of this 'knowledge', a sort of précis has remained ever since. All is One, All is Whole, and I need to just 'be'. [005474]

The following extracts are taken from a comprehensive account in which the correspondent tells of the consequences of an NDE, beginning with how her experience differed from the usual NDE pattern:

> I did not experience a tunnel, nor did anyone come to meet me. I did not see God or any recognisable person/spirit. Instead I was immediately and rapidly transported to a place of Great Light. ... I felt very welcome and safe and I 'knew' I was in the presence of the Divine. [005474]

She goes on to explain how the NDE led to a reappraisal of what really matters in this life,

> I became a new person and changed my whole life. I became much kinder, more compassionate and 'good'. I felt as though I had been handed a new set of values and beliefs on a plate. So I had to set about finding the lifestyle which would 'fit' these beliefs and values. [005474]

Religion and experience

For some people, spiritual experiences are related to religion – which may or may not be helpful. Childhood influences and upbringing stay with people throughout their lives. They may be accepted with gratitude or kicked against – temporarily or permanently – but they rarely quite disappear. This background plays an important role in how RSEs are interpreted and I recorded changes in relation to that initial worldview. For many, as in [000793] above, the terminology used to describe the experience is inevitably religious, but the experience is distinct from church-going or formal worship. Some people are supported by their religious institutions, while others either leave or remain on the outside. The correspondent below evaluates her connection with her religious institution as a connection with others on a spiritual level,

> I now think of public worship as of little importance in itself, except as it enables people to know and trust and love their fellow worshippers on a deeper level than would otherwise be possible, and hence to work

confidently with them where corporate action is required. The heart of religion is for me something deeply personal and independent of any formulations of it. [000344]

In the RERC archive, the religious background was given in the details of the account. In the first thousand accounts 87% recorded a Christian background. In the final thousand, as expected, fewer people, just 57%, had been brought up in that way. Indeed, many people explain that they did not receive help from within the church when seeking to understand their experience and descriptions of rejection of RSEs by clergy can be found in the archive. Some correspondents feel that their profound experiences are dismissed, and as a result they often leave religious institutions, many becoming spiritual but not religious (SBNR). Their experience seems to them a gift, and often unconnected to religious doctrine or ritual. In my research I found that the highest percentage of change from a Christian background was not to another religion, nor to no religion, but to SBNR, with 36% in the first thousand and 34% in the final thousand changing in this way. There is a wider trend, a general turn away from organised religion to a more spiritual approach to life in society as a whole (Hay, 1990, p. 61; Tacey, 2004; Heelas & Woodhead, 2005).

Hardy recorded only 3.87% reporting 'changes in religious belief' in the first three thousand accounts in the Archive (Hardy, 2006, p. 29), which is perhaps surprising, for as he said:

> It is only natural that a profound spiritual experience is likely to lead the recipient either to question former beliefs and perhaps replace them by others, or to see old beliefs in a new light or suddenly to become confronted with what appears to them to be an entirely new way of looking at the world and its relation to what they had previously only dimly thought of as something unreal and remote – something which they had hitherto conventionally called God. (Hardy, 2006, pp. 99–100)

Perhaps people remained nominally Christian, while expanding their understanding. Hardy considers humans to be spiritual by nature, with this expressed in a great variety of different religions and cultures:

> On Hardy's thesis, spirituality is not the exclusive property of any one religion, or for that matter of religion in general. Spiritual awareness could be signified … in secular and even anti-religious language amongst those who for historical reasons are alienated from religious culture. (Hay, 1998/2006, p. 23)

The correspondent below, despite being a self-confessed agnostic, describes this sense of the spiritual and how it flows out from her, leading her to a feeling of interconnectedness,

> I have come to the conclusion, after years of mental conflict, that I am an agnostic. (I no longer suffer from any guilt complex on this score.) However I do sincerely feel that there is some inner and outer source which seems to give me comfort and refreshment – and 'energy' – whenever I feel the need. …I feel there is some indescribable force within me and outside of me – ever present and all pervading. I am aware of it when I consciously relax mind and body, the effect being a sense of peacefulness together with rejuvenation – as though I am becoming blended with the universe. [000033]

Here her innate spirituality is expressed and the fruits of experience are accepted, giving her a sense of becoming one with the universe. The only mention of religion is her relief at having come to terms with being agnostic.

In the Archive there are many instances of people living in tune with the new understanding they have received from their experiences but who have no involvement with formal religion. These are people who find that church services do not resonate with them and who evolve their own private way to communicate with God. The fruits of these experiences seem to be a deeper awareness of the transcendent, but not expressed in religious observance. Such people do not form any kind of community, and in the example below, the point is made that they might not be counted when RSEs are analysed:

> I am venturing with very great diffidence to write to you to say that I believe a greater number of people have had similar religious experiences than is often realized. …we are rather a voiceless community, as we usually belong to…[no] specific creed or religious sect… It is not possible to put our belief into adequate words, …but to put it as clearly as possible we believe in an Infinite Mind which encloses & cares for everything both material & spiritual, & is the source of all Love, Truth, Wisdom & Beauty… The great teachers who founded the enduring religions of the world have all tried to express this Infinite Spirit, with greater or less success, but never, I think, to their satisfaction, as it is beyond finite expression;… I sometimes feel that the various churches are losing some of their appeal because they seem to lose sight of the Infinite in the finite doctrines & rituals of their particular persuasion. [000557]

Religion sets good against evil, acknowledging the existence of both, and there is also a darker side of RSEs. Not all are pleasant. I decided to explore whether the sense of ultimate reality was always beneficent. It is possible that people whose experiences were negative ignored Hardy's appeals as they felt that their experiences were of a different kind from what he was seeking, or were the kind of experience which they wanted to forget – or even had forgotten. I recorded negative consequences of experience as just 0.8% in the early accounts and 4% in the later ones. Previous research has focused experiences of evil rather than on negative consequences. Hardy found 4.5% reporting 'negative or destructive' accounts of a 'sense of external evil force as having initiative' (Hardy, 1979/2006, p. 28) in the first three thousand accounts. Hay and Heald recorded 12% of the national survey reporting an 'awareness of an evil presence' (Hay, 1990, p. 83). Only a small number of experiences of evil were found by Maxwell and Tschudin (2005, pp. 27–28) and 4.25% by Merete Jakobsen (1999). At the end of his book which focused on positive experiences, Peter Donovan briefly refers to suffering and to the grim realities of life as seeming 'to stand out against a background of what could have been or what ought to be' (Donovan, 1979/1998, p. 145) thereby turning thoughts toward God.

The negative experiences I found included premonitions of death of loved ones, feeling cold in haunted places and a sense of evil or oppressive forces. Some were countered by clinging to a Bible or through prayer, with good overcoming evil. But the following account left a lingering sense of the presence of evil spirits, a feeling that ultimate reality might have a divisive, malevolent aspect, rather than only the benevolence of interconnectivity. This was rare, but for this correspondent, was a real and lasting feeling,

> I awoke from a sound sleep and had overwhelming feeling of a presence in the room. The atmosphere felt very oppressive. I felt a strong sense of fear and forced myself to get up and put on the lights. I went from room to room and there was no living person there but this feeling persisted strongly. Again I resorted to prayer and gradually fell off to sleep with a rosary in my hand. I believe there are spirits or forces among us not always good that make themselves felt to the sensitive mind. [000038]

However, many more experiences of oneness seem to offer a vision of goodness and lead to altruism. In the following account, the relation between religious traditions and an awareness of interconnection is summed up and a practical outcome described,

> I am unable to accept the symbolism of any major world religion, and yet I always feel that there is something outside of myself outside of conscious thought. ...I find it difficult to describe my experience, only to say that it seems to be outside of me and enormous and yet at the same time I am a part of it, everything is. It is purely personal, and helps me to live and to love others. ...in some way because of this feeling I feel united to all people, to all living things. Of recent years the feeling has become so strong that I am now training to become a social worker because I find that I must help people in some way I feel their unhappiness as my own. [000663]

The following correspondent describes an experience of nature mysticism which led to her being overwhelmed by compassion. She then wonders whether, as humans evolve physically, we might also evolve spiritually as a result of spiritual experiences. This is an interesting and unusual conjecture, that if humans are innately spiritual, might this deepen over the generations – particularly if RSEs are accepted and valued. This may be considered a beneficial goal for individuals and society, particularly if altruism is a consequence. This an extract from the account:

> Surely history testifies that whilst it is still unhappily true that cruelty and ruthless selfishness still hold powerful sway in mankind, we do not accept as in centuries gone by the horrors done daily in the name of religion or 'divine right'. I believe man-kind seeks to improve his very 'being'. Is it possible that the wisdom of his descendants could be affected by 'physical' changes brought about in the genes as a result of spiritual experiences of the individual? [000464]

In the following account, the fruits of a mystical experience are long-lasting and clearly those of altruism:

> Fruits: This was experienced almost twenty years ago but I have never forgotten it. It changed my life, giving me a strong feeling of empathy for all the people around me and even all those I have never met. ... [from questionnaire]: it made me much more aware of the feelings and needs of other people. It made me realize that we were all part on [of] one great whole. I felt more responsible for the results of my words and actions. I realized I had a choice as to what I believed, my attitudes, my motivations. [004764]

Conclusion

The accounts of experiences quoted in this chapter were from people who were not academics, or clerics, or experts of any kind, but who were made aware of our interconnectedness with each other and with the world around us. This transformed them. For some this was triggered by a positive experience. Others went through a period of darkness and depression, which led to a reappraisal of themselves and their circumstances. Eventually they were able to find new meaning in life, form better relationships and thus feel a deep sense of wellbeing.

The benefits for humanity and the environment from a turn away from self-absorption to an acceptance of interconnectedness are boundless. This awareness has been shown to arise naturally, through experiences occurring with or without religious practice, but which frequently lead to an openness to the spiritual, however conceived. Some of our deepest experiences seem to bring a recognition that we and the whole universe are interlinked and this leads to love and compassion for our fellows and a deep concern for the environment.

We now have an awareness of the earth as a whole. All nations are affected by climate change, none is isolated. Nature is interlinked – even trees, long thought to be separate entities, are found to communicate beneath the ground through mycelium. The more we learn, the more we recognise the essential interconnectedness of the natural world, especially with an understanding of quantum entanglement. Science and spirituality, so long considered incompatible, are being brought into harmony. Gradually an understanding of interconnectedness is moving from being a mystical experience, to being accepted as a fact of life. People feel part of something much greater than themselves, part of the stream of life and the march of time.

Biographical note

Dr Marianne Rankin has for many years been involved with the Alister Hardy Trust, which supports the work of the Alister Hardy Religious Experience Research Centre (RERC) at the University of Wales Trinity Saint David in Lampeter.

Marianne is a linguist who lived in the Far East for about twenty years, working as a teacher; interpreter and translator; and freelance writer.

On her return to UK, she gained a Master of Studies in the Study of Religion at the University of Oxford and in 2021 at the University of Warwick, a PhD on *Researching the Fruits of Experience in the Alister Hardy RERC Archive*.

She has written on the Modern Hospice Movement, illustrated a book on Zen and is the author of *An Introduction to Religious and Spiritual Experience* (Bloomsbury, 2008).

Bibliography

Astley, J. 2020. *e*London: SCM Press.
Badham, P. 2013. *Making Sense of Death and Immortality*. London: SPCK.
Donovan, P. 1998. *Interpreting Religious Experience*. Oxford: RERC (original work published 1979).
Franks Davis, C. 1999. *The Evidential Force of Religious Experience*. Oxford: OUP (original work published 1989).
Happold F.C. 1990. *Mysticism, A Study and an Anthology*. London: Penguin Books (original work published 1963).
Hardy, A.C. 1985. *The Significance of Religious Experience*. Lampeter: RERC 2nd Series Occasional Paper 12.
Hardy, A. 2006. *The Spiritual Nature of Man: A Study of Contemporary Religious Experience*. Lampeter: RERC (original work published 1979).
Hay, D. 1990. *Religious Experience Today*. London: Mowbray.
Hay, D. 1994. The Biology of God: What is the Current Status of Hardy's Hypothesis? *The International Journal for the Psychology of Religion*, 4, 1, 1–23.
Hay, D. 2006. *Something There: The Biology of the Human Spirit*. London. Darton, Longman & Tod.
Hay, D., with Nye, R. 2006. *The Spirit of the Child: Revised edition*. London: Jessica Kingsley Publishers (original work published 1998).
Heelas, P. and Woodhead, L., with Seel, B., Szerszynski, B. and Tusting, K. 2005. *The Spiritual Revolution: Why Religion is Giving Way to Spirituality*. Oxford: Blackwell Publishing.
Hick, J. 1999. *The Fifth Dimension: An Exploration of the Spiritual Realm*. Oxford: Oneworld.
Jakobsen, M.D. 1999. *Negative Spiritual Experiences: Encounters with Evil*. Lampeter: RERC: 3rd Series Occasional Paper 1.
James, W. 2002. *The Varieties of Religious Experience: A Study in Human Nature*. London: Routledge (Special Centenary Edition, original work published 1902).
LeShan, L. 2003. *The Medium, the Mystic, and the Physicist: Toward a General Theory of the Paranormal*. New York, NY: Helios Press (original work published 1966).
Maxwell, M. and Tschudin, V., eds. 2005. *Seeing the Invisible: Modern Religious and Other Transcendent Experiences*. Lampeter: RERC (original work published 1990).
Moody, R. 1976. *Life after Life*. Covington, GA: Bantam (original work published 1975).

Parti, R. with Perry, P. 2016. *Dying to Wake Up: A Doctor's Voyage into the Afterlife and the Wisdom he Brought Back.* London: Hay House.

Peacocke, A. 2001. *Paths from Science towards God: The End of all our Exploring.* Oxford: Oneworld Publications.

Polkinghorne, J. 2005. *Quarks, Chaos and Christianity: Questions to Science and Religion.* London: SPCK (original work published 1994).

Rankin, M. 2008. *An Introduction to Religious and Spiritual Experience.* London: Continuum.

Roe, C. 2020. Clinical Parapsychology: The Interface Between Anomalous Experiences and Psychological Wellbeing. In: Schmidt, B. and Leonardi, J., eds. *Spirituality and Wellbeing: Interdisciplinary Approaches to the Study of Religious Experience and Health.* Sheffield: Equinox, pp. 44–63.

Sartori, P. 2014. *The Wisdom of Near-death Experiences: How Understanding NDEs Can Help us Live More Fully.* Oxford: Watkins Publishing.

Sartori, P. and Walsh, K. 2017. *The Transformative Power of Near-death Experiences: How the Message of NDEs Positively Impact the World.* London: Watkins Publishing.

Shushan, G. 2016. Cultural-linguistic Constructivism and the Challenge of Near-death and Out-of-body Experiences. In: Schmidt, B., ed. *The Study of Religious Experience: Approaches and Methodologies.* Sheffield: Equinox, pp. 71–87.

Tacey, D. 2004. *The Spirituality Revolution: The Emergence of Contemporary Spirituality.* Hove: Routledge.

van Lommel, P. 2010. *Consciousness Beyond Life: The Science of the Near-death Experience.* New York: HarperCollins (original work published 2007).

Yaden, D.B., Haidt, J., Hood, R.W. Jr., Vago, D.R. and Newberg, A.B. 2021. The Varieties of Self-transcendent Experience. *Review of General Psychology*, 21, 2, 143–160.

4 Julian of Norwich and spiritual depth: Spiritual experience and relational intimacy

Robert Fruehwirth

Introduction: At peace in oneself?

In the 14th century, in Chapter 49 of her *Revelations of Divine Love*, the famed English mystic and theologian, Julian of Norwich, wrote: 'When the soul is a peace in itself, suddenly it is one-d to God, because in (God) is found no wrath' (Tr. Swanson, 1988, Ch. 49).

This is extraordinary. In a spiritual culture in which the goal of the spiritual, and human, life was expressed as 'union with God', Julian is saying that what allows such union is the soul being at peace in and with itself. All of this follows from Julian's surprising discovery of a God without wrath, whose cherishing love is what sustains us in our being and is constantly at work with us to slake our wrath, reconciling us home to our substantial reality where God already is (see esp. *Revelations*. Ch. 47–49). The problem of the spiritual life is not that we are divided from God, or that God is angry with us, but we are divided against ourselves, where God in love has eternally established Godself.

Writing this about a medieval mystic seems strangely modern. Julian appears to be foreshadowing the 1960s when she insists that the main spiritual problem is not the judgement or anger of God but self-alienation and self-rejection, a wrathful opposition to a depth of our being where God in love already holds us in union with Godself.

Asserting this, however, begs another very modern type of question: how, exactly, is my soul to come to be at peace in itself? How do I get past being divided against myself? How do wrath, unhappiness, and resentment get slaked?

From monastery to person-centred therapist

For myself, this question of 'how' became focal during my two decades in a monastic community devoted to Julian of Norwich. Julian was suggesting that the aim of a monastic vocation was not pleasing or placating an angry God, but the slaking of wrathfulness in myself, coming to be at home at peace in my being, widely acceptant in my felt everyday existence and embodied self. I could understand all of this, yet I still experienced self-rejection and deep unhappiness about myself and the world. How was I ever to be healed? What would allow me to come home to myself in acceptance and peace?

My monastic vocation faltered as I searched for a deeper, wider connection with humanity. I left the monastery in my early 40s, and immersed myself in the writings of Carl Rogers, whom I had gradually begun to appreciate in my last years in the monastery through connections with the Norwich school of person-centred counselling brought into being by Brian Thorne, then deeply involved with Julian of Norwich as with counselling (see Thorne, 1998, pp. 105–115). As I was trained in the UK, in Norwich, in person-centred counseling, I discovered in Rogers' theories of positive personality change a clear theoretical understanding of how self-acceptance happens, how a certain quality of relationship with a self-accepting and significant other facilitates one's own coming home to oneself.

Through conversations with Brian Thorne, Lay Canon at Norwich Cathedral, then Chair of the Friends of Julian of Norwich, and internationally known as an authority on Rogers' 'person-centred' approach, I began to see how Rogers' therapeutic model gave me clarity on an under-appreciated aspect of Julian. I had meditated for years on the quote with which I started this essay. I understood that self-acceptance was the doorway to closeness with God. But Rogers helped me to see that, for Julian herself, as evidenced in her writings, what made possible widening self-acceptance was precisely the quality of relationship offered to her in the course of the mystical experiences and her life following.

Julian's spirituality is entirely relational. Her writings are the record of a human person growing into self-acceptance (and thus, automatically, closeness to God) through the experience of relational intimacy which, in her case, came from a perceived Divine Other. Rogers defined what was necessary and sufficient in any healing relationship: empathic understanding, unconditional acceptance, and authenticity (Rogers, 1957). This is precisely what Julian tells us she experienced of God, and it is the burden of this essay to track her experience of this and how it allowed her to develop.

Exploring Julian's spirituality of relational intimacy

To explore this relational process in Julian I will first provide a brief introduction to Julian herself. Then I will trace Julian's process from self-rejection in wrath to self-acceptance through the relationship she felt she had with God through her mystical experiences. Along the way, we will observe Julian rejecting three common ways of attempting to be at peace with self and the world apart from a healing relationship. These non-relational ways might be described as follows:

1. *Self-perfection:* Julian rejected the hope of being at peace in herself through approximation to, or growth towards, an idealised self.
2. *Transcendence and Denial:* Julian rejected a powerful draw towards a spirituality of transcendence in which one finds peace in oneself through an escape from self and world.
3. *Systematic Comprehension:* Julian labours through more than ten chapters of her *Revelations*, seeking a comprehensive understanding of why God allowed sin and suffering. She seeks to get to self- and world-acceptance through an understanding of the *purpose* of the painful and negative aspects of reality. In the end, Julian explicitly rejects the quest for such intelligibility and learns to rely instead on relational trust in profound unknowing.

It should be noted that a fourth strategy for self-acceptance, the epicurean management of externals and cultivation of pleasant experiences to enjoy a lack of conflict, external or internal, was not possible in the medieval world in which Julian lived. The plagues, violence, famine and cultural cataclysms of late medieval England made the creation of epicurean remove from all pain and suffering unlikely.

Epicurean spirituality is, however, one of the dominant spiritualities in the developed world. We seek to manage externalities, threats and pleasures to secure a more ready peace in ourselves, finding feelings of contentment and wellness along the way. This spirituality combines with the drive to self-perfection and the drive to transcendence and denial mentioned above.

We will return to a consideration of this epicurean spirituality of managed pleasantness at the end of the essay, in a wider application of Julian's spirituality to the global ecological crisis. For now, it is enough to note that, seeking to give her life to God, Julian rejected the relatively epicurean life in a wealthy Benedictine convent and chose the harsher solitude, restriction and vulnerability of the anchorhold.

Throughout this essay, I will refer to Julian's work as a whole as the *Revelations*, always citing the Long Text, as opposed to the earlier Short Text, by chapter unless otherwise noted. For clarity, I will refer to the sixteen discrete experiences of God that Julian identified in her *Revelations of Divine Love* as 'showings': the first showing, second showing, etc, including the chapter numbers from the Long Text when referenced. The modern translation used in quotations is *Lesson of Love* by John-Julian Swanson (1988). Quotes will be referenced by the chapter number in the Long Text.

Julian of Norwich

Julian lived from around 1343 to 1416 and spent most of her adult life as an anchorite attached to St. Julian's Church on a side lane in Norwich, England.

An anchorite took vows, like an enclosed contemplative nun, to give their life to God in prayer. However, these vows were not made in a convent under an abbess, but under a bishop and in a strictly solitary form of religious life. Anchorites lived and prayed in solitude in anchorholds, small apartments built on the side of a parish church, sometimes with a walled garden (Watkins, 2005, p. 5). This combination of solitude, nearly continual prayer, and restriction of movement was the essence of anchoritic life.[1]

Norwich at the time boasted several anchorites; Julian, as one of them, would have been regarded as something like a holy woman-in-residence for the parish. Julian's connection to the parish and world around her likely came through three windows, common for anchorites, one into the church for worship, another to the lay sisters who served her physical needs, and another to the outside world for the offering of counsel (Swanson, 2005, p. 39).

In her time Julian was renowned for her excellence as a spiritual director (Watson, 2005, p. 6; Swanson, 2005, pp. 32–34). While the parish priest bore the authority of the Church and the Sacraments over people's lives (and indeed after-lives), Julian offered a different sort of authority, the authority of someone who knew God experientially. The anchorhold not only gave Julian 'a room of her own' (Law, 2003) in which to contemplate her experience of God; it also gave her, as a woman, an authority to speak about God to ordinary Christians (Watson, 2005, p. 6).

Almost everything we know about Julian herself comes from her writings (Watson, 2005, pp. 4–6). For the sake of our exploration of Julian's process, I am going to follow Julian's direct advice to her readers *not* to get invested in figuring out who she, historically, was. Julian hoped that her sharing of her inner process in her experience of God would serve as the means for the opening of wisdom and love in her readers, by the direct action of the Holy Spirit (*Revelations*, 8). We will proceed thus by careful attention to Julian's process and seek, as noted, moments of contact with Carl Rogers and Person-Centred theory.

Contextually it should be noted that Julian lived through a cataclysmic, almost apocalyptic time – the Black Plague killing up to a half of the population of Norfolk, causing the collapse of social hierarchies and systems, accompanied by church schism and corruption at the highest levels, and also frequent famine, social unrest followed by brutal violence, and the Church martyring proto-protestants in Norwich itself (Jantzen, 2000, pp. 3–13).

From seeking perfection to relying on relationship

Desperate for God to do something: The youthful Julian

At the very start of her *Revelations* Julian tells us about a desire for three spiritual gifts that she had in her youth, some years before her mystical experiences. She says:

> This creature had previously desired three gifts from God: the first was memory of His passion; the second was bodily sickness in youth at thirty years of age; the third was to have from God's gift three wounds. (Ch 2)

Julian goes on to explain why she wanted these 'gifts'. First, she wanted to have a 'bodily sight' of Jesus's passion so that, like 'Mary Magdalen and with the others who were Christ's lovers' (ibid.), she could have a full consciousness of his suffering and suffer with him. She aspired to be like the saints of God, confirmed in a love that suffers with the Beloved, and then to live with a 'more true consciousness of the Passion'.

Second, Julian wanted a sickness severe enough that she would believe she was dying so that she 'would be purged by the mercy of God and afterwards live more to the honor of God' (ibid.).

Third, she wanted three spiritual wounds: of compassion, contrition and longing for God. The metaphor of three spiritual wounds was in conscious imitation of the three sword blows to the neck of St Cecilia in her martyrdom (as Julian writes in the Short Text, see Watson, 2005, pp. 64–65). She wanted compassion, contrition and longing for God to be existentially real for her, and conceived of these virtues in terms of death-dealing violence that, to continue the metaphor, would kill off her self as she experienced it.

Much has been written to make these desires seem less strange by placing them in the devotional context of Julian's time (Fruehwirth, 2016, pp. 4–7). For our purposes it's important to see how Julian's desire for these gifts reveals that she started her adult life in a highly problematic relationship to herself, craving three extraordinary divine interventions to metaphorically kill off her old self so that she could realise the kind of heavenly self she aspired to.

To put this in therapeutic terms, Julian felt a painful gap between who she wanted to be and how she was, and as she felt completely unable to bridge this gap, she sought divine intervention – paraphrasing the famous sonnet of John Donne – to batter her heart, break, blow, burn, and make her new.

Similar to the language of famous Q-studies engaged by Carl Rogers (Rogers, 1967, pp. 225–242), Julian felt a painful gap between her ideal self and her actual self. It is precisely this gap between the real and idealised self that Rogers and his colleagues hypothesised as the driver of psychological pathology. We identify with idealised and exalted selves because this allows us to give ourselves positive self-regard. The problem with this strategy is that our experientially real selves do not match these exalted self-pictures. The result is that denial and distortion of experience are required, a hostility to and rejection of ourselves as we actually are to retain a sense of identity with the ideal self. Positive therapeutic movement comes, however, not in the self getting closer to its ideal self, but in becoming less idealistic, softening and thus being more easily attuned to the flow of experience.

Julian before her mystical experiences was not a soul at peace in herself, but a soul craving a violent intervention against herself from a divine power, from outside. Behind this, there is an inarticulate presumption: 'I can be at peace in myself and close to God if I achieve an ideal-enough self. Or, if I cannot achieve this, at least I can hope to see myself progressing towards it. Then I can give myself positive regard. But since I cannot even see linear progress, I need God to intervene.'

At home in the muddle: The mature Julian

In striking contrast to this youthful state is a passage in the *Revelations*, written fifteen to twenty years following Julian's mystical experiences when Julian was likely in her early 50s.[2] We find in the mature Julian a woman at ease in a self that is not close to the ideal, and is not even making progress towards that ideal! Julian is acceptant of what she describes as a *muddled, experiential, dynamic, and varied* self that she cannot understand. She is also frank in not expecting any progress towards a spiritual idea, any climbing of a supposed 'ladder of perfection' to a better state. She writes:

> All we who shall be saved, for the period of this life, have in us a wondrous mixture both of well and woe: we have in us our Lord Jesus arisen; we have in us the misery of the misfortune of Adam's falling. Dying, we are steadfastly protected by Christ, and by His gracious touching we are raised in certain trust of salvation. And by Adam's falling we are so fragmented in our feeling in differing ways (by sins and by

various pains, in which we are made sad and blind as well) that scarcely do we know how to obtain any comfort… And thus is this mixture so wondrous in us that scarcely do we know about our selves or about our fellow Christians how we hold out, because of the wonderment of these different feelings – except for that same holy assent that we consent to God when we sense Him, truly willing to be with Him with all our heart, with all our soul, and with all our strength…*And thus we remain in this muddle all the days of our lives.* (Ch 52, emphasis mine)

In this mature description of herself, Julian experiences herself not in terms of a real self painfully divided from a desired ideal self. Instead, she describes herself, and all of us, as containing a 'wondrous' and confusing muddle of both ideal and real self at the same time, both a fragmented, suffering, dying Adam and a blissful Christ. Both of them are us.

The only stabilising element – and what gives Julian the capacity to stay comfortably in this dynamic, without seeking to escape into, say, a Christ-self, is a relationship with the divine Other who accepts her unconditionally, as she is. While there is no sense of ever 'getting better' or 'getting more like Christ' there is every sense of being able to allow this experiential flow of opposites in herself within a relationship in which all of her is loved. As she writes further in the same chapter, her comfort in this muddled and confusing state is God with her in three ways that she experienced in the showings:

(God) wills that we trust that [God] is everlastingly with us, and that in three ways: He is with us in heaven, true [human being] in His own Person drawing us upward (and that was shown in the spiritual thirst); and He is with us on earth, leading us (and that was shown in the third showing, where I saw God in a point); and He is with us in our soul eternally dwelling, ruling and taking care of us. (Ch 52).

Here we find the mature Julian approximating characteristics of Rogers' notion of the 'Fully Functioning Person' (Rogers, 1967, pp. 187–191) in being fully attuned to her moment-by-moment experience and able to accept it all. Julian is capable of a broad openness to her actual self-experience, from Adam's sin and death all the way up to Christ's human union with God in bliss and power. She expects to continue to suffer, sin and die, and also to experience delight, virtue and glory. She does not grade or judge her experience within a conceptual system that rejects some of herself and values other parts of herself.

The thesis of this paper is that it was the relationship that Julian experienced with God in her mystical experience that facilitated this positive personality change from more rigid, judgmental and self-rejecting to free-flowing, less condemning and more self-accepting. While it is not possible here to survey the whole of Julian's mystical experiences,[3] we can look to just the very first of the sixteen showings to gauge the kind and quality of relationship that she experienced with God. Using the first showing in this way makes sense because it is this showing, Julian says, that contains the essence of them all.[4] It is like a prologue in which the whole of what God will be offering Julian is present, if in seminal form.

Showing one: An authentic relationship of empathy and unconditional acceptance

God's homely loving

The showings begin with Julian, gravely ill, having a vision of the passion of Christ as she gazed at a crucifix:

> In this [first] showing I suddenly saw the red blood trickling down from under the garland, hot and freshly and most plenteously, just as it was at the time of His Passion when the garland of thorns was pressed onto His blessed head. Just so, I conceived truly and powerfully that it was He Himself (both God and man, the Same who suffered thus for me) who showed it to me without any go-between. (Ch 4).

This image of the suffering humanity of Jesus, symbolised in the blood dripping down 'plenteously' from the crown of thorns is for Julian a revelation of the unconditional compassion of God for us (*Revelations*, Ch. 18). Because God in love tolerates no separation from us, God experiences our human experience as God's own – a kind of Divine empathy. (*Revelations*, Ch. 51). Our human self-experience becomes part of God's self-experience in Jesus, all the way into godlessness and death.

But like all true empathy, God For Julian is not lost in God's experience of us. God knows our experiences as God's own, but also remains secure in God's eternal joy. Thus a second layer of the first showing is one of eternal joy. As Julian wrote:

> And in the same (first) showing suddenly the Trinity almost filled my heart with joy. (And I understood it shall be like that in heaven without end for all that shall come there.) For the Trinity is God, God is the Trinity; the Trinity is our Maker, the Trinity is our Keeper, the Trinity

is our everlasting Lover... (And this was shown in the first revelation and in all of them, for whenever Jesus appears, the blessed Trinity is understood, as I see it.) (Ch 4)

In this very first showing, containing, as Julian notes, the essence of all the showings, Julian is initiated into a relationship characterised by divine vulnerability to her in unlimited compassion, along with an eternal, transcendent security – at the same time! The experience is dual-layered. This is an empathic relationship in which God has already unconditionally accepted Julian in love and demonstrates this to Julian in the image of dying on the cross, and at the same time rejoices at having paid the price to secure such sustained and total connection with her.[5] Here is empathy. Here is Unconditional Positive Regard.

Finally, what moves Julian *most* in this first showing is not the showing itself, but how it was shown, as a direct and intimate self-sharing of God's own experience. Julian has a sense of Jesus himself directly opening his inner experience to her, making it available to her, even as, as an experience of compassion for humanity, it is an experience of Julian herself in God. As she says, 'I conceived truly and powerfully that it was He Himself (both God and man, the Same who suffered thus for me) who showed it to me without any go-between.' (Tr. Swanson, 1983, Ch. 4). Julian has a sense of immediate and open contact with Christ, and how he in love experiences her.

Julian's Middle English word for this close intimacy and love of God, this direct familiarity and sharing of selves, is 'homeliness' (Watson, 2005, p. 147 and notes on translation, p. 146). As she writes later a few chapters later, reflecting on the first showing:

> Of all the sights it was most comfort to me that our God and Lord, who is so worthy of respect and so fearsome, is also so plain (homely) and gracious; and this filled me almost full with delight and security of soul. For the greatest fullness of joy that we shall have, as I see it, is the marvelous graciousness and friendliness (homeliness) of the Father who is our Creator, in the Lord Jesus Christ who is our Brother and our Savior. (Ch. 7)

Positive change from self-acceptance

Julian's request for outside divine intervention to create in her an ideal self so that she can be more approving of herself is familiar to most therapists. People come to therapy because they do not like the state they are in and feel unable to get out of it on their own. They desire an outside intervention to put them in a better state. Little do they suspect that the person-centred therapist, far from offering a diagnosis and a solution, is going to offer, ideally, a quality of relationship – empathic, acceptant, authentic – in which the client will be able to accept themselves more widely. The paradox that person-centred therapy depends on is precisely that self-acceptance releases a capacity to change, whereas the refusal to accept oneself (in Julian: wrath) merely locks one into self-conflict. Carl Rogers described it this way:

> I find I am more effective when I can listen acceptantly to myself, and can be myself. I feel that over the years I have learned to become more adequate in listening to myself; so that I know, somewhat more adequately than I used to, what I am feeling in any given moment... One way of putting this is that I feel I have become more adequate in letting myself be what I am. It becomes easier for me to accept myself as a decidedly imperfect person, who by no means functions at all times in the way in which I would like to function. This must seem to some like a very strange direction in which to move. *It seems to me to have value because the curious paradox is that when I accept myself just as I am, then I change.* (Rogers, 1967, p. 17)

We have already seen that Julian explicitly credits her ability to stay in the free-flowing *muddle* of human experience, including all the good and all the bad, to the presence and relationship offered by God through all her mystical experiences and seen with special clarity in the very first showing. She can say she accepts herself not because she has achieved a spiritual idea, but because God has already known and accepted her, intimately, more than she knows or experiences herself.

Showing 8: Tempted to false transcendence

For Julian, a relationship with Christ of the kind described in the previous section, while enormously consoling, reassuring and joyful, also led to distress. In the first eight showings in her *Revelations*, we watch Julian's journey into intensifying awareness of Christ's sufferings, which is also, for Julian, an awareness of her pain, and indeed the suffering of creation (*Revelations*, Ch. 18). It is as if Julian, unable to experience herself directly, can experience herself in *another's* acceptant experience of her. She does not look into a mirror to see herself but gazes on the suffering body of Christ, and therein sees and experiences herself.

Her experience of Christ's suffering, and his of hers, and so of her own, reaches its climax in the eighth showing. Julian's imagery is graphic:

> The blessed body dried all alone a long time, with the twisting of the nails and weight of the body (for I understood that because of the tenderness of the sweet hands and of the sweet feet, and by the large size, cruelty, and hardship of the nails, the wounds grew wider), and the body sagged because of the weight by hanging a long time and the piercing and wrenching of the head and the binding of the crown, all parched with dry blood, with the sweet hair and the dry flesh clinging to the thorns, and the thorns to the drying flesh. And in the beginning while the flesh was fresh and bleeding, the constant settling of the thorns made the wounds wide. (Ch. 17)

So severe is this experience that Julian, in her words, 'repents' of ever having asked to be so close to Christ, which is to say, ever having to be so close to herself as she experiences Christ's experience of her. The process towards self-acceptance, whether religiously or otherwise, can involve encountering the suffering we have hitherto avoided. Julian writes:

> And all the other pains, because of which I saw that all I can say is too little, for it cannot be told! That showing of Christ's pains filled me full of pain, because I was well-aware that He suffered only once, though He wished to show it me, and fill me with awareness as I had before desired. And in all this time of Christ's pains I felt no pain except for Christ's pains. Then I thought, 'I knew but little what pain it was that I asked for,' and like a wretch I repented me, thinking that if I had known what it would be, I would have been loath to have prayed for it, for it seemed to me that my pains went beyond any bodily death. (Ch. 17)

As readers of Julian, we thus watch Julian moving in and out of self-acceptance, in and out of a desire to be with Christ. The pain here is too great, even when mediated by the body of a loving Other bearing it with her. Closeness to God demands a wider openness to self but this is precisely what sin and suffering make so difficult. We are in opposition to our own experience, in conflict with our reality, divided against ourselves.

Julian's backing out of intimacy with Christ (and with herself) leads to an explicit temptation to take flight from historical, embodied, suffering experience altogether. This is a temptation, not uncommon in religious circles, to a transcendental spirituality that finds peace in self through a flight from the world and time and the self's own experience (Gatta, 1987, p .72). Julian declares that this temptation came to her as a discrete proposal to look away from the crucified Christ and look straight to heaven.

> At this time I wished to look up from the Cross, and I dared not, for I was well-aware that while I gazed on the cross I was secure and safe; therefore I would not agree to put my soul in peril, because, aside from the cross, there was no protection from the horror of demons. *Then I had a proposal in my reason (as if it were like a friend) which said to me, 'Look up to heaven to His Father.'* And I saw well with the Faith that there was nothing between the cross and heaven that could have distressed me. Either it was appropriate for me to look up, or else to answer. (Ch. 19, emphasis mine)

This is the temptation. Julian responds:

> I answered inwardly with all the powers of my soul and said, 'No, I cannot, for Thou art my heaven.' (This I said because I wished not to look up, for I had rather have been in that pain until Doomsday than to have come to heaven otherwise than by Him, for I was well aware that He who bound me so painfully, He would unbind me when He wished.) …And that had been a learning for me that I should evermore do so, choosing only Jesus for my heaven in well and woe. (Ch 19).

Julian chooses to stay in the loving, empathic, acceptant relationship with the divine Other, even if this means having to stay with the pain of her own experience. She stays with a 'trust in the process', as a therapist might say – though for the moment this means great pain.

In Chapter 55 of the *Revelations*, Julian tells us that what made this choice possible. At the same time she was suffering in union with Christ and herself, she also felt, mysteriously, another stream of experience – one of joy, happiness and union with goodness:

> These two parts (of suffering and bliss) were seen and experienced in the eighth showing, in which my body was filled with the experience and memory of Christ's passion and His death – and furthermore, with this was an ethereal feeling and secret inward vision of the high part that I was shown at that same time (when I could not on account of the intermediary's suggestion look up into heaven), and that was because of the powerful vision of the inner life, and this inner life is that exalted essence, that precious soul, which is endlessly rejoicing in the Godhead. (Ch. 55)

Here is precisely the mystery of an authentic relationship. While it allows a more honest and healing journey into the suffering of the self, it sustains the journey at the same time with an 'ethereal' sense of rightness, even a secret rejoicing, a mysterious inner sense of rightness and goodness.

Julian thus rejects the temptation to find peace in flight from herself, in a spurious transcendence. She rejoins the divine Other as her 'heaven' whether that means well or woe. The relationship, and the process it unfolds has absolute priority.

Showing 13: Living in nonsense

Thus far we have seen Julian opening to a more acceptant relationship with herself, and thus drawing closer to God, because of her relationship with the divine Other who has already accepted her unconditionally; she has demonstrated total empathic eagerness to know her experience within Godself. We have seen how this allows Julian to settle into a widely varying self-experience, without any need even for the prospect of 'getting better'. What holds her, what gives her security and assurance, is the relationship itself. In all this, Julian is settling into the flow of her experience, good and bad, painful and delightful, in the assurance of the Other's presence and care. It is a relationship, not self-perfection, not escape from suffering into a transcendental escape, that is widening Julian's capacity to be at peace in herself, and thus close to God.

The *Revelations* show Julian going through one final challenge in her journey to being at home in herself and at home with God: the suffering that is not so much in her but in the world around her, and how she perceived God's way of responding to our suffering.

In the passage quoted at the very start of this essay, indicating that Julian's one-ness with God came through being at peace in herself, there is evidence that this 'being at peace' includes not just her relationship with herself, but being acceptant of the world as it is, and at peace with God's way of working in the world for its redemption. As Julian wrote:

> I saw full certainly that all our endless friendship, our place, our life, and our being is in God… But we are not blissfully safe in possessing our endless joy until we are wholly in peace and in love – that is to say, *fully gratified with God and with all His works and with all His judgements, and loving and peaceable with ourselves and with our fellow Christians and with all that God loves, as love pleases. And this God's goodness carries out in us.* (Ch. 49, emphasis mine)

This is a tall order: being 'fully gratified with God and all His works and with all his judgements...and with all that God loves, as love pleases.'[6] For Julian, 'God's works' include the work of creation and redemption, thus the total of human history. This passage is reminiscent of an earlier showing, Showing 3, in which Julian perceives God's joy permeating each moment, each atom of creation, and herself being invited, indeed tested, to join God in this joy:

> And all this He showed most blessedly, meaning this: 'See, I am God. See, I am in everything. See, I do everything. See, I never lift my hands from my works, nor ever shall, without end. See, I lead everything to the end I ordained for it from without beginning by the same Power, Wisdom, and Love with which I made it. How would anything be amiss?'
>
> Thus powerfully, wisely, and lovingly was the soul tested in this vision. Then I saw truthfully that it was appropriate that I needs must assent with great reverence, rejoicing in God. (Ch. 11)

If such a being at peace with the world as God has allowed it to be seems impossible to us, if outrage at how things are must be sustained for our sense of security and moral clarity, we should take note that it also seemed impossible to Julian. So much is dreadfully wrong; there is too much suffering. It is precisely this question, about the world outside herself, and the agony God has allowed in it, that breaks the bliss Julian had in God in showings 9 through 12. The question about the suffering of the world, and God allowing it all, forces a protest from Julian.

> After that, the Lord brought to my mind the yearning that I had for Him in the past, and I saw that nothing stood in my way except sin (and thus I observed universally in us all). And it seemed to me that if sin had not been, we would all have been pure and like to our Lord as He made us, and thus, in my folly, before this time I often wondered why, by the great foreseeing wisdom of God, the beginning of sin was not prevented, for then, it seemed to me, all would have been well.
>
> But Jesus (who in this vision informed me of all that I needed) answered by this word and said: 'Sin is inevitable, but all shall be well, and all shall be well, and all manner of thing shall be well.' (Ch. 27)

Julian is clear that her concern about the sin, above, is not limited to moral failing. It comprises all the pain of creation:

> In this unadorned word 'sin,' our Lord brought to my mind generally all that is not good, and the shameful despising and the uttermost tribulation that He bore for us in this life, and His dying, and all the pains and sufferings of all His created things, spiritually and bodily. (Ch. 27)

In the majestic words so often quoted from the *Revelations*, God reassures Julian that sin, while inevitable, will not stop God from eventually making all things well: 'Sin is inevitable (ME: behovely), but all shall be well, and all shall be well, and all manner of thing shall be well.' In other words, there is terrible suffering now, and terrible wrong, but all things are within a process of well-making that God will carry out. Julian, however, resists such easy comfort:

> But in this showing I remained watching generally, sorrowful and mourning, saying thus to our Lord in my meaning with full great fear: 'Ah! Good Lord, how can all be well considering the great damage that has come by sin to Thy creatures?' (Ch. 27)

While we can't here trace the entire debate that Julian has with God about this[7] we can define (1) exactly what Julian is seeking here, (2) how the divine Other responds to Julian and (3) what Julian's conclusion is.

1. *What Julian seeks:* What Julian is seeking is comprehension. She seeks intelligibility in God's allowance of evil and pain. She wants God to provide her with an intellectual framework to make sense of the sin, pain, and 'great damage' she sees in the world. She wants God to explain how all that seems so wrong could be a part of God's loving, all-powerful relationship with us. If she can understand why God has allowed sin and suffering, or how God is going to make it well, then with this long view, she can be at peace with the sin and the suffering and more easily rest in God.
2. *How God responds:* God responds in two ways to Julian. The first is by offering examples of how various wrongs have been taken into grace-filled processes to make for greater glory and goodness. For example, she is reminded how sin has been turned into greater good in the lives of the saints (Ch. 38). This is not so much an explanation for the sin and suffering of the world, as an invitation to trust that God can make a greater good out of what is not well. Julian responds to this invitation to trust with more protest, offering up more extreme examples of pain, such as the possibility of eternal damnation (Ch. 32). Finally, God asserts baldly to Julian that how God is going to make all things well is a secret and that God is intentionally not

showing it to her for her good (Ch. 36). This is accompanied by a deeper affirmation that the loving God Julian has experienced so exquisitely in the showings can and will make all things well. Julian even realises that the more she tries to 'figure God's secret out' like a math problem, the further she will be from living with God. This is critical:

> It is God's will that we have great regard for all His deeds that He has done, for He wills thereby that we know, trust, and believe all that He shall do, and evermore it is necessary for us to leave off involving ourselves with what the Deed shall be (that will make all things well), and desire to be like our brethren who are the saints in heaven who wish absolutely nothing but God's will, then shall we rejoice only in God and be well satisfied both with His hiding and with His showing, for I saw truly in our Lord's meaning that the more we busy ourselves to know His secrets in this or any other thing, the farther shall we be from the knowledge of them. (Ch. 33)

In other words, the more we search for a theoretical comprehension of suffering within a larger process that makes 'sense' of God's allowance of it and finds 'sense' in how it can be part of a greater good – the more we search for this, the farther we will get from the actual truth which God intentionally hides from us. What is asked of us is trust in the process without comprehension, without knowing, and this trust is what aligns us more with God and allows us to see how things are.

3. *Julian's conclusion:* Julian's conclusion is one of radical honesty about the world as it is, and continued faith in a God of love who is at work in each moment for the well-making of all things. But since we don't know *how* God is going to make all this world well, let alone why God allowed suffering in the first place, Julian invites us into a state of radical unknowing. The world as it is and faith in a God of all-powerful love make no sense together. There is no understanding, no intelligibility here, and any theorising we do either diminishes God's love or God's power or it minimises the horror of suffering. You might say that Julian invites us into a way of non-sense. This is not a nihilistic nonsense, cracking jokes into the void. It is the nonsense of being held open to the pain of this world exactly as it is, with sustained compassion and love for this world, and with sustained faith that God is at work in everything for final well-being.

The posture described here is analogous to that of Jesus on the cross: open to the world as it is, choosing to trust in God, and witnessing to the love of God, without understanding. There remains a sense, a flow, energy and warmth of God's presence and care, and there remains the horrendous suffering of self and world, right alongside each other.[8] We are invited to remain, simultaneously, in touch with both, and to make room for both inside our awareness.

Epilogue: Julian's place in the ecological crisis

For Julian, creation and ecology were not problems. She mentions hazelnuts, herrings and rain along with blood; she sees all of creation linked to the suffering of Christ, and all of creation washed in his blood, but never is there a concern about a rightful human relation to the non-human world. The problem of human beings disintegrating in sin and wrath and despair, and to a lesser extent, the problem of human society in a fallen world: these were her concerns. There is, however, a way to connect this chapter to the overarching theme of this book.

First, it is reasonable to assume that human beings who have been formed from the inside-out by the kind of relationship with a divine Other that Julian describes will be less inclined to the consumerism and greed that is destroying the human biosphere and causing ecological disaster. We might reasonably hope that this kind of spiritual formation would allow people to live less greedily, less fearfully and more free from materialistic compulsions. The aim of life would not be to create an epicurean enclosed garden, a gated community, where suffering and poverty could be externalised, where threats could be so managed that feelings of contentment could more easily arise, where entertainments could be offered with increasing, passive absorption and even the self becomes a project, physical and spiritual, of technological management.

As noted in the introduction, this kind of epicurean spirituality, which the author experiences as the default, dominant spirituality in the United States, is a combination of escapism and perfectionism. It hopes to bring the 'soul to being at peace in itself' and thus, in Julian's terms, close to God, by inner and outer managed perfectionism while using the power of wealth to keep suffering and humanity at bay. This gives a 'spiritual feeling' to consumers when the perfect house, sofa, or new phone is acquired, while suffering and vulnerability, and the rest of humanity, are kept out of awareness. Sitting with an expensive scotch in a quiet house, tastefully decorated in beige and grey almost like a zen centre, everything in order, there can arise momentary feelings of peace and contentment, general wellness. The problem is that such cocooning in wealth, aesthetics and technological management demands huge exploitation of the world and pretends at separation from the human plight and condition. It lacks a compassionate being-with; it also lacks honesty.

Secondly, if we are headed into our cataclysmic times, as it appears we are, with climate change and increasingly limited resources causing violent upheavals in political systems and driving military conflicts, inspiring ever more ruthless hoarding of resources by the powerful, thus creating yet more class conflict and the dissolution of social bonds – if this is where we are, then it appears that we need something beyond just living a pretty good materialistic life as a basis for feeling good about ourselves, for being at peace in ourselves and thus close to a sense of ultimate goodness, God. As our life expectations and material wellbeing might well decline from previous generations, we need something more than myths of progress or fantastical distractions in consuming technologies to stave off resentment, rage and hatred.

This is where the spiritual formation of the kind Julian invites seems wellnigh essential for the survival of human dignity in a world of cataclysmic change and violence, polarising conflict and declining material standards of being (declining ideally to a sustainable plateau!). Julian invites us into a spiritual formation based on a relationship with a divine Other that creates at the centre of who we are a sense of wholeness and a promise of eventual well-making, despite everything that we experience in our world. She invites us into a relationship with God who births in us a relational joy, an interplay, living and intimate, that embraces everything from Adam's curse to Christ's bliss.

Contemplating all this, the author is reminded of the Dutch Jew Etty Hillesum, chiding her neighbors for safeguarding their vacuum cleaners and dining sets as the Holocaust closed in, all the while neglecting to safeguard the presence of the Holy in their souls. (Woodhouse, 2009, p. 50). Julian invites us into a spiritual formation where presence and joy, the loving and dying of God, established as the existential centre of our selves, enables us to live honestly, compassionately and with dignity and hope. In turbulent times, we safeguard and are safeguarded by this relationship as the source of our final assurance and self-worth. This is Julian's gift to the coming generation of Christians and spiritual seekers, who will have to live through the cataclysms that are likely to come: security and assurance of wellbeing not based on material goods, heroic self-images, freedom from suffering, or conceptual understandings of a chaotic world, but based in a God of unqualified love who accompanies us in our experiences who lives and dies, and lives, at the heart of who we are.

Biographical note

The Rev. Robert Fruehwirth MA has journeyed with Julian for 35 years, first as a monk in an Anglican Religious Order, The Order of Julian of Norwich, then in his training and work as a Person-Centred Counselor and his ministry as Priest Director at the Julian Shrine in Norwich, UK. He now serves as the rector of an Episcopal parish in North Carolina, in the United States.

Notes

1 For an extensive treatment of medieval anchoritic life, see Grace Jantzen's Julian of Norwich, Mystic and Theologian (Jantzen, 2000, pp. 28–50).
2 There is some speculation about the ordering and timing of long and short text. In this essay I adopt the standard view of Jantzen (2000, p. 3) and Watson (2005, pp. 1–3).
3 This I have done with an eye towards therapeutic process and the emergence of self acceptance (Fruehwirth, 2016).
4 'We can never leave off wishing nor longing until we have Him in fullness of joy, and then can we wish for nothing more, for He wills that we be occupied in knowing and loving until the time that we shall be fulfilled in heaven. And for this purpose was this lesson of love shown (along with all that follows, as you shall see) – *for the strength and the basis of all was shown in the first vision*' (Tr. Swanson, *Lesson*, LT Ch 6, emphasis mine).
5 This is the theme of showing 9. See *Revelations*, 22–23.
6 See Showing 3, Ch 11, for a similar expense of challenge.
7 See Fruehwirth (2016, pp. 73–81).
8 See Chapter 10 of Karen Kilby's fascinating book, *God, Evil and the Limits of Theology – Julian of Norwich, Hans Urs Von Balthasar and the Status of Suffering in Christian Theology* (Kilby, 2020) for an exploration of how the desire to make the world and its suffering intelligible draws one away from the Christian Gospel; it involves theology in some kind of compromise.

Bibliography

Fruehwirth, R. 2016. *The Drawing of this Love: Growing in Faith with Julian of Norwich*. Norwich: Canterbury Press.
Gatta, J. 1987. *Three Spiritual Directors for our Time: Julian of Norwich, The Cloud of Unknowing, and Walter Hilton*. Cambridge, MA: Cowley Publications.

Law, S. 2003. *A Room of Her Own: Julian, Creativity, and Prayer*. Norwich: The Friends of Julian of Norwich.

Jantzen, G. 2000. *Julian of Norwich, Mystic and Theologian*. New York: Paulist Press. In this essay in an undated reprint by Whipf and Stock Publishers.

Kilby, K. 2020. *God, Evil, and the Limits of Theology*. London: T&T Clark.

Rogers, C. 1957. The Necessary and Sufficient Conditions of Therapeutic Personality Change. *Journal of Consulting Psychology*, 21, 95–203.

Rogers, C. 1967. *On Becoming a Person*. London: Constable and Company.

Swanson, J.-J. 1988. *A Lesson of Love: The Revelations of Julian of Norwich*. London: Darton, Longman & Todd.

Swanson, J.-J. 2005. *The Complete Julian*. Brewster, MA: Paraclete Press.

Thorne, B. 1998. *Person-Centred Counselling and Christian Spirituality: The Secular and the Holy*. London: Whurr.

Watson, N. and Jenkins, J. 2005. *The Writings of Julian of Norwich*. University Park, PA: Pennsylvania State University Press.

Woodhouse, P. 2009. *Etty Hillesum, A Life Transformed*. London: Continuum.

5 Beloved on the earth: Buddhist and person-centred perspectives on the ecological crisis

Becky Seale

We are currently living in a geological era which many scientists are calling the 'Anthropocene' (Lewis and Maslin, 2015); a term defined by the huge impact human beings have had on the ecosystems of our planet. Our planet has been in existence for approximately four and half billion years and if time were represented as a day, we have only been here for the last four seconds (Macy and Johnstone, 2012). During this short amount of time, however, human beings have had a dramatic and long-lasting impact. Most pressingly, we find ourselves on a rapidly-heating planet with many ecosystems being destroyed and currently there are predictions that we are facing the first human-induced mass extinction of living species on the Earth (IPBES, 2019). The devastating effects of human activity on the planet have been recognised for many years (Meadows et al., 1974), yet efforts to halt environmental destruction have had little effect. The causes of our eco-crisis are multilayered and simple solutions such as stopping the burning of fossil fuels will not be enough alone. Human societies are complex and such simple responses have so far seemed impossible to implement. The responses needed, however, are not only technological but also political, social, psychological and spiritual and require personal, communal and systematic change (Loy, 2018). Harth (2021, p. 142) writes that emotions too are 'essential motivational drivers for actions related to climate change' and so the starting point for this chapter has been through reflection on my feelings and emotional responses to the eco-crisis.

I write as a human being at a particular time in history in which my awareness has been shaped by some significant events. As a teenager towards the end of the Cold War, the fear of nuclear disaster woke me up in the mornings with a pit in my stomach and Chernobyl felt too close to us in rural England. I was lucky to have grown up in the countryside where I could play all day in the beechwoods of the Chiltern Hills. We would be gone all day without anyone worrying about where we were or what we were up to. In the summer

I would visit family by the sea in Wales near where I live now. Today, I am close to the estuary where I can watch the tides and sunsets across the water; I feel most alive when I'm swimming in the sea and walking along the coastal path. By the time I went to university, I was unfashionably worried about the ozone layer and the greenhouse effect, but throughout my life I have gone on to find other people who feel as concerned as I do and I have made many lifestyle choices which could give me strong 'green credentials'. A few years ago I joined in with the exciting energy and buzz of climate activists in central London. I joined multi-faith groups in walking meditation in Trafalgar Square and sitting vigils on Westminster Bridge, surrounded by the chaos and noise of protesters in stand-offs with the police. For a while, it felt purposeful and proactive. Now, I watch from a distance as protesters disrupt and anger those around them and I'm unconvinced about the utility of these actions.

In Zen, there is a tradition of the 'koan': an unanswerable question or rather a question that can't be answered through logic or 'knowing' but instead requires an altered state of knowing. We may not find an answer to the question but rather gain new insight or understanding (Brazier, 1995). Koan-like, my inquiry at the heart of this chapter has grown from my unanswered and unanswerable questions about the eco-crisis: what can I do to respond to the knowledge that human beings are having such a devastating effect on our beloved Earth? I find myself in a place of not knowing; a moment of stasis and inaction as I struggle with the uncomfortable feeling that I should be doing more. Pihkala's (2022) taxonomy of climate emotions highlights the range of feelings which may be experienced in relation to the ecological crisis, from eco-anxiety to 'solastalgia', a term which specifically relates to distress related to the environment (Albrecht et al., 2007). All of these responses are worthy of exploration yet a key question that interests me here is the nature of what it means to be a person in the context of what we have done to the planet. If I and other human beings don't do something to fix this problem we have created, and if as a species we don't take the action needed to stop it, does that make us fundamentally selfish and uncaring beings? If this is so, how do I feel about myself and my fellow human beings?

I am particularly interested in the notion of blame, shame, responsibility and the ability to respond to the environmental crisis. As a person-centred counsellor, I am also concerned with cultivating wellbeing, and there is no more important aspect of wellbeing to consider than that of our place in the natural world in the face of this crisis. The environmental crisis may also be considered as much a spiritual challenge as a technological or economic one (Loy, 2018; Pihkala, 2018), in that it requires an awareness of our being part of something larger than our individual selves. My reflections also include my Buddhist practice, which I see as an extension of a person-centred perspective (Seale, 2020). I consider how a Buddhist philosophy cultivates an awareness of a connection with, rather than separation from, all that exists; and how both approaches offer some insight into our nature as human beings in addressing our predicament.

My reflections in considering the question of how to respond to the enormity of our challenge are influenced by heuristic (Moustakas, 1990) and narrative inquiry (Etherington, 2020) with a focus on stories and meaning-making. Moustakas's (1990) methodology involves a phenomenological exploration (Sultan, 2019) requiring an immersive and intuitive process of reflection; an aspect which also aligns closely with a person-centred philosophy. Douglass and Moustakas (1985, p. 39) propose that heuristic inquiry is a 'passionate and discerning personal involvement in problem-solving, an effort to know the essence of some aspect of life through the internal pathways of the self'. I therefore hope this inquiry will shed light on the essence of some aspects of our predicament that will have some wider resonance and applicability to others. Along with the objective reality of scientific data which must be understood and responded to, I also consider the power of stories to influence and guide human experience which must also be understood if as human beings we are to navigate our way through environmental catastrophe. For Etherington (2004), our values, beliefs and influences become part of the story of research and she proposes there is a value in telling stories to 'reach readers on many different levels' (2020, p.80). I am writing from the inside out and I am unable to separate the story I tell from the time and context in which I tell it. Whilst I question a postmodern rejection of objective scientific 'truth,' and wonder what impact such a rejection has had on debates about climate change, I also recognise and value the importance of subjective experience and write here as a human being alive at this particular time in history; contemplating the end days of humanity and all life on Earth.

It may seem reasonable to assume that the escalation of the ecological crisis is due to human indifference, apathy or lack of care. Weintrobe (2021) describes modern, Western neo-liberal culture as a 'culture of uncare' with many of us denying or minimising the seriousness of our predicament. For Weintrobe (2021, p.13), the psychological roots of climate change lie in 'a rigid psychological mindset' in which we believe that we can have whatever we want. This echoes the views of Pope Francis (2015) who asserts that human actions leading to our ecological crisis are underpinned by selfishness, greed and an obsession with consumerism. According to the Climate Psychology Alliance (2022), the key 'challenge lies in the belief that, as a species, we are different and special compared to other species; that nature is a resource for us to use.' These perspectives resonate with how I feel at times both towards myself and towards others, yet I also hear chastisement in them which I suspect may ultimately be counterproductive (Harth, 2021). This may tell only part of the story about human beings and it may be worth considering whether there are underlying causes for humanity's 'rigid mindset' and selfishness. In turning to person-centred and Buddhist philosophies, I explore other layers and deeper causes that may tell a different story about human beings.

Person-centred perspectives

Weintrobe's (2021) discussion of the psychological roots of the climate crisis is approached through a psychoanalytic perspective which frames psychological process as a struggle between caring and uncaring parts of ourselves. Human beings have both an equal capacity to love and for 'ruthless destructiveness' (Weintrobe, 2021, p. 12) and our task as adult human beings is to learn to master our narcissistic drives and rein in the part of us that doesn't care. In contrast to psychoanalytic perspectives, the person-centred approach to counselling and psychotherapy, based on humanistic philosophy, has a more optimistic view of human nature. The concept of the 'actualising tendency' (Rogers, 1959, p. 195) is defined as 'the inherent tendency of the organism to develop all its capacities in ways which serve to maintain or enhance the organism'. As Tudor and Worrall (2006, p. 87) write, this is an 'organic and natural metaphor' at odds with the 'earlier inorganic or mechanical metaphors' of psychodynamic or behavioural approaches to psychotherapy. It is perhaps this mechanistic worldview, which perpetuates the idea that human beings can control nature, that underlies our ecological crisis (Bazzano, 2013; Duncan, 2023). As a philosophy which primarily sees human beings as inseparable from the natural world, a humanistic and person-centred approach may align well with an ecological perspective.

For Rogers (1959), the actualising tendency is the primary motivational force for human behaviour and hence a key feature of person-centred therapy is the lack of necessity to steer clients towards any particular way of being. As Freire (2001) emphasises, there is no need for therapists to *do* anything to effect change in the client but rather to trust in this tendency for growth. Whilst the person-centred approach does not deny the negative aspects of human nature, Rogers (2013, p. 24) rejects the psychodynamic view in emphatically stating that he finds 'no evidence of innate destructive tendencies, nor a necessity of keeping human nature under control'. In person-centred psychology, a 'fully-functioning' or psychologically healthy person is a 'congruent' one; someone who is authentic and open to their experience as it is in the moment (Rogers, 1959). Rogers' theory suggests that we lose the ability to trust in our experience though, through internalising values from others around us; that is, some experiences become valued as acceptable and some unacceptable in relation to social and relational expectations. This disconnection, arising from what Rogers terms the development of 'conditions of worth' (1959), leads not only to a lack of trust in ourselves but also a primary disconnection between experience and our being in the world. In his later work, Rogers (1980) considers a wider understanding of the actualising tendency to describe a formative tendency which extends to a sense of connection with the natural world and beyond to the Universe. Our disconnection from the natural world therefore may be viewed in terms of our 'incongruence' or disconnection from ourselves and our organismic experience (Ottiger and Joseph, 2021).

The implications of this philosophy in the context of a response to ecological awareness and concern for the environment could suggest that the behaviour which leads to the destruction of our natural environment can be understood through this concept of incongruence, rather than selfishness or narcissistic entitlement (Weintrobe, 2021). In terms of person-centred theory, therefore, the ability to cultivate the conditions that enable the development of greater congruence or authenticity may consequently enable the development of greater environmental sensibilities. In person-centred theory, Rogers (1959) identifies the necessary and sufficient conditions for therapeutic change to occur and to enable clients to move from incongruence to congruence. These conditions include the relational qualities of a person experiencing genuine acceptance and empathic understanding from another human being. As part of this process, our conditions of worth are understood to 'dissolve', which enables greater self-acceptance and thus the development of greater congruence. It is the aspect of acceptance of the person, often described as experiencing 'unconditional positive regard' for the other, however, that is considered *the* curative factor in therapy (Bozarth, 1998) and the distinctive feature of the approach (Freire, 2001). When human beings feel accepted and deeply understood by another in this theory, our 'positive and forward-moving core' is revealed (Mearns and Thorne 2000, p. 61).

On evil

The notion of being able to experience unconditional positive regard towards all human beings can be very challenging when there is so much evidence of destructive human behaviour in the world. In person-centred theory, however, the ability to accept others unconditionally is something that is more likely to arise naturally with empathic understanding of the experience of others. For those of us working in the field of therapy, it is therefore important to seek first to understand, and to explore and question our beliefs and assumptions about human nature if we are to be of help to others. The possibility of qualities such as 'evil' being inherent to human beings does pose a particular challenge. However, it may be considered a 'category error' to conflate humans' actions with their intrinsic being (Worsley, 2005, p. 148). The fact that we may commit evil, selfish or destructive acts does not necessarily make us so. Robinson (2019) shows some understanding of this when she suggests it is the denial of climate change that is 'malign and evil' rather than those doing the denying.

The concept of evil may be seen as an estrangement from our actualising tendency or the deprivation of love, not only love of others but of ourselves (Schmid, 2010). Thorne (in Mearns and Thorne, 2000, p. 63) proposes that destructive or evil behaviour in human beings is the result of being 'not yet able to recognise the essential wonder of our own natures and to live it out in the world'. The theory of incongruence sees the actualising tendency as something that becomes thwarted or inhibited rather than an inner struggle between good and evil, with an emphasis more on human potential rather than deficit or moral weakness' (Mearns and Thorne, 2000). Destructive aspects of human nature are accordingly viewed as the result of the absence of more positive relational experiences rather than an inherent fixed quality.

Person-centred practitioners may be considered naive in having such positive views of human nature. By failing to acknowledge our own or our clients' destructive behaviour and personalities, May (in Mearns and Thorne, 2000, p. 62) argues that person-centred practitioners are 'wilfully blind to the "shadow side" of human nature'. Rogers (1961, p. 27) was aware of such criticisms of his approach in emphasising that he does not simply take a 'Pollyanna view' of human beings that denies the cruelty and destructive side of human nature. As Thorne (Mearns and Thorne, 2000, p. 63) argues, transformation is possible not through 'avoiding evil but by engaging with it and by disarming it through the power of relationship where spirit meets spirit'. The paradox at the heart of the person-centred approach is that change occurs through the acceptance of aspects of our nature which might be deemed as unacceptable (Freire, 2001); there is a need therefore to face our own shadow or 'evil' in order to accept ourselves. It is this notion which in practice echoes the first noble truth in Buddhism: that of fully knowing or understanding suffering (Batchelor, 1997).

Applying Buddhist perspectives

For Zen monk Thich Nhat Hanh (2021, p.12), learning the 'art of happiness' also requires us to learn the 'art of suffering'; the more we learn about and understand the roots of our suffering, the more we can overcome them. This is essential, he proposes, in order to become fully present as we confront the enormity of the planet's predicament. Buddhist teaching does not directly focus on the notion of 'evil' other than considering greed, ill-will and delusion as the three poisons or roots of what could be termed 'evil' (Loy, 2018). It is through understanding how these qualities lead to suffering that these 'poisons' can be transformed into generosity, compassion and wisdom. Wisdom, Loy (2018) suggests, includes a recognition that our wellbeing and the wellbeing of others and the Earth itself are not separate things. Generosity involves being able to offer unconditional 'open-hearted kindness to others' (p. 166); a notion that clearly resonates with the person-centred concept of unconditional positive regard. These qualities are cultivated not only for moral or ethical reasons, however, but because they lead to a reduction of suffering: our own as well as others'. The cultivation of these qualities also connects with a higher part of ourselves which is in Buddhist terms called '*buddhata*' or our buddha nature. For Brazier (1995, p. 34) this concept is the common ground between humanism and Zen: that is something 'essentially trustworthy at the core of the person'. Loy (2018, p. 56) also echoes person-centred philosophy in describing buddha nature as an 'energetic, self-organizing organism'. For Armstrong (2022) buddha nature is an expression of existence itself, which again implies a quality intrinsic to not only human nature but all that lives. Brazier (1995, p. 34), however, considers the differences in the two concepts from a Buddhist perspective: buddha nature is not a fixed entity and may be understood more as 'self-transcending' rather than self-actualising. In terms of developing a greater ecological awareness, this calls for moving away from a *person*-centred emphasis to one that decentres the person (Bazzano, 2013); something Loy (2018, p. 106) regards as waking up to the 'illusion of separation'. It is through this realisation of our connection to all that exists, that human self-centredness can be transformed.

Brazier (1995) warns of a tendency in therapy to encourage clients to focus on their own needs, suggesting that therapy culture encourages selfishness. He argues that therapy becomes a 'handmaiden of consumerism' (p. 203) and therefore could imply that a focus on the self in therapy exacerbates the causes of the environmental crisis. Welwood (2000, p.207) argues however that both emotional and psychological work is needed in order for us to ground ourselves in a 'personal way of relating to life' for a spiritual connection to have any authenticity. 'Soulwork', Welwood (2000, p. 16) asserts, requires us to 'come down to earth' before we can engage in what might be a spiritual surrender of the self. As Zen master Dogen advised, 'to study the self is to forget the self' (Batchelor, 1997, p. 91) and the study of the self is multifaceted. Learning to understand the self may be a necessary step in developing greater awareness of the inner experience of ourselves as embodied beings before being able to overcome our desire and craving.

The second of the Buddhist noble truths has been termed as having the capacity to release our cravings (Batchelor, 2011). Craving or desire for material things which then leads to overconsumption is a significant underlying cause of human destructive behaviour. But as Batchelor (2011) points out, the noble truths are not intended to be dogma, and ridding ourselves of desire is not something that can happen through forcing ourselves to do so. Undoubtedly some effort is required in order to make changes to our behaviour, and from a Buddhist perspective this is viewed as putting in the 'right' kind of effort. Finding a balance in terms of 'right effort' or 'right action' is something that can be difficult to achieve, however, and requires the ability to develop a sensitivity and awareness of our inner process (Burbea, 2014). It is perhaps important to consider carefully the motivations underlying our actions if they are to be helpful and for Nhat Hanh (2021, p. 81), the 'quality of action depends on the quality of being'. As human beings we have a tendency towards feeling both inferior and superior and the work for us is to recognise that we are neither exceptional nor flawed. It is important to recognise, therefore, that action borne from either a sense of inferiority or of knowing best may be just as unhelpful as inaction. Actions based on guilt or chastisement of ourselves or others may be equally unfruitful.

It is worth recognising perhaps that we can't make ourselves or other human beings *be* a certain way, or be other than we are, any more than we can make a plant grow or be a different type of plant. Rather than forcing ourselves to change, both Buddhist and person-centred philosophies stress the need to offer the right conditions for growth and both approaches urge self-acceptance and understanding; if we don't respect ourselves, 'it will be difficult to respect others or the Earth' (Nhat Hanh, 2021, p. 97). It may be that respect for the Earth is as much about what we don't do, rather a letting go and a letting be that allows the natural world to grow and regenerate without human actions (Bazzano, 2013). Human beings have, after all, done too much already.

Underlying motivations

Using language to describe human beings as fundamentally selfish, evil or narcissistic is perhaps counterproductive and as Bregman (2020, p. 134) fears, 'cynicism can become a self-fulfilling prophecy'. A cynical view would also suggest that environmental concerns are purely utilitarian, in the same way that acts of charity could be viewed as selfish because it feels good to do them. Neville (1999, p. 69) questions this view by suggesting that caring for the planet is not simply a question of morality but rather an 'expression of our identity'. This view is also supported by Bregman (2020, p. 384), who points out it is irrelevant whether we base our actions on altruism or self-interest, 'Doing good typically feels good because it *is* good'. In terms of person-centred theory, this may be seen as expression of our congruent being or in Buddhist terms, our buddha nature.

Disconnection from our inherent interconnectedness with all that is the Earth, the Universe and the Cosmos (Nhat Hanh, 2021) may be considered a key psychological cause of the environmental crisis. As Nhat Hanh asserts (2021, p. 14), 'we are the environment, we are the Earth' and so what we need is love, understanding and compassion, for ourselves and our fellow beings. Craving, which is considered at the heart of suffering in Buddhist terms, underlies the experience of addiction which many experience in modern society and drives much of our overconsumption. According to Hari (2022, p. 276), we are living in the midst of an 'attention crisis' and we 'can only solve the climate crisis if we solve our attention crisis.' Again, as individuals, we may feel personally responsible for the distractions we face from social media and the smartphone culture. We may blame ourselves for our weakness yet smartphones and social media have been expressly designed for us to find them irresistibly addictive. Whilst Hari (2022) points out that these aspects of modern society are greatly impeding our ability to join together to find collective solutions to the world's crises, this is a collective as well as an individual concern. It is worth noting that there is much evidence to suggest that addictive behaviour in general is strongly related to trauma experiences (Maté, 2018), which further indicates that it is not always moral fibre that human beings lack.

Society, culture and the trauma of disconnection

The person-centred approach has been criticised for a focus on individualism (Holdstock, 1993; Neville, 1999) as has therapy in general (Brazier, 1995) and this is perhaps a symptom of an emphasis in the Western world on individualism and autonomy, which could also underlie views of human selfishness. Environmental approaches also tend to emphasise individual actions and solutions to environmental problems such as recycling, not flying and other consumer choices. Welwood (2000, p. 4) theorises that psychologies of ego in the West and egolessness in the East represent two different aspects of human nature and that we need both aspects to fully realise the 'potentials inherent in human existence'. Human wholeness, he writes, is essential for the planet and requires us to bring both sides of our nature together.

Mearns and Thorne (2000, p. 56) suggest that it is the organisation of human societies that has led to us losing touch with our 'humanity and the humanity of others' and there is much evidence to show that human beings can live in constructive relationships with the natural world implying that environmentally destructive behaviour is not an inevitably human quality (Bregman, 2020). Many cultures have co-existed with their natural surroundings for centuries and many continue to do so (Ottiger and Joseph, 2021). Bendell (2023) conjectures that the story of humans being innately destructive encourages our separation and argues that it is specific historical events rather than innate human nature that have led to this separation. Bendell (2023) goes on to argue that it is patriarchal culture that encourages shaming and blaming as well as emotional disconnection. It is our culture, he contends, that has taught us how to be in the world and which ultimately has led to the ecocide the planet is facing. He also calls for moving beyond the view of the inherent destructiveness of human beings as this can enhance our fear and sense of feeling unsafe in the world. After all, as Pinker (2011) argues, there may be much evidence to suggest that human beings and human societies are becoming far less violent as they develop despite our perceptions, therefore these fears may be self-perpetuating and our perceptions worth questioning.

Disconnection from our land and the natural world may be viewed as the result of a 'deep legacy of systematic broken attachment and oppression', leading to a traumatic severance from our environment (Duncan, 2023). The environmental destruction we are currently facing, Duncan writes, (p. 20) may be the result of the 'culmination of centuries of alienation from nature' which is linked to trauma 'which is so endemic it's hard to see it for what it is'. If, as he suggests, the lives we are living today are the result of 'hundreds of years of the human soul living in exile', then it would not be surprising if we find our current situation somewhat overwhelming and not easily corrected. Bendell (2023) concurs with this view by highlighting that many human beings are being coerced to accept the economic systems in which we live today and many people and cultures have been violently killed in the process.

In terms of person-centred theory, we could be seen to be living a cultural 'condition of worth'; a collective sense of unworthiness that may both cause and sustain our current challenges. Loy (2018) notes that many human beings carry a sense of lack and not being good enough and argues that it is this feeling that feeds our desire for things or power; a desire that can never be satisfied. Blaming ourselves and others, though, will only reinforce our sense of worthlessness. Nhat Hanh (2021) urges us to recognise that it is not that our world leaders don't want to do something, it is more that they can't: they don't know how to deal with their own pain and suffering. Figueres (in Nhat Hanh 2021, p. 215) warns that 'the moment that you engage in the blaming games and demonizing…you've lost your game'. Harth's (2021) study supports this view by exploring the impact of cultivating positive views of ourselves rather than eliciting blame or guilt to motivate change in relation to the ecological crisis. It may be that societies which value 'aggressive competitiveness and materialistic selfishness' (Mearns and Thorne, 2000, p. 62) make it unlikely that human beings will meet their potential; therefore an ability to address these values on a societal level may be necessary if we are to address the crisis overall.

There is much evidence to show that inequality in many of our societies has had a huge impact on mental and physical health and is also implicated in overconsumption as competition for social status is a significant driver for many consumers (Pickett and Wilkinson, 2009). Another facet of the impact of living in an unequal society is evident in Schor's (1998) research which highlights the human propensity to overconsume as a result of societal pressures and a desire to keep up with what we see others around us having. Children in particular are susceptible to this kind of social influence and Schor's (2004) work shows how they are targeted as consumers at a time in their lives where belonging is particularly important. The commercialisation of children hence is a huge factor in overconsumption in modern society. It is questionable whether children can be held responsible for overconsumption when huge amounts of money are ploughed into advertising, turning them into consumer addicts. It may therefore be unreasonable to blame ourselves for our selfishness when so many aspects of our culture and society are designed and shaped for us to behave in these ways. Meadows (2004, p. 261) writes that rather than needing new things, we need 'admiration and respect' and instead of trying to fill needs for 'identity, community and self-esteem', we need instead 'challenge, love and joy'.

Beyond blame

Whilst there is much value in understanding subjective phenomenological experience, there may be dangers also in making assumptions about personal perceptions without objective evidence. Bregman (2020) highlights a human tendency towards negativity bias in our thinking and presents a strong case against inherent selfishness concerning environmental destruction. He considers it 'utterly unrealistic' (p. 381) to view human beings as selfish or destructive. Although humans are undoubtedly responsible for the potential destruction of life on Earth, it may be worth considering whether we are to blame: at least as individuals and as Bendell (2023) urges, we perhaps need to forgive ourselves instead. Lerztman (2013, p. 130) considers apathy in the face of climate change to be a symptom of 'difficult and conflicting affective states' which may alternatively be a sense of eco-paralysis experienced by people who care *too* much. Underneath the mask of apathy, writes Pihkala (2018), people have profound feelings. Considerable evidence suggests that people do care deeply about the environment (Davis and Levi, 2021), which again indicates a need to question whether human selfishness and narcissism are fundamental causes of the destruction of the environment. Many people have other pressing concerns in their lives and it may be hard to contribute to action on environmental issues for those struggling to get their most basic needs met (Nhat Hanh, 2021). It could be seen as somewhat of a luxury to be worrying deeply about environmental issues which are not always impacting on daily life and which may seem far off in the future (Harth, 2021; Lertzman, 2013).

As Bregman (2020) suggests, 'If we believe most people are decent and kind, everything changes.' Whilst it may not be difficult to believe that human beings are always worthy of respect, believing the story that human beings are innately in need of being controlled in order to stop destroying the planet may also not be a helpful approach. When I view my fellow humans with distrust and see others doing the same, it seems inevitable to me that fear and distrust will grow. In contrast to the Judeo-Christian concept of 'Original sin', Nhat Hanh (1995, p .44) instead puts forwards the Buddhist view that we all carry negative seeds within us such as of violence and hatred. At the same time, however, we also carry a 'seed of compassion within us' (Nhat Hanh, 2021, p. 113), and it is the circumstances and conditions we find ourselves in that will determine which seeds grow more vigorously. This metaphor echoes a person-centred and humanistic view that, as with all beings in nature, our conditions determine how we grow. If the seed of violence is watered, then violence will prevail, Nhat Hanh (2021) writes, and if the seed of compassion is watered, then compassion will flourish. There is perhaps a tendency for human beings to polarise qualities such as good and evil; selfish and caring; inferiority and superiority; and yet, as Welwood (2000) and Nhat Hanh (2021) imply, our true nature both accepts and transcends these qualities. It may paradoxically be through acceptance of them even that we become able to transcend them. It is necessary perhaps to recognise and embrace all aspects of human nature and as Welwood (2000, p. 5) suggests, it may be 'essential for the planet' that we do so, to 'discover our human wholeness'. Worsely (2005, p. 156) also asks us not to push away these different aspects of what it means to be human. Denial of the potential to be destructive or, in the case of ecological destruction, uncaring and selfish, also denies our humanity. Acceptance of ourselves and others means accepting all parts of ourselves. Welwood (2000, p. 285) considers that it is our true or 'absolute nature' which 'allows a universal compassion' to grow. I recognise that it is human acts of selfishness and destructive ways of being that are ultimately harming all that we have on the planet and these aspects are part of our nature. However, as I have explored here, there may be some ways to understand or explain these aspects, such as inequality in societies, trauma and the deprivation of love. Human beings, after all, also have an immense capacity to be caring, compassionate and loving beings.

Conclusion: What the world needs now

Climate anxiety is increasing particularly amongst young people (Clayton and Karazia, 2020) and therapists hold an important role in providing support for others as we face whatever this future holds; something we can only do if we have explored our own emotional responses (Totton, 2023). Totton (2023, p. 74) writes that 'ecologically aware psychotherapists and counsellors need to prepare to be among those who act as therapists to the human race, as it increasingly wrestles with its grief, fear, anger and guilt'. Macy (2007, p. 123) echoes this when she writes that to 'heal society, our psyches must heal as well'. The greatest healing may come not from curing an illness but in coming to terms with it and thus healing demands our unconditional presence: accepting all parts of our humanity (Welwood, 2000).

My interest in this chapter has been an exploration of the intrinsic nature of human beings which emerges from my reflections after a lifetime of concern for the natural world and through questioning my responsibility: that is, my ability to respond. I have reached a point in my life where I no longer know what to do and question whether there is anything that I can do; and underlying this position I find myself in is a feeling of responsibility and self-blame. There are feelings of frustration and powerlessness at being able to effect so little change; like watching a cup that is about to fall, I can't quite catch it before it crashes to the ground. I have considered here person-centred views of human nature and motivations and some connections with Buddhist teachings in order to consider how to respond. Buddhist teachings, however, suggest that there is a need simply to respond appropriately; instead of telling us *what* to do exactly, the teachings offer a guide for *how* to do it (Loy, 2018). Nhat Hanh (2021, p. 81) writes that 'Sometimes you don't do anything but you do a lot. And sometimes you do a lot and you don't do anything'; ill-considered actions can be counterproductive.

Environmental action can range from making changes in consumer choices to engaging in direct political action. However, to be psychologically adaptive, it is important to stay engaged emotionally as well as to develop compassion and care for others and a connection with the natural world (Andrews and Hoggett, 2019). It is perhaps *how* these actions are undertaken that is as important as what action is taken and ecological activism can become itself a spiritual path (Loy, 2018).

Blaming and judgment can be seen as maladaptive responses (Andrews and Hoggett, 2019) and therefore viewing our fellow humans with compassion and understanding is an important aspect of addressing the ecological crisis. In person-centred theory, as I have discussed here, incongruence or disconnection from nature is a symptom of our lack of acceptance of our organismic experience. This lack of acceptance is borne from a lack of regard for our inherent worthiness and it is this very feeling of lack that can lead human beings towards the overconsumption that is damaging the Earth we so depend on.

Etherington (2020) highlights the role of stories in giving meaning beyond the local and personal context; stories can be healing. How we make sense of and understand events in our lives and the meanings we give to them can transform and heal; soothe and calm; inspire as well as destroy and as Solnit (2023) writes, we need new stories about our environmental crisis. The story of human selfishness is one I have particularly wanted to address here as I suggest it is one that both creates and perpetuates environmental breakdown. The intrinsic values of human beings include the importance of shared community and compassion and there is perhaps a need to develop more shared positive stories about human beings and our communities for effecting change; we must create 'tales of joy' rather than the ones of 'terror' – so often a theme in social and environmental activism (Harré, 2023, p. 38). There is a human tendency towards 'othering': dividing those of us who care, the goodies, from the careless baddies causing all the evil and destruction in the world as well as a strong sense that 'others can't be trusted' (ibid.). It is important to move beyond this and recognise that these qualities belong to us all. Shohet (2023, p. 44) writes that fear 'is the source of all pollution' and fearing the range of our feelings in response to environmental breakdown as well as fearing our fellow human beings may ultimately be our downfall. There is an urgent need to 'cultivate an empathy with our fellow human beings that transcends national, political, racial and other ideological boundaries as well as a sense of responsibility – and love – towards the "myriad things" of nature' (Armstrong, 2022, pp 80–181). Underlying the selfishness and the overconsumption that is driving our environmental crisis lies a lack of understanding and acceptance of the entirety of what it means to be a human being. Nhat Hanh (2021) advises that there is first a need to find inner stability through finding a quiet space within. 'Once we have peace, we are clear enough and calm enough to see the way forward', he writes (p. 53). There is no need to force ourselves to act but rather the right and appropriate action will naturally arise from the space we have cleared within. As poet Martha Postlethwaite (2019) writes, 'Only then will you know how to give yourself to this world so worthy of rescue.'

The combined philosophies of the person-centred approach and Buddhist practice offer respectively a psychological and spiritual path which are both needed to support our actions. They offer a shared understanding of the intrinsic nature and motivations of human beings; that we do not need to be compelled to care but rather our capacity to care and love for all beings and our beloved Earth arise naturally through the realisation of our interconnectedness with all beings and our planet.

Biographical note

Becky Seale is a lecturer in counselling at Coleg Sir Gâr on the University of Wales Trinity St David validated foundation degree and BA in counselling in Ammanford, Wales, UK. Becky's interest in the person-centred approach to counselling and her Buddhist practice formed the basis for her MA in counselling practice in 2015. She has also had a keen and active interest in environmental issues throughout her life.

Bibliography

Albrecht, G., Sartore, G.M., Connor, L., Higginbotham, N., Freeman, S., Kelly, B., Stain, H., Tonna, A. and Pollard, G. 2007. Solastalgia: the Distress Caused by Environmental Change. *Australasian Psychiatry: Bulletin of Royal Australian and New Zealand College of Psychiatrists*, 15, 1, 41–55.

Andrews, N. and Hoggett, P. 2019. Facing up to Ecological Crisis: A Psychosocial Perspective from Climate Psychology. In: Foster, J., ed. *Facing up to Climate Reality: Honesty, Disaster and Hope*. London: Green House Publishing, pp. 155–172.

Armstrong, K. 2022. *Sacred Nature*. London: Penguin.

Batchelor, S. 1997. *Buddhism Without Beliefs*. London: Bloomsbury.

Batchelor, S. 2011.*Confession of a Buddhist Atheist*. New York: Speigal and Grau.

Bazzano, M. 2013. One More Step: From Person-Centered to Eco-Centered Therapy. *Person-centered and Experiential Psychotherapies*, 12, 4, 344–354.

Bendell, J. 2023. *Breaking Together: A Freedom-Loving Response to Collapse*. Bristol: Good Works.

Bozarth, J. 1998. *Person-centered Therapy: A Revolutionary Paradigm*. Ross-on-Wye: PCCS Books.

Brazier, D. 1995. *Zen Therapy*. London: Robinson.

Bregman, R. 2020. *Humankind: A Hopeful History*. London: Bloomsbury.

Burbea, R. 2014. *Seeing That Frees*. West Ogwell: Hermes Amara.

Clayton, S. and Karazsia, B. 2020. Development and Validation of a Measure of Climate Change Anxiety. *Journal of Environmental Psychology*. 69.

Climate Psychology Alliance. 2022. *Handbook of Climate Psychology*. Available at: www.climatepsychologyalliance.org/index.php/component/content/article/climate-psychology-handbook?catid=15&Itemid=101 (accessed August 2023).

Davis, R. and Levi, S. 2021. *A Crisis in Common: How Eco-Anxiety is Shared Across Our Country*. Available at: https://globalfuturefoundation.com/reports/a-crisis-in-common/ (accessed May 2025).

Douglass, B.G. and Moustakas, C. 1985. Heuristic Inquiry: The Internal Search to Know. *Journal of Humanistic Psychology*, 25, 3, 39–55.

Duncan, R. 2023. What Your Biology Teacher Didn't Teach You: Reclaiming a Western Indigenous Relationship With Nature for a Post-Mechanistic World. In: Aspey, L. et al., eds., *Holding the Hope: Reviving Psychological and Spiritual Agency in the Face of Climate Change*. Monmouth: PCCS Books, pp. 7–25.

Etherington, K. 2004. *Becoming a Reflexive Researcher: Using Ourselves in Research*. London: Jessica Kingsley Publishers.

Etherington, K. 2020. Being a Narrative Researcher. In: Bager-Charleson, S. and McBeath, A. eds., *Enjoying Research in Counselling and Psychotherapy: Qualitative, Quantitative and Mixed Methods Research*. London: Palgrave Macmillan, pp. 73–93.

Francis, P. 2015. *Laudato Si' – On Care for Our Common Home*. Vatican: Vatican Press.

Freire, B. 2001. Unconditional Positive Regard: The Distinctive Feature of Client-Centred Therapy. In: Bozarth, J.D. and Wilkins, P., ed. *Rogers' Therapeutic Conditions: Evolution, Theory and Practice*. Ross-on-Wye: PCCS Books, pp. 145–154.

Hari, J. 2022. *Stolen Focus*. London: Bloomsbury.

Holdstock, T.L. 1993. Can We Afford Not to Revision the Person-Centred Concept of Self? In Brazier, D., ed. *Beyond Carl Rogers*. London: Constable, pp. 29–52.

Harré, N. 2023. Towards a Sacred Framework. In: Aspey, L. et al., ed. *Holding the Hope: Reviving Psychological and Spiritual Agency in the Face of Climate Change*. Monmouth: PCCS Books, pp. 33–41.

Harth. N. 2021. Affect, (Group-Based) Emotions, and Climate Change Action. *Current Opinion in Psychology*, 42, 140–144.

IPBES. 2019. *Global Assessment Report on Biodiversity and Ecosystem Services of the Intergovernmental Science-Policy Platform on Biodiversity and Ecosystem Services*, ed. E.S. Brondizio, J. Settele, S. Díaz, and H.T. Ngo. Bonn: IPBES Secretariat.

Lertzman, R.A. 2013. The Myth of Apathy: Psychoanalytic Explorations of Environmental Subjectivity. In: Weintrobe, S., ed. *Engaging with Climate Change: Psychoanalytic and Interdisciplinary Perspectives*. Hove: Routledge, pp. 117–133.

Lewis, S. and Maslin, M. 2015. Defining the Anthropocene. *Nature*, 519, 171–180.

Loy, D. 2018. *Ecodharma: Buddhist Teachings for the Ecological Crisis*. Somerville: Wisdom Publications.

Macy, J. 2007. *World as Lover, World as Self*. Berkeley, CA: Parallax Press.

Macy, J. and Johnstone, C. 2012. *Active Hope: How to Face the Mess We're in with Unexpected Resilience and Creative Power*. Novato, CA: New World Library.

Maté, G. 2018. In: *the Realm of Hungry Ghosts: Close Encounters with Addiction*. London: Penguin.

Meadows, D. et al. 1974. *The Limits to Growth*. New York: Universe Books.

Meadows, D., Randers, J. and Meadows, D. 2004. *The Limits to Growth: The 30-Year Update*. Chelsea, VT: Chelsea Green Publishing Company.

Mearns, D. and Thorne, B. 2000. *Person-Centred Therapy Today: New Frontiers in Theory and Practice*. London: SAGE.

Moustakas, C. 1990. *Heuristic Research: Design, Methodology and Applications*. London: Sage.

Neville, B. 1999. The Client-Centred Eco-Psychologist. *The Person-Centered Journal*, 6, 1, 59–74.

Nhat Hanh, T. 1995. *Living Buddha, Living Christ*. London: Rider.

Nhat Hanh, T. 2021. *Zen and the Art of Saving the Planet*. London: Penguin.

Ottiger, A.S. and Joseph, S. 2021. From Ego-centred to Eco-centred: An Investigation of the Association between Authenticity and Ecological Sensitivity. *Person-Centered & Experiential Psychotherapies*, 20, 2, 139–151.

Pickett, K. and Wilkinson, R. 2009. *The Spirit Level: Why More Equal Societies Almost Always Do Better*. London: Penguin Books.

Pihkala, P. 2018. Eco-Anxiety, Tragedy, and Hope: Psychological and Spiritual Dimensions of Climate Change. *Zygon*, 53, 2, 545–569.

Pihkala, P. 2022. Toward a Taxonomy of Climate Emotions. *Frontiers in Climate*, 3, 738154.

Pinker, S. 2011. *The Better Angels of Our Nature: Why Violence Has Declined*. New York: Viking.

Postlethwaite, M. 2019. *Addiction and Recovery: A Spiritual Pilgrimage*. Minneapolis, MN: Fortress Press.

Robinson, M. 2019. Climate Change Denial is a Malign Evil. Available at: https://theelders.org/news/climate-change-denial-malign-evil (accessed August 2023).

Rogers, C.R. 2013. The Basic Conditions of the Facilitative Therapeutic Relationship. In: Cooper, M. et al., *The Handbook of Person-Centred Psychotherapy and Counselling*, 2nd edn. Basingstoke: Palgrave MacMillan, pp. 24–28.

Rogers, C.R. 1959. A Theory of Therapy, Personality, and Interpersonal Relationships: As Developed in the Client-Centered Framework. In: Koch S., ed. *Psychology: A Study of a Science. Vol. 3. Formulations of the Person and the Social Context*. New York: McGraw Hill, pp. 184–256.

Rogers, C. 1961. *On Becoming a Person*. Boston: Houghton Mifflin.

Rogers, C. 1980. *A Way of Being*. Boston: Houghton Mifflin.

Schmid, P. 2010. The Person and Evil. In: Leonardi, J., ed., *The Human Being Fully Alive*. Ross-on-Wye: PCCS Books, pp. 128–148.

Schor, J. 1998. *The Overspent American*. New York: Harper Collins.

Schor, J. 2004. *Born to Buy*. New York: Scribner.

Seale, B. 2020. Compassionate Presence: Buddhist Practice and the Person-Centred Approach to Counselling and Psychotherapy. In: Schmidt, B. and Leonardi, J., eds., *Spirituality and Wellbeing: Interdisciplinary Approaches to the Study of Religious Experience and Health*. Bristol: Equinox, pp. 225–243.

Shohet, R. 2023. How Green is Your Mind? In Aspey, L. et al., eds. *Holding the Hope: Reviving Psychological and Spiritual Agency in the Face of Climate Change*. Monmouth: PCCS Books, pp. 42–50.

Solnit, R. 2023. If You Win the Popular Imagination, You Change the Game: Why We Need New Stories on Climate. *The Guardian*, 12 January 2023. Available at: www.theguardian.com/news/2023/jan/12/rebecca-solnit-climate-crisis-popular-imagination-why-we-need-new-stories (accessed August 2023).

Sultan, N. 2019. *Heuristic Inquiry*. London: Sage.

Totton, N. 2023. Rewilding Hope. In: Aspey, L. et al., eds., *Holding the Hope: Reviving Psychological and Spiritual Agency in the Face of Climate Change*. Monmouth: PCCS Books, pp. 68–75.

Tudor, K. and Worrall, M. 2006. *Person-Centred Therapy: A Clinical Philosophy*. Hove: Routledge.

Weintrobe, S. 2021. *The Psychological Roots of the Climate Crisis*. London: Bloomsbury.

Welwood, J. 2000. *Towards a Psychology of Awakening*. Boston: Shambhala.

Worsley, R. 2005. The Concept of Evil as the Key to the Therapist's Use of Self. In: Joseph, S. and Worsley, R., eds., *Person-Centred Psychopathology: A Positive Psychology of Mental Health*. Monmouth: PCCS Books, pp. 146–157.

6 Spiritual experiences and counselling

William West

Introduction

In this chapter I will be drawing on my own spiritual experiences as well as other people's and considering how to make sense of this and how it can be usefully explored within a counselling and psychotherapy setting. My life has been changed for the better by my own spiritual experiences. For many years, between the age of about 20 and 40, I did not have a religious home as such or a very clear sense of how to process these experiences and locate them within a faith setting. It is not surprising on reflection that many such experiences, for me, occurred in nature.

For many people spiritual experiences are very positive, and like me, often life-changing. However, they can have a downside, especially when mental health issues are involved. Many people in the health and therapy world still have polarised views – seeing such experiences as always either healthy or crazy.

It is much better to view such experiences through the lens of 'what does this do for this person?' and 'what support might they need?' In other words to put the experience into the context of the client, their life and their needs. Given that over half of us in Britain have such experiences from time to time we deserve a more a nuanced approach. Indeed, Hay and Hunt (2000) found in their survey that 76% of their respondents reported having spiritual or religious experiences.

Britain and many parts of the West could well be viewed as post Christian. Church attendance is at an all-time low. For instance, in the Census Survey of 2021, 'For the first time in a census of England and Wales, less than half of the population (46.2%, 27.5 million people) described themselves as "Christian", a 13.1 percentage point decrease from 59.3% (33.3 million) in 2011' (Office for National Statistics, 2022). This does not mean that less people are having spiritual experiences, or consider themselves to be 'spiritual' but that they are less likely to be a member of a religious group. This suggests that many of the people struggling with such experiences would not likely seek religious help.

This may not be a bad thing given the history of religion and its sometimes unhelpful support for people struggling with spiritual experiences. However, it does mean that the support offered by secular therapists will vary in its acceptance, knowledge and valuing of such experiences.

What are spiritual experiences?

Firstly, to many of us the words 'spiritual' and 'spirituality' are very important. A minority of people have no acceptance of spirituality and make sense of their lives without the need to use this word. In some ways this does not really matter, in others ways it is a crucial issue. I remain committed to discussing issues associated with the words spiritual and spirituality and respect both the people who use these words and those who do not.

For some users of the words 'spiritual' and 'spirituality', they are always linked with the word 'religion', for some even interchangeable. For many people religion is the word used to describe the buildings, the organisation, the staff whilst spirituality is what faith means to the individual believer. In Britain today many people are spiritual but not religious.

In the therapeutic context it is useful to think about spirituality in terms of: (a) experiences that people have they refer to as 'spiritual'; (b) the beliefs that have in relation to their spirituality; (c) the value system explicit or implicit they have in relation to their spirituality; and (d) finally where this all fits in with organised religion or not (West, 2012).

We can usefully expand this notion of spirituality and spiritual experiences within a therapeutic context and say that:

1. It is rooted in human experiencing and meaning making rather than abstract theology.
2. It can be experienced as embodied.
3. It can involve linking with other people and the universe at large.
4. It may well involve non ordinary or altered states of consciousness.
5. That active engagement with spirituality tends to make people more altruistic, less materialistic and more environmentally aware.
6. It deals with the meaning that people make of their lives.
7. It faces suffering and its causes.
8. It relates to God/Goddess/Divinity and ultimate reality.
9. It often uses the word 'soul' or 'higher self' though I experience my higher self or soul as deep within me rather than 'higher'.
10. People exploring their spirituality may use techniques such as prayer, meditation, contemplation, mindfulness, yoga and Tai Chi,

even if some of these practices may be taught in a non or aspiritual way or context. (adopted from West, 2012: 14).

Possible challenges

Inevitably challenges can arise for the counsellor when working with their clients' spirituality, faith and spiritual experiences. Broadly these fail into three categories:

1. clients' spiritual and religious issues;
2. spiritual issues arising within the session;
3. spiritual issues arising for the counsellor from their work with the client.

It is important not to make assumptions about the meaning making that clients will be engaged with in relation to their spirituality. If they are part of a religious faith again not to jump to conclusions. There is a range of opinions both with any faith group and the client themselves may or may not agree with the dominant opinion or creed. In my experience religious clients can be very cruel and judgmental on themselves and their behaviour despite the emphasis in most religions on (self) love, compassion and forgiveness. As a supporter of LGBT+ rights I have difficulties with religious groups that will not welcome nor marry LGBT+ people.

At times the counselling session can have a strong spiritual feel to it that either or both client and counsellor may be aware of. These can often occur in moments of deep silence which have been explored in Rogers' concept of presence (1980) and in Thorne's Tenderness (1991).

Rogers describing his experience of presence: 'I find that when I am closer to my inner intuitive self, when I am somehow in touch with the unknown in me, when perhaps I am in a slightly altered state of consciousness in the relationship, then whatever I do seems to be full of healing. Then simply my presence is releasing and helpful... I may behave in strange and impulsive ways in the relationship, ways which I cannot justify rationally, which have nothing to do with my thought processes... At these moments it seems that my inner spirit has reached out and touched the spirit of the other... Profound growth and healing energies are present' (Rogers in Kirchenbaum and Henderson, 1990, p. 137). It seems clear to me that Rogers is describing a deep spiritual connection with the client and being open to creative and intuitive ways of responding to the client's issues.

Thorne talking about his notion of tenderness writes: 'It seems as if for a space, however brief, two human beings are fully alive because they have given themselves and each other permission to be fully alive. At such a moment I have no hesitation in saying that my client and I are caught up in a stream of love. Within this stream there comes an effortless or intuitive understanding and what is astonishing in how complex this understanding can be' (1991, p. 77). Thorne is, like Rogers, describing a deep and spiritual connection with the client and not being afraid to use the word 'love'. To my mind this is love as 'agape'. Also, like Rogers, Thorne sees the connection as having an intuitive element to it.

However, this deep and intuitive work does not have to be seen as spiritual and Mearns and Cooper's (2005) concept of relational depth is an alternative way of framing such work. Cooper describes relational depth as 'A sense of connectedness and flow with another person that is so powerful that it can feel quite magical. At these times, the person feels alive, immersed in the encounter, and truly themselves; while experiencing the other as open, genuine and valuing of who they are' (2013, p. 71).

Another non-spiritual view of a deep and therapeutic connection between counsellor and client can be found in Gendlin's notion of the 'felt sense' – 'The felt sense that I also call the edge of awareness is the centre of the personality. It comes between the conscious person and the deep universal reaches of human nature where we are no longer ourselves. It is open to what comes from these universals but it feels like "really me"' (Gendlin, 1984, p. 81). Gendlin does not use the word 'spirituality' in relation to his felt sense. To my mind he is talking about what many other people would see as 'spiritual' but I respect his choice of language. To me, it is the experience and its impact on us that is important and not the words we choose to apply to it.

I have written in detail elsewhere about my work with a Sufi client (West, 2004b) where we reached a silent spiritual depth that had a strong impact on both of us. He later spoke of his concerns about the 'spiritual intimacy' that was occurring between us. This led me to wonder that I might have crossed the line from counsellor to spiritual director but when I raised it with the client he said that he already had spiritual guidance and had come to me for counselling. What was also striking for me at the time was that the spiritual depth I allowed myself to reach with him was familiar to me from my time in the silence of Quaker Meetings but I also knew I had to hang on to being his counsellor and not just give over to the silence. Also, when I broke the silence and spoke to him it did not immediately pull me out of this spiritual depth. I found this surprising. I later found that these silences are familiar to Sufis as well as Quakers.

I personally have wrestled for some years with the mysteries of suffering and I do not think there is a cognitive solution! It can seem so unfair that a particular client or family member or close friend has to face particular sufferings. I am challenged by the question: why them? So being present to what seems like unfair sufferings remains a spiritual challenge for me which is only solved albeit temporarily in a quiet spiritual experience, often in a church. I know some counsellors feel that God is present in their therapy rooms (West, 2004a). I could not and can not make this claim. However, I do feel at times that I am helped in my work with clients. Very occasionally, I have felt the presence of the loved one of someone recently bereaved which I have usually taken as a sign that they are ready to talk about the person who has died.

More recently I have noticed that therapy and academic work has deepened my own need for spiritual solitude and contemplation which could be part of an aging process but also suggests a need for self care to enable me to be most present.

My own spiritual experiences

I have decided to share some of my own spiritual experiences here. Partially because I have had them for over 50 years now(!). Also because they are not that dramatic in themselves; more in their impact on me. So I guess I am seeking to flag up spiritual experiences as not always earth-shattering as events but life-changing in how we can make sense of them. Also, having lived with their impact on me for years, there is a potential for an autoethnographical approach; indeed, I would like to invite people to see such events as common-or-garden for many of us. Think of a spectrum with people at one end not having any such experiences; then people who have a few; next, people like me in the middle with many but relatively mild ones; and at the other end people having intense experiences that can go on for days and really shake them up and challenge their mental health and wellbeing. Lucas in her book (2011) courageously shares her own experiences and their powerful impact on her.

When I have a spiritual experience, time stands still; I feel I am in the depth of my being and feel connected to all things, and everything makes sense in that moment. I have discussed elsewhere in some detail some of my own most vivid spiritual experiences (West, 2021), but what particularly stands out now is how my connection to nature is often a key element in my own spiritual experiences and spiritual journey. For example, following the breakup of a relationship in my early twenties I moved into a bedsit and was very miserable. One day in the nearby park I came across a tree in blossom and something lit up inside me in response to that tree. This was a turning point in my suffering and showed the possible impact of nature on me and my wellbeing. These experiences continued and continue for me. They do not just happen in times of misery! They can emerge from love – agape – when I am feeling fine and then contact with nature spiritually uplifts me even more.

Besides being moved by my contact with nature I also found that spiritual experiences could occur to me in holy places, in mediation and in pauses between yoga positions on spiritually led classes. So, I learnt to sit quietly in churches, cathedrals, synagogues and to wait. And quite often spiritual experiences would happen; not always and not necessarily in the way I might expect. But never frightening. Many times, I would be moved to tears by such experiences. There is much involved in these experiences as they do feel like they put me in touch with a deeper sense of who I am – my soul if you will – and awaken a desire in me to lead a better life. This is no claim to spiritual enlightenment on my part merely that nature does help me to be a better person. So, for example, I posted this recently on Facebook, 'I arrive and settle in the chapel and there is the lovely sound of our pianist RuiYing Wang playing through today's hymns. I suddenly feel deeply at peace – my un/usual anxieties and fears have melted away for now. I am touched by a sense of gratitude for I am in a holy place within and without' (23 October 2022).

Having had these experiences of being transformed by connecting to nature and to holy places it was a challenge for me to find a religious group where these experiences and the sense I made of them was acceptable and indeed welcomed. I spent 20 years wrestling with my membership of the Church of England and whether I could accept the Nicene Creed; some Sundays I could, some not. When I stumbled across Quakers I found their gathered silence inviting and their lack of a creed helpful. More recently I have moved on to Unitarians, who are a liberal, arguably Post-Christian, faith that again does not ask its members to sign up to a creed and where spiritual experiences can happen for me.

How does counselling understand and work with spiritual experiences?

Counselling, like psychology, has a mixed and varied response to spirituality and spiritual experience. This is curious as modern counselling has its roots in religious pastoral care and people of faith played, and continue to play, a significant part in the development of modern counselling (McLeod, 2009). It is too easy to take a binary attitude to spiritual experiences, seeing them as always good and healthy or always harmful. It is not unusual for people to have mental health issues mixed in with their spiritual experiences and beliefs. It is too easy for the counsellor to view their client's ideas and experiences through their own lenses. This is especially so in relation to spirituality and faith.

It is crucially important that counsellors are aware of their own stance on spirituality, spiritual experiences and religious faith. This, of course, can change over time and is inevitably affected by their work as counsellors. Of course, this is also true regarding ethnicity, class, gender, sexuality, disability and age. Jonathan Wyatt reminds us that, 'When I am clear about my faith and comfortable with it – whatever it looks like – then that is good. I know what I think. I know what I believe and I know what I do not believe. I know what my values are, or I know that I don't know. Then, when I am like that, I can listen to clients' (Wyatt, 2002: 182).

Some time ago I realised that like Brian Thorne said I did not want to leave my soul outside of the counselling room. In the counselling room I was white, male, educated, healthy, middle-class, old and a person of faith. I hoped I could be whatever was of use to my clients, but I do know on the nonverbal level they would be picking up and processing a lot of information about me – maybe not always accurately. So I could not not be who I am with them in the room. But I did not have to impose who I am on them. For those who are regularly working with clients and issues of faith arise for them or for you, then I would recommend you receive regular one-to-one supervision from an experienced supervisor who is open and supportive of this work. And if none of your clients ever address any spiritual issues then consider how one may be shutting them down without realising it.

There is a real challenge in talking about spiritual experiences, which for many of us are beyond words and may occur in altered states of consciousness. So to talk about them is a real demand on us. Firstly, to put into words that which we may well have experienced as beyond words. Secondly, as soon as we use words, we are encultured. So our words and concepts come from our culture, both societal, community and individual. This is a particular challenge for a counsellor who might find a client drawing on Christianity, Judaism, Islam, Hinduism, Sikhism, Buddhism, paganism or a more generalised and/or specific spiritual viewpoint. To journey with any client as they share important aspects of their life can often be a challenge and something as fundamental to many of us as spirituality, faith and religion is a big ask.

Having said that, just being a counsellor is a big ask! So in my years of counselling I have worked with many people from many backgrounds very different to mine. The challenge has always been how I can be in the room with this other person and let them occupy the space with me and share their story when they are ready. And they may be very comfortable in their faith and the challenges they face may come from, say, their sexuality or ethnicity and so on.

I guess faith has been, and still is, so important to me, such a hard-won safe place to find, that I am well tuned into picking up on such issues when they arise for other people. Obviously, it is important not to impose one's own agenda on clients when working as a counsellor. Again, this is where effective supervision can be a great help. And it is curious how clients can often seem to raise issues that are important to us(!). But maybe their very raising of such issues highlights their importance for them rather than them unconsciously following our needs. Or perhaps synchronicity can be occurring. The client might well be raising issues that are important to them and to us. Again, the unpicking of this is important.

When spiritual experience becomes spiritual emergency

Spiritual experiences can be relatively easy to process as a one-off event; or can occur from time to time; or can seem part of something bigger that could be called spiritual awakening or spiritual emergence or emergency. Assagioli (1986), the founder of the transpersonal approach to therapy called *psychosynthesis* suggests that there were four stages in a person's spiritual awakening: (1) crises preceding the spiritual awakening; (2) crises caused by the spiritual awakening; (3) reactions following the spiritual awakening; and (4) phases of the 'process of transmutation' of the personality in which higher or my spiritual levels of self-realisation can be achieved.

These higher spiritual levels were spelled out by Wilber in his spectrum of consciousness model (1979), in which he usefully explores the differing roles that the therapist or helper uses according to which level the client is at. Wilber's model is helpfully simplified and explored in relation to counselling and psychotherapy by Rowan (2005). It is useful to think at what level a client may be at spiritually and thereby what type of helper and what type of intervention they might need. Wilber usefully provides a notion that sometimes we are only peaking a particular level of consciousness and not able to remain at that level.

Grof and Grof (1991) offered an expanded view of spiritual awakening which they referred to as spiritual emergence/emergency. This highlights that a speeding up of the spiritual emergence process can result in a spiritual emergency. They identify ten forms of spiritual emergence. These include: shamanic crisis; awakening of kundalini energy; peak experiences; increase in psychic or intuitive experiences; past-life experiences; near-death experiences and possession (further explored in West, 2000).

Lucas (2011) draws on her own and other people's experience of spiritual emergency which she says can be triggered by many things including loss of faith or a loved one, intense spiritual practices or even childbirth. She describes moving successfully through spiritual emergency in three phases: one, coping with the crisis by looking after body, mind and spirit – she highlights the use of Mindfulness; two, making sense of it all – seeing it as a Hero's journey; three, going back into the world which may well present its own challenges.

Rather than getting lost in the theory of spiritual awakening/emergency, I think it is important to see these experiences as potentially healthy and developmental. However, they can be overwhelming and people can need 24-hour support during an intense phase. There may also be specific mental health issues mixed in. But it is important to see spiritual awakening/emergency as potentially healthy. Unfortunately, some therapists will consider all such experiences are either healthy or crazy. A better position put forward by Lukoff (1985) was to view this as a spectrum with healthy spirituality at one end and psychosis at the other. The client could be potentially at any point on this spectrum. The key issue was what kind of support they need. And, of course, their position on this spectrum can change over time, and not necessarily always for the better.

Chris Jenkins (2006) did some ground-breaking research into clients' experiences of having their spirituality denied in therapy. He describes one client's experience of this in a mental hospital setting:

> Imagine being in a psychiatric unit, so ill and confused you aren't even sure of the year. Imagine as the confusion begins to subside, having one source of clarity, an awareness of divine care and love. Imagine meeting your therapist and mentioning this and seeing her reaction, noticing your medication has been increased…and is increased whenever you talk about your spiritual awareness. Then being in a therapy group when another patient names their sense of God, the group shutting then up and hearing, at the break, the patient being told: 'Don't talk about that stuff in here, you'll never get out.' (Jenkins, 2011, p. 29)

So, to find her way out of the mental hospital this client had to learn how to play the game, how not to mention her spirituality, however important to her. Jenkins (2011) also explores the experiences of clients receiving help outside of hospital care, 'In certain circles…religion and spirituality don't come into it. You know it's just not talked about or addressed,…it embarrasses people,

people don't like to talk about things like that, and certainly psychotherapy fits into that milieu…where I come from if you say that you are a Catholic, it's the same as saying you are stupid' (Jenkins, 2011, p. 31).

The ongoing relevance of spiritual experiences and their part in the climate emergency

As I write this (in August 2023), we have had a heatwave and fires in Southern Europe and fires in Canada and the USA; severe floods in China, Greece, Libya; melting ice caps; and ocean temperature are the hottest ever. The future direction of the Gulf Stream is under question, as is the hope that global average temperature will not rise above 1.5 degrees. It is becoming clear that the victims of the climate emergency are more likely to be poor people and people living in the South. Already, then, social justice is linked to the struggle to minimise the impact of the climate emergency.

I struggled with the impact of Climate Change on me; I felt like I was not doing enough and not enough was happening. I persuade my minister for us to co-lead a group on Climate Conversation at which people were invited to share their experiences, including those active in specialist work such as solar panels and home insulation. Curiously, this group has reduced my anxiety levels so I am able to be more effective!

I do think that the only hope for the future of the human race is a change of consciousness away from individualism, which remains popular in the USA and the West as a whole, to a sense of interconnectedness between people and between people and the planet. This position has been highlighted in two recent books by Maria Curtis (2023) and Karen Armstrong (2023). As Maria Curtis expresses it, 'Let us continue to occupy our place in space and time, not as plunderers and exploiters but with gratitude and humility, aware of our interconnectedness and interdependency with the Earth, her land, her rivers and oceans, her air, and all her creatures. Let us preserve the natural world as the primary revelation of the divine' (2023, p. 16).

Armstrong advises us: 'We need to cultivate the veneration of nature that human beings carefully cultivated for millennia; it we fail to do this our concern for the natural environment will remain superficial…. It is not a question of believing religious doctrine; it is about incorporating into our lives insights and practices that will not only help us to meet today's serious challenges but change our hearts and minds' (2023, pp. 18/20).

This brings to mind an important insight that gradually occurred to me when I settled down with Quakers in their collective silence in 1991 and realised that I was walking less heavily on the planet and also asking less from my personal relationships. These changes in me had been made possible by the nourishing impact on the spiritual side of me by Quaker worship. In those early days I could feel its effect on my energy system for several days after a service. So, for a while I used to attend twice a week to feel topped up.

So spiritual experiences, especially when they embody this sense of interconnectedness with the planet, with creation, need to be welcomed, and people having these experiences need our support. As Grof and Grof remind us, 'People who are involved in the process of spiritual emergence tend to develop a new appreciation and reverence for all forms of life and a new understanding of the unity of all things, which often results in strong ecological concerns and greater tolerance toward other human beings' (1991, p. 235).

Lucas (2011) argues that we are seeing a global spiritual emergency and she uses an interesting phrase, 'dark night of the globe', which echoes the individual spiritual crisis that can be seen as 'dark night of the soul'. The individual crisis can be misdiagnosed as depression and likewise we can deny our part in the climate emergency that is occurring.

Conclusion

As McLeod states: 'The emotional task of the twenty-first century will be around learning to cope with the fact that the planet, the ground on which we stand, will in many ways become unable, as a result of human action, to sustain the way of life to which we have grown accustomed' (2009, p. 656.) Indeed, the biggest challenge facing the human race is arguably the Climate Emergency we are now in, which clearly threatens our future and that of other sentient beings. Healthy spiritual experiences could well be a key factor in addressing climate issues. Counsellors and others who assist and support individuals and communities in their soul journeys could have a key part to play if they have the skills to work effectively with clients addressing issues that arise around spirituality and spiritual experiences.

Biographical note

William West is a Visiting Professor in Counselling and Spirituality at the University of Chester, where he supervises a number of PhD and doctorate students who share his interests in spirituality, faith, diversity and culture. William is a Fellow of the British Association for Counselling and Psychotherapy. His most recent book (2021), co-edited with Greg Nolan, was *Extending Horizons in Helping and Caring Therapies*.

Bibliography

Armstrong, K. 2023. *Sacred: How We Can Recover Our Bond with the Natural World.* Dublin: Vintage.

Assagioli, R . 1986. Self-realisation and Psychological Disturbance. *Revision,* 8, 2, 21–31.

Cooper, M. 2013. Experiencing Relational Depth in Therapy: What We Know So Far. In: Knox, R., Murphy, D., Wiggins S. and Cooper, M., eds. *Relational Depth: New Perspectives and Developments.* London: Bloomsbury Academic, pp. 62–76.

Curtis, M. 2023., ed. *Cherishing the Earth – Nourishing the Spirit.* London: Lindsey Press.

Gendlin, E.T. 1984. The Client's Client: The Edge of Awareness. In: Levant, R.F. and Shlien, J.M., eds., *Client-Centred Therapy and the Person-Centred Approach: New Directions in Theory, Research and Practice.* New York: Praeger, pp. 76–107.

Grof, S. and Grof, C., eds. 1991. *Spiritual Emergency: When Personal Transformation Becomes a Crisis.* Los Angles: Tarcher.

Hay, D. and Hunt, K. 2000. *Understanding the Spirituality of People Who Don't Go to Church.* Nottingham: Nottingham Centre for the Study of Human Relations.

Jenkins, C. 2006. A Voice Denied: Clients' Experience of the Exclusion of Spirituality in Psychotherapy and Counselling, PhD thesis, University of Manchester.

Jenkins, C. 2011. When Client's Spirituality is Denied in Therapy. In: W. West, ed. *Exploring Therapy, Spirituality and Healing.* Basingstoke: Palgrave MacMillian, pp. 28–47.

Kirchenbaum, H. and Henderson, V., eds. 1990. *The Carl Rogers Reader.* London: Constable.

Lucas, C.G. 2011. In: *Case of Spiritual Emergency: Moving Successfully Through Your Awakening.* Forres: Findhorn Press.

Lukoff, D. 1985. The Diagnosis of Mystical Experiences with Psychotic Features. *Journal of Transpersonal Psychology,* 17, 2, 155–181.

Mearns, D. and Cooper, M. 2005. *Working at Relational Depth in Counselling and Psychotherapy.* London: Sage.

McLeod, J. 2009. *An Introduction to Counselling,* 4th edn. Maidenhead: Open University Press.

Office for National Statistics (2022). Religion, England and Wales: Census 2021. www.ons.gov.uk/peoplepopulationandcommunity/culturalidentity/religion/bulletins/religionenglandandwales/census2021 (accessed 25 September 2023).

Rogers, C. 1980. *A Way of Being.* Boston: Houghton Mifflin.

Rowan, J. 2005. *The Transpersonal: Spirituality in Psychotherapy and Counselling.* London: Routledge.

Thorne, B. 1991. *Person-Centred Counselling: Therapeutic and Spiritual Dimensions.* London: Whurr.

West, W. 2000. *Psychotherapy and Spirituality: Crossing the Line Between Therapy and Religion.* London: Sage.

West, W. 2004a. *Spiritual Issues in Therapy: Relating Experience to Practice.* Basingstoke: Palgrave.

West, W. 2004b. Humanistic Integral Psychotherapy with a Sufi Convert. In: Richards, P.S. and Bergen, A.E., eds. *Casebook for a Spiritual Strategy in Counseling and Psychotherapy*. Washington, APA.

West, W. 2012. Addressing Spiritual Issues in Counselling and Psychotherapy. *Thresholds*, Winter, 12–17.

West, W. 2021. Hymns to the Silence. *Journal of Critical Psychology, Counselling and Psychotherapy*, 21, 2, 78–84.

Wilber, K. 1979. A Developmental View of Consciousness. *Journal of Transpersonal Psychology*, 11, 1, 1–21.

Wyatt, J. 2002. 'Confronting the Almighty God'? A Study of How Psychodynamic Counsellors Respond to Clients' Expressions of Religious Faith. *Counselling and Psychotherapy Research*, 2, 3, 177–184.

Part III
Bringing the human being into relationship with the environment

7 How is the marriage of Heaven and Earth going? Spirituality, health and the environment in Brazil

Marta Helena de Freitas

Introduction

Brazil is one of the world's largest countries. Its territorial expanse measures 3,287,953 square miles, extending from the Amazon basin and rainforest to the north of South America, down to the huge vineyards of Rio Grande do Sul and the gigantesque waterfalls of the Iguaçu River in the extreme south. The last demographic census (Brazil, 2023) informs that the population grew by 56% over ten years. Today the country is home to over 203 million people, who are brown (45.3%), white (43.5%), black (10.2%), indigenous (0.83%) and yellow (0.4%) and, for the most part, adult (64.4%) and female (55.7%). It indicates there is a prominence of Catholics (56.7%), followed by Evangelicals (26.9%), Spiritists (1.8%) and followers of Afro-Brazilian religions (1.0%). Those who adhered to indigenous religions were situated in the midst of 'other religions' (4.0%), while 9.3% of the population claimed they had no religious affiliation and 0.2% don't know or did not declare belonging to any religion (Brazil, 2025).

This grouping of geographical and cultural characteristics, added to the vicissitudes of its historical process and the contemporary socio political reality, leaves the country in a paradoxical situation vis-à-vis the world regarding its role in the environmental equilibrium on Earth: at the same time that it is considered to be the country with the greatest biodiversity on the planet, and one of the foremost countries in terms of global food production, it has been accused of not duly caring for its large expanse of forest, promoting an increase in carbon concentrations in the atmosphere and negatively impacting the planet's average temperatures. Curiously, the accusations levelled against the country have been formulated by both spiritual/religious leaders and by international scientists. Thus, for example, in 2017, the President of the Pan-Amazonian Ecclesial Network (REPAM) reported how much the Amazon rainforest was being threatened, destroyed and continuously degraded. Pope Francis, in 2019, predicting the impacts of the destruction of Amazonia on the planet, convoked a Synod of Bishops for that region and condemned the 'blind and destructive mentality that prioritises profit over justice', denouncing the profound crisis generated by the continuing human intervention in the region, motivated by the 'culture of disposal' and by the 'mentality of extractivism' (Secretaria Geral dos Sínodos dos Bispos, 2017, p. 2). Also in 2019, 602 European scientists, together with two indigenous groups, the Coordination of the Indigenous Organisations of the Brazilian Amazon (COIAB) and the Articulation of Indigenous Peoples of Brazil (APIB), published a manifesto article in the journal *Science* calling for the EU's trade with Brazil to be sustained.

Given this initial contextualisation, it is clearly important to address the psycho-sociocultural aspects involved in the relationship between religiosity, spirituality, health, wellbeing and the environment in this country, whose beginnings were marked 'by the confluence and welding of Portuguese colonisers, with their Christian theology, the indigenous inhabitants of the forests and plains, with their brand of shamanism, and black Africans, with their orishas' (Freitas, 2013, p. 262). These 'newcomers' (Ribeiro, 1995/2009), with their syncretic, singular culture, were gradually joined, over the course of history, by great waves of immigrants from other continents and countries, as well as Europeans. Considering the responsibility globally assigned to Brazil today with regard to its role in the preservation of wellbeing across the entire planet, it has to be acknowledged that the scope of the topic in question extends well beyond its own borders. In fact, in recent years, academic and scientific interest has grown in the study of the relationship between environmental conservation and spirituality, whether it be from a psychological perspective or a multicultural one. In Brazil, however, studies of this kind are still in their infancy, although a number of initiatives have emerged in the field of the sciences of religion and environmental psychology in dialogue with other areas like sociology, anthropology and theology.

The aim of this chapter is to contribute to the understanding of the topic based on a phenomenological input, initially addressing some historical aspects that have marked the relationship between the country's native peoples and those who came later, as well as the contemporary implications for the relationship between human beings and nature. Subsequently, the psychological aspects involved in the specific features of the spiritual and religious systems that may have positive and/or negative impacts on global environment, wellbeing and health in general, and on this country in particular, will be addressed. Thirdly, by way of a more comprehensive illustration of this issue, an excerpt of the relationship between indigenous people and health professionals will be addressed, based on studies whose results illustrate the confluences and conflicts between indigenous cosmology and medical science. Lastly, we shall present and discuss the challenges and implications of the health policy situation for indigenous people in Brazil, and for the population in general, relating to cultural identity, physical and mental health, and the environment.

Brazilians and the environment: Historical and contemporary aspects

> On one occasion, in Sweden, I was taken to the North Pole where the *Samis* (Eskimos) live. The first question their leader asked me was: 'Do Brazilian Indians marry heaven and earth?' I answered: 'But of course they marry heaven and earth because of that marriage all things are born.' To which he replied: 'So they are true Indians. Our brothers and sisters here no longer marry heaven and earth, that is why they have confused ideas and are always fighting. Marrying heaven and earth means keeping together God and nature, man and woman, the old and the young, work and play, life and death. That way everything stays in harmony. And we are happy.' (Boff, 2022)

The affirmative response about the marriage of Heaven and Earth given by the theologian Leonardo Boff to the *Samis* leader in Sweden, as can be seen in the epigraph above, is indeed valid for the Indians in Brazil. The same cannot be said, however, for the relationship with the rest of the population. After all, it cannot be said that Brazilians, as a whole, still marry Heaven and Earth. And this is nothing new! This rift between the way the indigenous people and the rest of the population live dates back to the time when the process of colonisation began, when the 'white man' arrived, with the aim of conquering land, accumulating wealth, imposing their language and spiritual values. Indeed, to better understand the meaning of the aforementioned metaphor insofar as it relates to the indigenous peoples of Brazil, it should be explained that, in the Portuguese language as it is spoken today in Brazil, the same word '*céu*', is used to refer to both 'Heaven' and 'sky'. Similarly, the same word '*terra*' is used to mean both 'Earth' and 'land'. Thus, to say that Brazil's Indians still 'marry heaven and earth' is valid for both meanings: that of joining and bringing closer together 'sky and land', and that of reuniting and integrating 'Heaven and Earth'.

Numerous ethnographic writings describe the way of life of the indigenous peoples of Brazil and in the Americas in general. In fact, these writings attest to a way of life in which there is no dissociation between human beings and other living creatures in nature and the universe in general. Thus, interaction between humans and the relationship between humans and animals, plants, rivers, stars and all the other elements that make up the existential universe, constitute a kind of relational network, where the common link between beings is established by a kind of 'universal background of the cosmos' (Viveiros de Castro, 2008, p. 94). Thus, in the various indigenous mythologies, and also in the forms of life reported by them or by ethnographers, a kind of radical assumption is evident in which humanity permeates all other beings with whom they have a relationship, characterising what some scholars call 'animism', while others use the expressions 'presumption or preconceptual intuition (the plane of immanence, as Deleuze might say) that the universal background of reality is the spirit' (Viveiros de Castro, 2008, p.33).

Unfortunately, it may be said that the history of the settlement on Brazilian territory of those who still marry Heaven and Earth is, in truth, a story of depopulation (Vainfas, 2007). After all, when the process of colonisation began on Brazilian soil at the dawn of the 16th century, the existing native population was home to millions. Today there are less than 300,000 indigenous people (Brazil, 2023). This depopulation over a period of five centuries was not only characterised by the numerical reduction in native peoples but also by the cruel tendency to strip away their cultural identity, depriving them of their customs, traditions, values and ways of fostering spirituality. 'The very term employed to call them "Indians", was the result of a mistake by Columbus, the "discoverer" of America, who believed he had discovered the Indies, the "other world", as he said, in his voyage in 1492' (Vainfas, 2007, p. 37) on his way to the new continent. Moreover, this term competed with others then used by the colonisers. As Vainfas (2007) highlighted, the Jesuits, for instance, imbued with the missionary purpose that inspired them, called the natives 'gentiles' or even 'pagans', taken to be synonyms for 'governed by the devil', applied to those who did not partake of the Christian principles then imposed by the system of Catholic catechesis.

On the other hand, in parallel with the indigenous depopulation throughout its five centuries of history, Brazil was being settled by many other peoples. So, on the conveyor belt of the process of colonisation, its vast territorial expanse, originally inhabited by native peoples, came to be mainly occupied by people from the Western world: Europeans, in the shape of colonisers, and Africans who came to Brazil as slaves, bought and sold by Europeans and, later on, emancipated. Subsequently, during the 19th and 20th centuries, as a result of its migratory policies, the country received large waves of Orientals, particularly Arabs, Japanese and Chinese, or Euro-Orientals as is the case of the Russians and Turks. Each of these peoples brought with them their own lifestyles and religions, making their mark and influence on the cultural formation of the Brazilian. Thus, the Brazilian population, despite its linguistic unity, is characterised by an enormous cultural variety and ways to cultivate spirituality. These may vary, ranging from the Africanity of the saints and orishas to Russian orthodoxy, from India Buddhism to evangelical fundamentalism, or from Ayahuasca rituals to Roman Catholicism. In other words, despite the cultural and religious hegemony initially imposed by the Portuguese colonisers, and there being no lack of massacres and bloodbaths in territorial and ideological disputes over the course of the five centuries of this country's history, Brazil differs from the USA, for example, where the Anglo-Saxon, protestant hegemony was inexorably imposed (Vainfas, 2007). At the same time, all of those 'foreigners' who began settling in the country also became Brazilians, as if 'neutralising' the impact of their 'Cultural Babel' journey, a situation described by Vainfas (2007, p. 15) as: 'a "mystery of the prosperous" in the mirror, whose decipherment is a challenge for the next millennium'.

Curiously, this 'mystery of the prosperous' may date back to Amerindian mythology, described by Lévi-Strauss in a passage reproduced as an epigraph to the book *La chute du ciel: paroles d'un chaman yanomami*, by Kopenawa and Albert (2010, p. 5). In the aforementioned mythology, the French anthropologist identifies the ideological schemes of those native peoples who were already predicting the joining, for better or for worse, of two pieces of humanity, originating from the same creation. Thus it predicts for both a 'solidarity of origin' which is transformed into a 'solidarity of destiny'. By not dissociating his people's destiny from that of the rest of humanity, the Yanomami shaman knows that it is not only the Indians who would be threatened by unfettered economic greed but also the white people. Thus everyone would be 'dragged into the same catastrophe, unless they understood that mutual respect is the prerequisite for each one's survival' (Lévi-Strauss, in Kopenawa and Albert, 2010, p. 5). The 'mystery of the prosperous' is illustrated in even greater detail at the end of the cited paragraph:

> Desperately struggling to preserve their beliefs and rituals, the Yanomami shaman contemplates working for the good of all, including the cruellest of his enemies. Formulated in the terms of a metaphysics that is no longer ours, this conception of human solidarity and diversity, and their mutual implication, is striking in its grandeur. For it falls to one of the last spokesmen of one of so many societies on the path to extinction through our actions to state the principles of a wisdom which we are still too few to understand is also crucial to our own survival. (Lévi-Strauss, in Kopenawa and Albert, 2010, p. 5, translated by Nicholas Elliot)

Turning our attention to the present day, the Yanomami situation described by Lévi-Strauss is more topical than ever. After all, expansion of illegal mining in Amazonia in the last four years has caused hundreds of deaths on the largest Indigenous Territory in Brazil, exactly where these peoples live. The greed and the mistakes of a vast section of humanity, which insists on cultivating a life stoked by liberal individualism at the expense of the collective, threatens to sweep away the 'mystery of the prosperous' from the national and global mirror. If the immense territory of Brazil, the fertility of its soil, the abundance of natural resources and the cordiality of its people are treated as signs of potentiality and national wealth, a large part of which remains unexplored, the lack of care provided to its native peoples threatens to wipe them away inexorably.

Psychology, spirituality and caring for the environment

§ 220 CURA [Care]: When *Cura* [Care, Worry] was crossing a certain river, she saw some clayey mud. She took it up thoughtfully and began to fashion a man. While she was pondering on what she had done, *Jove* [Jupiter] came up; *Cura* [Care] asked him to give the image life (breath), and *Jove* readily granted this. When *Cura* wanted to give it her name, *Jove* forbade it, and said that his name should be given it. But while they were disputing about the name, *Tellus* [Mother Earth] arose and said that it should have her name, since she had given her own body. They took Saturn for judge; he seems to have decided for them: *Jove*, since you gave him life (breath) take his soul (spirit) after death; since *Tellus* offered her body, let her receive his body; since *Cura* first fashioned him, let her possess him as long as he lives, but since there is controversy about his name, let him be called homo (human being), since he seems to be made from *humus* (earth). (Gaius Julius Hyginus, 2007)

The myth in the epigraph, a widely-known fable by Hyginus, taken from Herder by Goethe, shows Care as pre-dating mankind, whether in its spirit, infused by Jupiter, or in its body, imparted by the Earth. At the same time as it is pre-ontological, originating and constituent. Care is also the common thread that knits human beings together, in both its material and immaterial aspects, and keeps it alive, before its spirit returns to the *Deus Pater*, Lord of the Heavens, and its body returns to Mother Earth, Lady of the Wet Soil. To put it another way, without Care human beings would not exist. Curiously, this interpretation of the myth finds support in both philosophy and theology. It shall be no different in the understanding of psychology, science and profession that it has Care as its axiological foundation. Especially when considering its semantic field and respective etymology, the Latin word *cogitare*, which in its transitive form, in addition to caring, means thinking, attending, reflecting, being concerned. Based on this perspective of care for human life and with the world it inhabits, how can psychology contribute to an understanding of the relationship between spirituality, religiosity, environment and ecology?

But first, possible answers to the question above will require some conceptual clarification. The recent field of psychology that deals with relationships between human behaviour and the 'environment' defines this term very broadly 'to include all that is natural on the planet as well as social settings, built environments, learning environments and informational environments' (DeYoung, 1999, p. 223). To achieve its purpose and really understand and adequately deal with human-environment interactions, whether global or local, as underlined by DeYoung (1999, p. 223), this field of study and the practice of psychology must adopt 'a model of human nature that predicts the environmental conditions under which humans will behave in a decent and creative manner'. The author stresses the importance of an interdisciplinary approach, such that this model makes it possible to conceive, manage, protect and enhance the human being/environment relationship, promoting increasingly healthy conditions of life, and in its biopsychosocial aspects. It is necessary to add here the spiritual and religious dimension, frequently neglected by contemporary psychological sciences, despite its unquestionable relevance in the structuring of mental structuring and in the mediation between man and the environment. Indeed, these topics have been more adequately addressed by the field of psychology which it has been convention to designate as 'Psychology of Religion' and, more recently 'Psychology of Spirituality' (Paloutzian and Park, 2021). Accordingly, an effective contribution of psychology to the topic in question requires a meaningful, interdisciplinary dialogue between environmental psychology and the psychology of religion and spirituality, also liaising with other fields of knowledge, in particular philosophy, theology, anthropology, sociology and ecology. This dialogue is addressed here, applying a phenomenological perspective.

The possibility of studying, understanding and making pronouncements on the potential positive or negative impacts of human beings' religiosity and/or spirituality on the environment, must necessarily address the understanding of the relationships, distinctions and connections of the two terms, spirituality and religiosity, as well as their correlate, religion. Etymologically, the term spirituality, which derives from the Latin word *spiritus*, refers to the notion of the 'breath of life', characterising vital fluidity. From a phenomenological perspective, this movement of existential vitality and fluidity is associated with the experience of an active human being, capable of reflecting, seeking and finding meaning in that which is beyond him and situated at the heart of the big questions about life, existence and all that surrounds him (Freitas, 2024). These questions are formulated, in general, by the common person, but also by the religious one, by the philosopher, by the scientist: 'Where did we come from?'; 'Where are we and what are we doing here?'; 'Where are we going to?' If these questions have always gone hand in hand with human existence, they tend to take on special forcefulness in dramatic, threatening situations, whether on the individual or the collective plane, as has been seen recently in the existential crises triggered by the pandemic.

This conception of spirituality is rooted in the Husserlian notion of intentionality, derived from the scholastic *intentio* of Brentano, which always defines conscience as awareness of something, even in that which is ill-considered, when the intentio proceeds in the direction of the object. It is in this flux of 'heading towards something', as happens with the phenomenological rotation of the look (Husserl, 1990), that the immanent and originating, essential trait of spirituality is constituted, inasmuch as it drives the search for meaning. Defined thus, spirituality may be applied to all human beings, regardless of the object towards which their conscience points in the search for existential meaning: whether situated on Earth – the nature of its beings; in the heavens and its stars – God, Jehovah, Buddha; or even in their own acts of thinking and understanding – philosophies, ideologies, science…

In order to effectively understand spirituality and its destinies by including the way these affect the relationship with the environment, it will also be necessary to understand its impulsion for the objects that serves to its purpose. The belief in a transcendent, sacred, creative, infinite, ultimate dimension, or one which is beyond human being, has become one of the forms of response that accompanies humanity, historically and geographically, in all the known cultures. The name of religiosity has been assigned to this destiny of spirituality, invested in the belief in an object that transcends human beings themselves and to which are attributed special characteristics or powers (sacred, creative, omnipresent, omnipotent, etc.).

Naturally, responses to the big questions about meaning may be sought in a variety of ways, whether through contact with nature or art, or even in philosophy or scientific activity, as has already been stated. However, for a significant majority of the population, Brazilians in particular (Brazil, 2023), these answers also manifest themselves by adhering to the belief in a transcendental dimension. Thus, when exposed to adverse, limiting or even incomprehensible situations, 'these people, engaged in the search for meaning for what they experience, are going to look for answers to their anxieties in a dimension which transcends them, promoted by the belief in a supreme being, force or energy, capable of providing answers and delivering solace, serenity, resilience and/or hope' (Freitas, Leal and Nwora, 2022). But not simply to search for solace. Also, when faced with the mysterious, the surprising, the overwhelming, the marvellous, the human being is led to experience this encounter of signification in an inexplicable force that surpasses him and overtakes him.

As for religion, this is a phenomenological concept reserved for when specific forms of experiencing and elaborating religiosity are collectively shared and, in this process, they become hierarchical, social groups (e.g. the Christian religions), or they characterise the cultural identity of a people (e.g. indigenous religions). In this regard, the term 'religion', although it is always associated with the institutional aspect, characterising a more static dimension mired in tradition, dogma and doctrine, accompanied by a conception that is, at one and the same time, moral and normative, does not necessarily have to be placed in opposition to spirituality. Rather, it may be understood as one of the possible destinies of spirituality and religiosity, though not only these, since, being a collectively expressed response, it is intrinsically linked with other factors: political, economic, ideological... Therefore, by adopting a perspective of phenomenological understanding, rather than merely placing the terms (spirituality, religiosity and religion) in opposition to each other, one has to consider them in a kind of continuous line in which spirituality nurtures religiosity and religion. The latter, then, is understood to be a system of shared beliefs/answers about meaning, acquiring forms of doctrine and/or institutions over the course of the history of humanity, holding on to their specific attributes in accordance with the different cultures. Figure 7.1 illustrates this flow of continuity. This conceptual model favours a phenomenological understanding of the psychosocial mechanisms involved in the relationship between spirituality and caring for the environment, as explained below.

Without a shadow of a doubt, all the world's religions cherish values that affect the relationship of their followers with the environment. Thus they ask about the meaning of the universe, design systems for an understanding and explanation of the world, interpret the human condition on Earth, employ symbols and myths to celebrate the cycles of nature, and so on (Maçaneiro, 2016). All of them (Hinduism, Buddhism, Judaism, Christianism, Islamism, Spiritism, Afro-Brazilian and indigenous religions, among others) propagate dogmas and doctrines, contemplated in their sacred texts or rituals, where 'mystic elements intermingle with historical and cultural data, weaving a peculiar episteme of nature, where understanding or knowledge of a religious nature seeks to "reconnect" the biological and the spiritual, matter and transcendence' (Silva and Carmona, 2018, p. 85). It may be said that the diverse

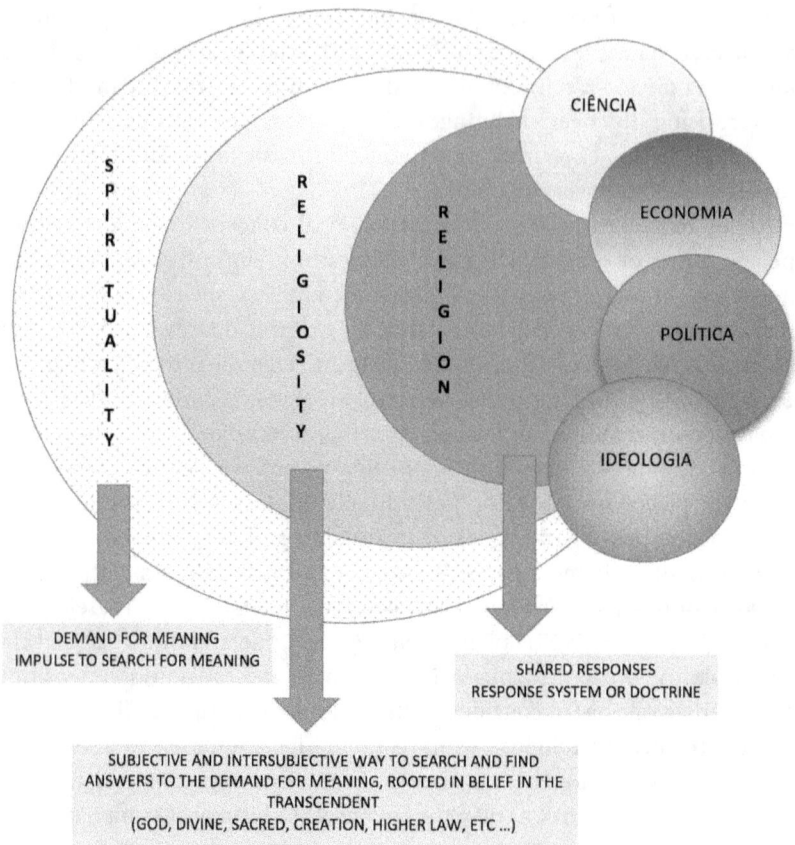

Figure 7.1 Spirituality, religiosity and religion: conceptual model inspired by phenomenology (Reproduced and adapted from Freitas, 2024)

forms through which nature makes its presence felt in religious thinking reflect the destinies of human spirituality and the specific configurations of the 'look of the eyes – the windows and mirrors of the soul', when directing itself towards the world around them, their vital ecosystem, in an effort to understand it, but also to properly administer interaction with it. Some authors indicate that the purpose of millennial religions would be to 'save' human beings from their four basic afflictions in the world: living, falling ill, growing old and dying. Thus they would provide guidance on how to achieve health, wellbeing, longevity, freedom and happiness. Strictly speaking, this would necessarily imply a harmonisation with the world around them. In fact, theological scriptures have shown religious traditions to be inspiring and even determinants of positive human action towards the preservation of the planet (Maçaneiro, 2016; Silva and Carmona, 2018). However, such a conclusion is controversial (Bratton, 2021). After all, the impact of world religions has been shown to be more complex throughout the history of humanity and also in the present day, as was noted for example in the brief outline presented above concerning the present situation in Brazil, one of the most religious countries in the world.

A recent, cross-sectional study exploring the interplay of environmental conservation within spirituality and with a multicultural perspective, developed by Omoyajowo et al. (2023), shows in fact that the majority of religious people agree that every human being has a duty to care for nature. Over 60% of these people are inclined to observe measures to care for the environment if their leaders lead by example, demonstrating a desire to become involved in the global conservation effort, as expressed in their prayers, meditations, fasting and the tangible care of other people, animals and the planet. Other studies (e.g. Eom et al., 2021) point out that the belief in a controlling God is associated with environmental guilt, which may also lead to greater support for environmental action. And there are others (e.g. Skalski et al., 2022) who show the potential of religion to promote changes in mentality, behaviour and policies in favour of ecological sustainability. In general, these studies show that religious involvement in environmental issues is on the rise. On the other hand, studies at the intersection of psychology of religion and environmental psychology have shown that the relationship between religiosity and care of the environment is not always so straightforward, requiring a more sophisticated understanding of the subjective and intersubjective mechanisms at stake, with regard to both individual and institutional actions.

As the results of an exhaustive examination of the set of psychological evidence related to the way religious momentum can affect environmentalism, both negatively and positively, Preston and Baimel (2021) group them into good and bad news. Thus, considering the climate question as a moral issue, religious values can both restrict and promote care with environmental issues. The bad news appears to be connected with a certain stereotype of right-wing Christians, in the USA in particular, whose stance appears to be more conservative, antiscientific, deniers of global warming and the impact of environmental interventions on the climate. In these groups, surveys have shown lower indices of religious indicators regarding environmental care. They also allege that those religions that tend to allay concerns about the environment in their followers are in general those that are far more committed to dominance over nature, or are even indifferent to it, frequently imbued with beliefs in a 'fair world', or in the 'end of the world', and other dogmatic expressions. These results are in accord with a study in environmental psychology conducted in Brazil (Diniz and Pinheiro, 2014), which found clear associations between anthropocentrism, environmental apathy and immediatism, accompanied by an absence of the practice of environmental care. Preston and Baimel (2021) also draw our attention to the fact that the majority of studies with a psychological slant on the topic at hand focused mostly on Judaic/Christian traditions and on Americans in particular. Even so, they reiterate the good news that, inter-culturally, diverse religious traditions around the world have offered support to concrete commitments to protect the natural world, either through the public cooperation of religious leaders with secular groups, e.g. United Nations Organization, or in other forms of religious engagement for sustainable development.

It can be seen, therefore, that the destinies of spirituality, being formatted through religion, can intermingle with issues of a political, economic or ideological nature. In this process, the generous expression towards the world materialises – or maybe not! Like the one illustrated in the extract from Lévi-Strauss reproduced in the book *La chute du ciel: paroles d'un chaman yanomami*, witnessing the sympathetic wisdom of the Yanomami shaman. The look, a prime example of spirituality, is a driver of meaning, as Marilena Chauí (1988, p. 34) shows us: 'The look teaches a generous thinking that, coming into it, leaves from it through the thinking of another who grabs it and proceeds with it. The glimpse, identity of the leaving and entering in itself, is the definition of the spirit.' However, allowing it to dogmatise, inwards or outwards, the look/spirit is dimmed. Thus, the religious impulse, by feeding, or not, off the essential fundament of spirituality – a person's generous look inwards and outwards, may highlight or dim environmental care.

Agreements and disagreements between Heaven and Earth in the context of health

> Only the spirits know how to tear harmful things from inside our body and throw them far away from us. They are immortal and very good at curing us. This is why we appreciate them so and have continued to make them dance to this day. Very long ago, before the white people's medicine had reached us, our shaman could only rely on the spirits to avenge their people, children, women, and elders. They drank the *yãkoana*, made their spirits come down, laid in ambush with them to attack the sickness and make it flee. Of course they did not always succeed and despite their efforts some children were devoured by the evil beings' diseases. This was no different from the white people's doctors, who sometimes attempt treatment with medicines that fail. After the shamans' work, our elders' wives, also very wise, used healing plants from the forest. They used them to rub and bathe the bodies of the sick

who had just escaped being devoured by the evil beings or the epidemic spirits. Unfortunately, few women today still know how to use these plants. People still think that only the *xapiri* [spirits of the Amazon rainforest] can truly cure them, but now they also count on the help of the white people's medicine. (Kopenawa, 2010, p. 175)

If the indigenous peoples' responses to climate change, upon the marriage of Heaven and Earth, tend to defy certain religious classes of the so-called civilised people, this is no different with regard to the categories of the sciences, in particular those of contemporary medicine. Again, as can be seen in the testimony of the Yanomami chief, in the epigraph, it is not necessarily the indigenous people who will reject what could effectively offer him white people's knowledge. Indeed, what has been frequently observed in hospital settings in Brazil is much more the difficulty of those dressed 'in white' to cast a generous and compassionate look over indigenous cosmology and its peculiarities with regard to healthcare (Freitas, Vilela and Nwora, 2023; Vilela and Freitas, 2022; Nwora and Freitas, 2020). And it cannot be said that this difficulty in understanding is explained solely by linguistic differences between the various indigenous dialects and the Portuguese language. It is true that these difficulties in translation also exist in communication between indigenous patients and attending health professionals. But the big problem of translation between them takes place at a much deeper level. It is existential in nature. It is of the same order as coined in the epigraph of the work of Merleau-Ponty (1964, p. 159), 'Eye and Mind'. The philosopher reproduces a statement of Cézanne: 'What I am trying to convey to you is more mysterious; it is entwined in the very roots of being, in the impalpable source of sensations.' This applies very well to what Kopenawa is attempting to convey to the civilised world in *La chute du ciel: paroles d'un chaman yanomami* (Kopenawa and Albert, 2010). The native Indian speaks of a place of those who inhabit the world around him, while medical science, learnt by the health professionals, talks of a place for those who 'manipulate things and give up inhabiting them' (Merleau-Ponty, 1964, p. 159).

Indeed, as demonstrated in the studies developed by Langdon (2014), a North American anthropologist based in Brazil for around 40 years, and a researcher into indigenous narratives, while Western medicine understands the health-illness process rooted in the principles of biomedicine, of natural causes and verifiable biological aspects through the tangible observation of universal physical symptoms, the millennial indigenous medicine is founded on a cosmology that embraces invisible forces, contextually combining spiritual, natural and human forces. Thus he attributes great importance to the role of the shaman, who, imbued with this ecocentric, as opposed to an anthropocentric perspective, can produce cures, involving the ecosystemic community. In other words, the shaman is the holder of a peculiar *ethos* that involves local knowledge and understanding and is expressed in a tribal and mythologically shared linguistic-genealogical structure in which the conception of health is not separated from spiritual harmony with nature and all the beings that inhabit it. His purpose, by seeking to cure disease, is to lead the sick individual and the community in which he is situated to re-encounter the correct path, in other words, that which returns to the cycle of equilibrium between Heaven and Earth. So this involves the use of the elements of nature (smoke, fire, water), as well as plants, animals, minerals, etc., always coupled with spiritual treatment.

It is the case that such practices tend to be rejected, ridiculed, scorned, misunderstood or even feared by health professionals in hospital settings, according to studies conducted in Brazil (Freitas, Vilela and Nwora, 2023; Vilela and Freitas, 2022). In turn, this can spark mistrust in the indigenous people in relation to scientific medicine. This mistrust usually happens most frequently and intensely when they do not identify in the procedures adopted (e.g. pills, surgery, aseptic techniques) any concern with the equilibrium and harmony between human beings and the cosmos. After all, as Langdon (2014) puts it, beyond the cure for their diseases, the cosmology of the natives requires an explanation of its 'why', always using as its basis the ecocentric instead of an anthropocentric principle.

From a phenomenological perspective, the conflict between these two epistemologies, contemporary Western medicine and the medicine of the indigenous tribes, may be better understood when taking into consideration the degree to which both are situated, each at diametrically opposed poles in relation to the place attributed to intentionality. The former, faithful to the parameters of objectivist Western medical science, seeks to understand and control the processes of health and illness according to the assumption that it will be necessary to divest both objects like the environment of any intentionality. As for the latter, which moves the cosmology of native peoples in their healthcare, is exactly the opposite: the more one attributes intentionality to objects and the surrounding world, the better one may understand the events and actions that can promote wellbeing or bring physical/spiritual suffering/illness.

In this basic difference between the two epistemologies, as very well put by Viveiros de Castro (2008), for scientific medicine 'the more one is capable of interpreting human (or animal) behaviour, shall we say in terms of energetic states of a neural network, and not in terms of beliefs, desires, intentions, the more one understands the behaviour' (pp. 40–41). Thus, the more the world becomes 'disheartened' and devoid of subjectivity, the more one knows it. And the greater the advances in science, the more 'everything will be able to be described through the language of physical attitude, and no longer intentional attitude' (Viveiros de Castro, 2008, p. 41). Meanwhile, for the indigenous people, 'good understanding' is that which is capable of interpreting all world events as if they were actions, the result of some form of intentionality. [...] For them, explaining is to go deeper into the intentionality of what is known, that is to say, to determine the 'object' of knowledge as a 'subject' (Viveiros de Castro, 2008, p. 42).

By identifying the world around it as endowed with intentionality, the medicine practised by the shaman is grounded on a kind of transcendence of the human being, in which his body is akin to a material expression (terrestrial) of something larger and spiritual (celestial) which also lives inside him. Fundamentally modelled on the lifeworld, together with nature and the beings that comprise it, and to which we relate, this epistemology assumes that being, in a human way, is to intentionally establish itself in a world of relations, always directed towards caring in its various forms: seeing and watching, sympathetic of the other; experiencing the pulsating rush of the future forged in what is usual but also in the sensitive listening of that which, albeit occult, is seen in diverse ayes; projecting fears, desires and annoying suffering, specific to living, and giving them meaning from a perspective of reciprocity with the environment. While this epistemology takes place in a world where all of nature's beings are also subjects, the medical model, which prevails in hospitals, follows the depleted epistemology of intentionality, as is so well described by Merleau-Ponty (1964, p. 159): 'Science is and always has been that admirably active, ingenious and bold way of thinking whose fundamental bias is to treat everything as though it were an object-in-general – as though it meant nothing to us and yet was predestined for our own use.'

It is necessary to stress, however, that the agreements and disagreements between Heaven and Earth in the context of health do not just occur with the care of the indigenous people. Interviews conducted with health professionals in hospitals and mental health services in Brazil (Freitas, 2020) show that conflict exists between a variety of spiritual/religious epistemologies and that which nowadays inspires the medical model, as long as it is firmly established on criteria of objectification in order to formulate diagnoses and treat all diseases. Phenomenologically speaking, this is nothing unusual. After all, not only the indigenous cosmology but also the human condition in general resist complete objectification, by harbouring an immediate and pre-reflexive contact with the world, based on the inexhaustibility of the human being in the face of cultural and symbolic meanings. On the other hand, studies involving healthcare professionals (Freitas, 2020) also show that even they are frequently struck by a kind of 'feeling of opaqueness in the world'. This sentiment, as recalled by Merleau-Ponty (1964, p. 159), used to characterise classical science which sought to combine their constructions with other operations capable of maintaining a 'transcendent or transcendental foundation'. Albeit in a form of unknown knowledge, those who are dressed 'in white', in health-related settings, appear to be aware of this. After all, in their ethical oath on graduation, they adopt the words of Hippocrates, the father of Medicine. It was he that, as the legend goes, stated, against every merely anthropocentric conception: 'There is a common circulation, a common breath. All things are related.'

Implications for environmental and health policies

> The forest is alive. It can only die if the white people persist in destroying it. If they succeed, the rivers will disappear underground, the soil will crumble, the trees will shrivel up, and the stones will crack in the heat. The dried-up earth will become empty and silent. The *xapiri* spirits [spirits of the Amazon rainforest] who come down from the mountains to play on their mirrors in the forest will escape far away. Their shaman fathers will no longer be able to call them and make them dance to protect us. They will be powerless to repel the epidemic fumes which devour us. They will no longer be able to hold back the evil beings who will turn the forest to chaos. We will die one after the other, the white people as well as us. All the shamans will finally perish. Then, if none of them survive to hold it up, the sky will fall. (Kopenawa, 2010, p. 8)

The recent Covid-19 pandemic was frequently interpreted as a literal fulfilment of a Yanomami prophecy. In Brazil and across the world, there was no shortage of editorials in scientific journals and book prefaces reproducing the words of Kopenawa, the shaman, often written as epigraphs. Today, it appears that the pandemia has been controlled. However, the number of wars are escalating and are spreading their tentacles across the whole planet. The media announces that the Doomsday Clock, updated by a group of nuclear scientists, is set to 90 minutes to midnight, the time of the end of the world. Given this reality, which is far within and beyond the colossal convergence of efforts to preserve the Amazonia, it is appropriate to end this chapter by leaving some reflexions based on what has been laid out herein, in respect of the implications for environmental policies and health in Brazil, and in the world.

One of the big challenges for public policies on preservation of the environment, all over the world, and in Brazil in particular, involves the ability of statesmen and institutions to combine competence and sensitivities, at the same time and to the same degree. Competence based on all the currently available technical and scientific understanding regarding environmental issues, both in terms of the biological/exact sciences and the human/social sciences, capable of proposing, stimulating and guaranteeing actions to promote and provide this knowledge to different cultures, races, nationalities, ethnic groups, and socioeconomic groups across the world. In turn, these competences cannot be sustained ethnocentrically by the glamorous and propagated, but reductionist, jargon of 'scientific neutrality'. This jargon, in addition to being seen as foreign to the human and ecological diversity of human life on the planet, is sustained on the false belief of omnipotence and anthropocentric centrality.

Beyond the necessary competence, it will be necessary to find a place for sensitivity in public policies seriously committed to the sustainability of the planet and the wellbeing of its population, considered here to be all creatures that inhabit it, including humans, but not restricted to them. With this sensitivity, the glamour will be supplanted by care for real beings, diverse and plural, with specific identities, deserving of a look that respects them as such, and which also characterises their own way of looking, its cultural identities, cosmologies and specific ways to cultivate their spirituality with the world around them.

Moreover, the importance should be stressed that this alliance between competence and sensitivity should also reach professional education in all areas of human understanding, from Medicine to Philosophy, Psychology to Theology, Physics to Sociology, Mathematics to Anthropology, but in particular the training of professionals in the area of health. This is the only possible prerequisite for obtaining coherence in the fulfilment of that which the World Health Organization and public health policies advocate for the native peoples of this country and across the world.

The implementation of the aforementioned policies does not necessarily need to be inspired by romantic or idealised models that deify the native peoples. Similarly, it is not necessary to adopt their cosmologies in place of their own spirituality/religiosity and far less to deny that anthropophagous indigenous people existed and still exist. But, who knows, with a better understanding of their customs of marrying Heaven and Earth, it may be possible to glimpse, even in the anthropophagous act, the denunciation of individualism. Ultimately, by adopting an anthropocentric perspective, as per the manifesto of Oswald de Andrade (1928): 'only anthropophagy unites us'.

Biographical note

Marta Helena de Freitas is a Brazilian psychologist, earned a master's degree and doctorate in Psychology (University of Brasília, Brazil), with postdoctorates in Psychology of Religion (University of Kent at Canterbury, UK), Intercultural Psychology (University of OPorto, Portugal) and Anthropology of Religion (University of Wales Trinity University Saint David – UWTSD, UK). She is professor and researcher in the Psychology Program at the Catholic University of Brasília, Brazil, with extensive technical and bibliographical production in the psychology of religion, and phenomenology. She also has a scholarship in Researcher Productivity with the National Council for Scientific and Technological Development (CNPq) in Brazil. She is also an Honorary Research Fellow at the UWTSD, in the UK, a member of the American Psychology Association (APA), and currently the President of the International Association for the Psychology of Religion (IAPR).

Bibliography

Andrade, Oswald de. 1928. Manifesto Antropofágico [Anthropophagic Manifesto]. *Revista de Antropofagia*, 1, 1. Available at: https://pib.socioambiental.org/files/manifesto_antropofago.pdf (accessed 25 January 2024).

Boff, Leonardo. 2022. *O casamento entre o céu e a terra: contos dos povos indígenas do Brasil*. São Paulo: Planeta do Brasil.

Brazil. 2023. *Censo Demográfico 2022: Identificação étnico-racial da população, por sexo e idade* [2022 Demographic Census: Ethnic-racial Identification of the Population, by Sex and Age]. Rio de Janeiro: Instituto Brasileiro de Geografia e Estatística (IBGE). Available at: https://biblioteca.ibge.gov.br/visualizacao/periodicos/3105/cd_2022_etnico_racial.pdf (accessed 17 January 2024).

Brazil. 2025. *Censo Demográfico 222: Religiões* [2025 Demographic Census: Religions]. Rio de Janeiro: Instituto de Geografia e Estatística (IBGE). Available at: https://biblioteca.ibge.gov.br/visualizacao/livros/liv102182.pdf (acessed 5 July 2025).

Bratton, S.P. 2021. *Religion and the Environment. An Introduction*. New York: Routledge.

Chauí, M. 1988. Janela da alma, espelho do mundo. In: Novaes, A., ed., *O Olhar*. São Paulo: Companhia das Letras, pp. 33–34. Available at: https://artepensamento.ims.com.br/item/janela-da-alma-espelho-do-mundo/ (accessed 22 January 2024).

DeYoung, R. (1999). Environmental Psychology. In: *Environmental Geology. Encyclopedia of Earth Science*. Dordrecht: Springer, pp. 223–224.

Diniz, R.F. and Pinheiro, J.Q. 2014. Environmental Care in Times of Sustainability: The Relationship between Pro-Environmental Commitment and Future Orientation. *Psico*, 45, 3, pp. 387–394.

Eom, K. et al. 2021. Religion, Environmental Guilt, and Pro-environmental Support: The Opposing Pathways of Stewardship Belief and Belief in a Controlling God. *Journal of Environmental Psychology*, 78, 101717.

Freitas, M.H. de. 2013. Religiosidade e saúde mental em imigrantes: a percepção de psiquiatras e psicólogos ingleses e brasileiros [Religiosity and mental health in immigrants: the perception of English and Brazilian psychiatrists and psychologists]. In: Freitas, M.H., Paiva, G.J. and Moraes, C., eds. *Psicologia da Religião no Mundo Ocidental Contemporâneo: Desafios da Interdisciplinaridade*. Brasília: UCB, pp. 257–274.

Freitas, M.H. de. 2020. Religiosity, Spirituality and Wellbeing in the Perception of Brazilian Health and Mental Health Professionals. In: Schmidt, B.E. and Leonardi, J., eds. *Spirituality and Wellbeing: Interdisciplinary Approaches to the Study of Religious Experience and Health*. Sheffield: Equinox, pp. 199–224.

Freitas, M.H. de. 2024. Destinos da espiritualidade na clínica psicológica: um modelo conceitual inspirado na fenomenologia [Destinations of spirituality in the psychological clinic: a conceptual model inspired by phenomenology]. In: Ribeiro, J.P. and Neubern, M., eds. *Fenomenologia: encontro marcado com a psicoterapia* (ongoing).

Freitas, M.H. de; Leal, M.M. and Nwora, E.I. 2022. Praying for a Miracle Part II: Idiosyncrasies of Spirituality and its Relations with Religious Expressions in Health. *Frontiers in Psychology*, 13, 1–11.

Freitas, M.H. de; Vilela, Paula Rey & Nwora, Emmanuel Ifeka. 2023. Religiosity and Indigenous Cosmology in a Brazilian Hospital Setting: The Challenges Faced by Health Professionals. *International Journal Of Latin American Religions*, 7, 46–77.

Hempel, L. 2021. Religion and the Environment. In: Schaefer, C. et al., eds. *Handbook of Environmental Sociology*. Handbooks of Sociology and Social Research. Springer, Cham, pp. 315–331.

Hyginus, C.J. 2007. Hyginus Fabulae. In: Apollodorus. *Apollodorus' Library and Higinus' Fabulae: Two Handbooks of Greek Mythology*. Translated, with introductions by Smith, S. and Trzaskoma, S.M. Indianapolis: Hackett, pp. 95–246 (original written in approximately 1000BC, translated from a 1872 edition.)

Husserl, E. 1990. *El Artículo de la Encyclopaedia Britannica* (translated and edited by Antonio Zirión). Mexico: UNAM (Original de 1927).

Kopenawa, D. and Albert, B. 2010. *La chute du ciel: paroles d'un chaman yanomami*. Paris: Terre Humain, Plon.

Langdon, E.J. 2014. Os diálogos da antropologia com a saúde: contribuições para as políticas públicas. *Ciência e Saúde Coletiva Rio de Janeiro*, 19, 4, 1019–1029.

Maçaneiro, M. 2016. 'Ética e Episteme: Contribuição das Religiões para a Ecologia'. [2016 Ethics and Episteme: Contribution of Religions to Ecology]. *Revista Encontros Teológicos*, 26, 1.

Merleau-Ponty, M. 1964. Eye and Mind. In: Wild, J., ed. *The Primacy of Perception*. Evanston, IL: Northwestern University Press, pp. 159–190 (original published in 1961.)

Nwora, E.I. and Freitas, M.H. de. 2020. Interventions in Indigenous Contexts: Vicissitudes and Perspectives. *Caminhos De Diálogo*, 8, 12, 126–140.

Omoyajowo, K. et al. 2023. Exploring the Interplay of Environmental Conservation within Spirituality and Multicultural Perspective: Insights from a Cross-Sectional Study. *Environ Dev Sustain*, 20, 1–29.

Paloutzian, R.F. and Park, C.L. 2021. *The Psychology of Religion and Spirituality: How Big the Tent? Psychology of Religion and Spirituality*, 13, 1, 3–13.

Preston, J.L. and Baimel, A. 2021. Towards a Psychology of Religion and The Environment: The Good, the Bad, and the Mechanisms. *Current Opinion in Psychology*, 40, 145–149

Ribeiro, D. 2009. *The Brazilian People: The Formation and Meaning of Brazil.* Gainesville, FL: University Press of Florida (original published in 1995).

Secretaria Geral dos Sínodos dos Bispos. 2017. *Documento preparatório do Sínodo para a Amazônia* [Preparatory Document for the Synod for the Amazon]. Available at: http://secretariat.synod.va/content/sinodoamazonico/pt/documentos/documento-preparatorio.html (accessed 17 January 2024).

Silva, C.A. Oliveira da and Carmona, R.M. 2018. As Ciências das Religiões e suas contribuições na Preservação Do Meio Ambiente (As Obras Da Criação) [The Sciences of Religions and Their Contributions to the Preservation of the Environment (The Works of Creation)]. *Revista Campo do Saber*, 4, 2, 83–94.

Skalski, S.B. et al. 2022. Relationships between Spirituality, Religious Fundamentalism and Environmentalism: The Mediating Role of Right-Wing Authoritarianism. *International Journal of Environmental Research and Public Health*, 19, 20, 13242.

Vainfas, R. 2007. História indígena: 500 anos de povoamento [Indigenous History: 500 Years of Settlement]. In: *Brasil: 500 anos de povoamento* [Brazil: 500 Years of Settlement]. Rio de Janeiro: IBGE, pp. 35–59.

Vilela, P.R. and Freitas, M.H. de. 2022. Lidando com a religiosidade indígena no contexto hospitalar. In: Dias, R.J. de Lima and Freitas, M.H., eds. *Sofrimento psíquico e sentido da vida no mundo contemporâneo: Contribuições da psicologia da religião*. Curitiba: CRV, pp. 45–70.

Viveiros de Castro, E. 2008. O chocalho do xamã é um acelerador de partículas/Se tudo é humano, então tudo é perigoso. [The Shaman's Rattle is a Particle Accelerator/If Everything is Human, Then Everything is Dangerous]. In: Sztutman, R., ed. *Encontros: Entrevistas com Eduardo Viveiros de Castro*. Rio de Janeiro: Azougue, pp. 26–49; 88–113 (original publications in 1999 and 2004).

8   *La Pachamama*'s soul: Understanding eco-spirituality through archetypal intersubjectivity

Hannah Armbrust

It was *Omama* who created the land and the forest, the wind that shakes its leaves, and the rivers whose water we drink. It is he who gave us life and made us many. (Kopenawa et al., 2023, p. 27)

Introduction

Spirituality is often thought of as existing only through religious practices. It, indeed, plays an essential role in faith-oriented rituals. But spirituality transcends space and time; it is a breath of life, an energy conduit that moves us towards meaningful practices. As a Jungian-oriented psychotherapist, I consider spirituality the key that opens the doors to the individuation process, or psychological integration. Spirituality is the bridge that connects the dynamic relationship between the psyche's conscious and unconscious processes.

The origin of the word spirituality is from the Latin *spiritus*, meaning 'breath', 'soul', a vital force that goes on *ad infinitum*. Spiritual practices are undoubtedly ritualistic; beyond the realm of morality, ritualistic practices are ancestral and deeply rooted in our collective consciousness. In psychotherapy, rituals such as constantly washing hands to reduce anxiety are seen as pathological. But other rituals such as saying 'hello' every time you see a stranger on the street is considered courteous. More traditional celebrations are found in religious practices, such as using words and actions to revere objects during a service or the festivals of rites of passage, are considered sacred. Spirituality energises individuals and entire communities because it carries meaning.

The Romanian historian of religions, Mircea Eliade, argues that we can see those rituals in connection with their respective spaces as sacred or profane. According to Eliade, the sacred manifests itself as a transcendent event, which the religious person sees as holy; he names the manifestation of the sacred a *hierophany*. The natural or profane world is part of the nonreligious person's reality due to the rejection of the sacrality of the space. The space, as a symbol of the cosmos, loses its meaning. It is desacralised. It is important to keep in mind that the terms religious and nonreligious do not necessarily refer to being part of a religious denomination. Again, when rituals in sacred spaces lose their meaning, the 'nonreligious man' lives a 'desacralized existence' or profane while preserving 'traces of a religious valorization of the world' (Eliade, 1959, p. 23).

Going shopping every Saturday morning, for instance, is an energising ritual taking place in a desacralised space (the shopping mall) and constitutes a profane spiritual practice (consumerism is a form of spirituality); others get thrilled by engaging in heated political discussions (political spirituality). What defines the sacred and the profane is the symbol; 'an existential and sacred space that has an entirely different structure, that admits of an infinite number of breaks and hence is capable of an infinite number of communications with the transcendent' – the Earth is the quintessential sacred space, the *Pachamama*, our 'universal mother and nurse' (Eliade, 1959, p. 57) – it is time to restore our sacred space and our relationship with Mother Earth.

While living in Virginia, I provided services as an intensive in-home therapist and used to drive up to the Blue Ridge Mountains to see my clients. I enjoyed the drive and felt a sense of belonging and awe when looking at the landscape, especially during the Fall (direct experience of the sacred; spirituality). Passing through villages, I often saw small churches where people gathered for services and social events that were meaningful for them (religion; not necessarily spirituality). Religion connects and builds community through meaningful microevents or religious rituals; spirituality, on the other hand, moves the community to individual and collective fulfillment through the direct experience of the sacred. In this chapter, I will explore one among many forms of spirituality, eco-spirituality, a practice that builds community by combining science and soul.

The prefix eco- derives from the Greek word *oikos* (house) and, along with the Greek suffix -logia (a field of writing or study), forms the word ecology, a branch of biology concerned with studying the relationships amongst living beings and their physical environment. I am particularly interested in understanding the meaning of those relationships and their ethical implications for the lives of all beings on this planet. I will begin by exploring key concepts of Jungian psychology and relying on the mythopoesis of the oral stories of some of the ancestral peoples of South America to examine how archetypal intersubjectivity, as an epistemology, can offer new insights into the ethical paths we can choose to restore human relationship with Mother Earth, for the Andean people, the *Pachamama*.

C.G. Jung (1969a) stated that the psyche is transpersonal. Its spiritual dimension produces sacred experiences revealed in myths and rituals that still hold on to their transcendent nature or through the numinous character of the symbol and the symbolic life. For Jung, 'myth is not fiction: it consists of facts that are continually repeated and can be observed over and over again' (Jung, 1969b, p. 409). Jung considered the study of myths a significant aspect of the foundations of analytical psychology and his personal life. Jung's self-inquiry, 'What is the myth you are living?' is paramount to his quest into mythological studies:

> I found no answer to this question, and had to admit that I was not living with a myth, or even in a myth, but rather in an uncertain cloud of theoretical possibilities which I was beginning to regard with increasing distrust. I did not know that I was living a myth, and even if I had known it, I would not have known what sort of myth was ordering my life without my knowledge. So, in the most natural way, I took it upon myself to get to know 'my' myth, and I regarded this as the task of tasks, for – so I told myself – how could I, when treating my patients, make due allowance for the personal factor, for my personal equation, which is yet so necessary for a knowledge of the other person, if I was unconscious of it? (Jung, 1956, xxiv–xxv)

Mircea Eliade says that 'the myth relates a sacred history' (Eliade, 1959, p. 95) – a mystery – a proclamation of what happened *ab origine*. It is in the mystery that we find the sacred. But what we have been experiencing for the last six decades is a process of radical desacralisation of the environment to feed the endless appetite of consumerism. By asking Jung's self-inquiry we may discover the root of our troublesome relationship with this planet. Questions such as 'What archetypal energy is leading my life, my choices?' or 'What type of direct experiences with the sacred I have had recently?' may help us to find out how our myth has contributed to the current environmental crisis. Is your myth congruent with the quest for eco-spiritual practices, or must it be revised and adjusted? Please note that for the purpose of this chapter, the words 'myth', and 'collective narratives' will be used interchangeably, meaning archetypal stories. The goal is to simplify our conversation without making it necessarily shallow but to prevent a radical shift from the focus on eco-spirituality.

A brief account of Jungian psychology

Eco-spirituality is a field where analytical psychology can integrate its key concepts, such as archetypes, the transcendent function and the unconscious. Following this line of thought, I will introduce the concept of archetypal intersubjectivity to explore how our relationship with the symbolic, with one another and with the environment utterly shapes us and how we can relate to all these meaningful aspects of life from an eco-spiritual perspective.

Carl Gustav Jung, a German-Swiss psychiatrist, was the first to use the concept of archetypes in psychology. He stated that all humans share a deeper layer of unconscious content, which is cross-cultural and phylogenetic; he named it the collective unconscious. Jung argues that archetypes are the contents of the collective unconscious and have no definite form but can be identified in mythologems and images that manifest archetypal motifs. The word archetypes comes from the Greek word *arkhetupon*, *arkhe* (primitive or archaic) + *tupos* (a model or form). The concept of archetypes and the collective unconscious are the most controversial concepts in Jungian psychology; they have been deemed as 'unscientific' and rejected by mainstream branches of psychology. Jung insisted that through dream analysis, and by studying archetypal motifs in myths, fairytales and fantasies, he could demonstrate the veracity of his claims. However, there is no empirical evidence to corroborate that.

For a long time, Freud received accolades for being the one who first introduced the concept of the unconscious in psychology. However, the idea of the unconscious was part of a broad discussion among psychologists in the *fin de siècle*. Freud's genius rests on systematising the use of the unconscious in treating trauma and other mental disorders, a method he called psychoanalysis. Freud and Jung had different views of the dynamic and structure of the psyche, the unconscious and the concept of 'libido', which for Jung was synonymous with energy and intentionality. In contrast, Freud initially thought of libido as a sexual drive. Both used dream analysis to access unconscious contents, though. It is important to note that Jung was not a disciple of Freud. From the beginning, Jung's view of the unconscious and psychic energy (the libido) was sharply distinct from Freud and more aligned with other contemporary philosophers and scholars, such as Schopenhauer and Hartmann (Shamdasani, 2003).

Jung asserted that he analysed hundreds of his patients' dreams and was able to find patterns associated with ancestral mythologies from different parts of the world, leading him to conclude that we all share a deeper layer of the unconscious – the collective unconscious – that goes beyond our living experience, and that archetypes are its contents. The universalisation of human experience and interpreting the meaning of archetypes from a Western-modern perspective is disconcerting. At a time when psychology was a young science and highly divided, Jung's goal was to make psychology a universal science. There are limitations to Jung's theories, and some have received harsh criticism from post-Jungians and non-Jungians alike. Looking at the collective or cultural unconscious from the archetypal intersubjectivity's perspective can serve as a pluriversal option to universality.

Archetypal intersubjectivity

Words name things, create paths to learning, understanding and making meaning out of relationships with one another, and the environment where we live, visit or interact with. The Austrian philosopher Ludwig Wittgenstein (1989–1951), who developed the concept of language-game, asserted that words create mental processes which lead to actions. However, a simple word or sentence is not enough to provoke a meaningful response, if 'the rule of the game' is not clear: 'A substantive makes us look for a thing that corresponds to it' (Wittgenstein, 2009, p. 85). Words, therefore, are the main component of epistemologies, a branch of philosophy concerned with the nature, origin and scope of knowledge. The invention of the words 'civilised' and 'savage' to categorise human beings, for instance, will lead to mental processes that will lead to assumptions of 'knowing' the ones defined as 'civilised' and 'savage'. These are ontological assumptions restricted to the Western worldview only, although imposed upon other cultures as a universal truth.

Archetypal intersubjectivity's epistemological assumption is that the essence of Being is intertwined and dependent on relationships. Those relationships are not restricted to other human beings, or to the environment, and include our relationship with the symbolic. Those relationships are archetypal, meaning, they have historicity (narratives or a system of communication) and carry ancestral emotions (ancestral brain networks) (Panksepp and Biven, 2012); they are based on intersubjectivity or interbeing (Plum Village, 2021).

Eco-spirituality: The archetypal ethos

Eco-spirituality is oriented by science, faith and eco-friendly practices. It is a spiritual path of self-integration to the environment achieved through understanding that all sentient beings are interrelated and interdependent.

Ernest Haeckel, the well-known German zoologist, and evolutionary biologist, coined the term *Oecologie* in 1866, and defined this new science as the study of the interrelationship of all sentient and non-sentient beings with the environment, and the impact of those relationships to one another; hence the term ecology (*oikos*, Greek word meaning house). Ecology has gone from a mere field of study of biology to a more comprehensive concept that includes other forms of knowledge. Haeckel, with this new scientific model of understanding how organisms are interdependent, began a process of changing the collective consciousness that generated a social, economic, political and spiritual movement. Here is the definition of ecology in Haeckel's words:

> By ecology, we mean the whole science of the relations of the organism to the environment including, in the broad sense, all the 'conditions of existence.' Each organism has among the other organisms its friends and its enemies, those which favor its existence and those which harm it. (Egerton, 2013)

Haeckel's ecology is in tune with the idea that we are interbeing, which is paramount to our discussion. Jung goes further than that when he asserts that the 'psyche is Nature itself' (Jung, 2002, p. 1). Although Jung used the word 'nature' in his statement, he implies that our connection with the environment transcends the physical world. Jung's words lead us to reflect on the depth of our alliance with the environment; we are soul-nature (psyche = soul) in our essence and urgently need to find healing through this alliance.

A relationship with Mother Earth that is based on the exploitation and domination of resources comes from a narrative that places human beings as 'superior' and separated from 'nature'. This relationship ignores scientific and spiritual perspectives. How can we restore our ancestral form of synergy with the planet? The change must come from learning to unlearn the current approach to life itself. We have, collectively speaking, a desacralised life, to paraphrase Eliade. To learn new forms of relationship with the environment, we need to unlearn the current predatory way to be on this planet. Changing from the domination narrative to a story founded in trust and interbeing, which will offer just and healthy perspectives of life on this planet, might take decades to accomplish. Still, without starting it now, it will not ever be possible.

Eco-friendly practices are based on:

1. The recognition of Earth's rights as a living organism which possesses a unique form of subjectivity and alterity (Boff, 2009).
2. The effort of using eco-friendly words which denote our interbeing relationship with all living organisms in the planet.

3. An eco-spiritual practice based on archetypal intersubjectivity.
4. A caring and empathic attitude towards all sentient and non-sentient beings.

The future of humanity depends on having another relationship with the Earth and all its inhabitants so that the planet maintains its biocapacity and can continue to be our good and generous Mother and common home.

'What is the myth you are living?'

I will examine a few indigenous mythologies' cosmovision (their perspective of reality or worldview) aligned with eco-spirituality's practices through the lenses of creation myths – 'the deepest and most important of all myths' – as stated by Marie-Louise von Franz (1995). In the following myths, we will be in touch with several archetypal images produced by the unconscious. They are not scientific facts, and we cannot comprehend them from a scientific point of view. Nevertheless, they are psychological facts worth exploring due to their eco-spiritual character; Franz says they 'are concerned with the ultimate meaning, not only of *our* existence but of the existence of the whole cosmos' (Franz, 1995, p. 1). Now, let's return to Jung's question, 'What is the myth you are living?' What provisional mindset has moved me away from eco-spiritual practice?

There are numerous creation myths among ancestral peoples. Those archetypal narratives often describe the interconnection between two realities, the sky and the earth realms. They have in common the archetypal idea of a creator or a powerful force that brought life in all its expressions to this planet. The creation myths describe the beginning of times when humans came after other beings were already living here. One of these narratives is the *Huni Kuin*[1] myth of the *Yusha Kuru*.[2] It teaches us that we came to this world from the sky and fell to the Earth from the top of a huge tree. From that point on, we became mortals and had to learn how to heal the sick. *Yusha Kuru* (Armbrust, 2023) was the healer who taught them how to become trees after death and serve as remedies for those who fell ill. *Yusha Kuru*'s myth inspires us to think of life and death as part of the same reality and that our existential purpose is to heal ourselves in an 'inter-action' with the environment. In the *Yusha Kuru* creation myth, the physical and spiritual experiences are integrated; there is no promise of leaving the planet after death (the Huni Kuin become trees after dying). *Huni Kuin*'s cosmovision summons us to find existential meaning by fostering life.

Another compelling creation myth is the story of the most important goddess of Andean mythology, the *Pachamama*, a powerful deity whose name can be translated as Mother Earth. She is the goddess of creation; all living beings came through her. The myth of the *Pachamama* is a narrative in which the essence is reverence and gratitude to Mother Earth. For the Andean people, having a harmonious relationship with the *Pachamama* is essential to material and spiritual growth. In this Andean creation narrative, the supreme being possesses a dual aspect. She nurtures and punishes all living beings according to their attitude towards her. In other words, by engaging in a predatory relationship with the *Pachamama*, suffering will inevitably come as the natural consequence of our acts. The interbeing aspect of life on this planet is an essential aspect of the Andean cosmovision.

The Judeo-Christian creation myth is also one of those archetypal stories. In the book of *Bereshit* – Hebrew expression meaning 'in the beginning' or the book of Genesis in the Western world, Moses describes how G-d (Elohim or YHWH), created the world in six days and took the seventh day (Sabbath) to rest. The first human being (Adam or *Ha-Adam*) was created after all other beings were already living on Earth. YHWH shaped or formed *Ha-Adam* of the dust of the earth (*ha-adamah*) according to YHWH's will and breath of life[3] (one of the two etymological roots of the word psyche is the verb 'to breathe' *psychein*). When the physical existence is no more, the body returns to earth (shaped of the dust) and the soul of human beings returns to G-d (breath of life, spirit): 'And the dust returns to the earth as it was, and the spirit returns to G-d, who gave it.'[4] Eco-spirituality is present in all religious practices whose aim is to promote life and the respect for all forms of life on this planet.

All the creation myths above reject the idea of separation from the environment while conveying the sense of interbeing. Through their archetypal narratives, ancestral peoples remind us that the basis of our relationship with the environment is solidarity and that trust is at the centre of such connection. The current environmental crisis is one of the consequences of the myth of separation championed by René Descartes's (1596–1650) dualistic theory of mind and body. Cartesian philosophy is founded on subjectivity – 'I think, therefore I am.' The 'I am' forms the spirit of rejecting interbeing (intersubjectivity) with the environment. Unfortunately, we live in the Cartesian myth of separation: the mainstream belief that has shaped the Western modern cosmovision.

Depending on where you live, environmental and social justice will look different. But the impact of climate change will haunt everyone; and ultimately, the effects of the inequalities we face as humankind will, somehow, hit your community. We live under the same roof, so to speak, and as Pope

Francis stated in his *encyclical*, the Earth is our Common House. There are two main roads leading to the future of this planet. One grounded on individual needs, economic growth, and the continual exploitation of this planet. This road is a form of spirituality fed by the thrill of consumerism and political fundamentalism; it has proven to be a failure. We face the dilemma of choosing between continuing to travel on such a destructive path or choose the unfamiliar but safe road of redeeming the sins we have committed against Gaia.

The archetypal ethos of eco-spirituality is about rescuing the sense of wonder and belonging, so well expressed in indigenous mythologies; and reigniting our spiritual connection to the *Pachamama* by reflecting on the concept of interbeing and archetypal intersubjectivity as the baseline of recognising Earth's rights and starting a new relationship with this planet. We cannot travel both roads, and we do need to look 'as just as fair' and ponder the difference between traveling the worn-out road of the Anthropocene or finding new forms of relationship with Mother Earth. In this historical moment of ecological disaster and two wars happening at the same time, we witness devasted communities crying for help, forests burning, apocalyptic floods, hurricanes and tornadoes as never seen before. The image of the world in the age of the Anthropocene is not comforting.

The invention of the word 'nature' associated with the word 'savage' culminating with the idea of civilised humans being separated from 'nature' serves the type of narrative based on the exploitation of land and labor. Such separation has political, economic, academic, religious and spiritual consequences. The work of a psychologist has also political implications in the sense of advocating for social justice and the psychological wellbeing of humans in their environment. We will need a new spirit to make changes possible; a form of consciousness or force that will move us towards working on a solution to the urgent problems we are facing.

Eco-spirituality: An earth-centred approach

The Brazilian philosopher and writer Leonardo Boff (2016) argues that we live in a period when the tension between two geological eras is confronting each other: The Anthropocene and the Ecozoic. The Anthropocene – a term coined by the ecologist Eugene Stoermer – is a human-centred geological age (Greek *anthropo*, meaning 'human', and *-cene*, meaning 'new'). In the past 60 years, the human impact on the planet has accelerated causing some irreversible harm to Mother Earth. The Anthropocene is also known as the age of plastic pollution: 'Plastic could become a key marker of the Anthropocene.

Earth is now awash with plastic – millions of tons are produced every year. Because plastic doesn't biodegrade, it ends up littering soils and ocean beds.'[5] According to Boff, the Anthropocene is based on the premise of separation and domination of nature; it is the dominant ontology responsible for the current social and ecological crisis: 'The will to dominate to accumulate and accumulate to consume in an unlimited way has created the perverse gap between the few rich and the many poor: social injustice.' Boff also says that the Anthropocene is the leading cause of the 'ecological injustice' we live in due to the 'mercilessly plundered ecosystems, without considering the limits of nature's non-renewable resources' (Boff, 2016, p. 11).

The term Ecozoid (Greek *oikos* 'eco' meaning 'house' and *zoikos* 'zoic' meaning 'pertaining to living beings') was coined by the ecologist Thomas Berry during the Eleventh Annual E. F. Schumacher Lectures, in Great Barrington, Massachusetts in October of 1991.[6] During this conference, Thomas Berry spoke about the risks to life if we continue to walk on the Anthropocene path:

> The human inhabitants of the Earth, came into this region with all the ambivalences we bring with us. Not only here but throughout the planet we have become a profoundly disturbing presence. In this region and to the north in southern Quebec, the native maple trees are dying out in great numbers due to pollutants we have put into the atmosphere, the soil, and the water.

Leonardo Boff believes that the Ecozoic is a sustainable alternative to our civilisation, which Boff calls 'the civilization of death' (Boff, 2016, p. 12). Although Boff and Berry are clear when criticising the Anthropocene and its demises, they still separated humans from the environment, and both use the word 'nature' to describe other forms of life. I consider this wording problematic because it alerts to the dangers and offers sound alternatives to our ecological crisis. However, the language they use is in tune with the belief in human exceptionalism. Since the 90s we have been talking about the dangers of the Anthropocene, and how our predatory behavior has put life at risk on the planet, nevertheless, we need a profound change in the way we feel-think about it. This profound change needs to come with eco-words that will lead to eco-epistemologies and eco-ontologies. Unless we present new ontologies, we will continue to think about 'us' and 'nature' as separate units.

I use an Earth-centred attitude as a base for eco-spiritual practices and clinical work. Recent studies show that environmental issues can have a significant impact on mental health. Climate change, pollution, the loss of biodiversity and ecological disasters can lead to extreme anxiety, eco-anxiety

(Coffey et al., 2021) and other trauma-related disorders. I will refrain from exploring the implications of using an Earth-centred approach in clinical work in this chapter and will continue to centre my attention on eco-spirituality instead.

An Earth-centred attitude requires an unlearning process (Jung, 2009). As a psychotherapist, I encourage my clients to learn to unlearn. And what I mean by unlearning is to reject a provisional ego-centred personality, which is one-sided, and aligned with the promises of the Anthropocene (consumerism, exploitation of the environment, accumulation of resources) to answer to summons of the soul (wholeness, spirituality, collaboration) – to Jungian therapists the soul is the psyche, and psyche is nature.[7] Jung was Earth-centred as we can see in this passage:

> Through scientific understanding, our world has become dehumanized. Man feels himself isolated from the cosmos. He is no longer involved in nature and has lost his emotional participation in natural events, which hitherto had a symbolic meaning for him. Thunder is no longer the voice of a god, nor is lightening his avenging missile. No river contains a spirit, no tree means a man's life, no snake is the embodiment of wisdom, and no mountain still harbors a great demon. Neither do things speak to him nor can he speak to things, like stones, springs, plants, and animals. He no longer has a bush-soul identifying with a wild animal. His immediate communication with nature is gone forever, and the emotional energy it generated has sunk into the unconscious. (Jung, 1955)

Contrary to Jung, I am optimistic about recovering the emotional energy we once had through our profound and intersubjective relationship with the environment. The archetypal meaning of this relationship is to find a sense of belonging by understanding that we are interbeing with one another and with the environment. Eco-spirituality encompasses ancestral wisdom and current knowledge; it is the foundation of an Earth-centred attitude in all human practices, the archetypal ethos of benevolence and care that we need to restore our sense of interbeing with the surrounding reality from an ecological cosmovision.

Pachamama's pain, an eco-ethics to urgent care

I wrote this chapter while experiencing a mix of grief, hope, joy and several emotions, which I don't find the right words to describe. As humanity, we are facing the loss of thousands of people every day due to two wars going on simultaneously, genocide in Sudan, mass shootings in the U.S. and, of course, an unprecedented environmental crisis. It was in the news recently that the city of Rio de Janeiro reached a historic heat index of 138 °F – the vast majority in Rio live on less than 200 dollars per month, and most cannot afford air-conditioning. People with low incomes are the most vulnerable and suffering the most from climate change. Life on Earth has become increasingly difficult and, to some extent, unbearable. How can we change this? There is no simple answer to this question; we live in a moment of extremes where people hold on to their beliefs so passionately that engaging in a constructive discussion about the current environmental crisis has become unviable. However, giving up and pretending that one day this crisis shall pass is not an option because sooner or later, each one of us will be affected by this ecological nightmare.

It is my wish that the collective pain will lead us to develop a sacred, thus meaningful relationship with the environment. As Jung once said while referring to how relationships, rather than going smoothly and free from conflicts, can be somewhat strained by what he called the tension of the opposites: 'There is no birth of consciousness without pain' (Jung, 1954, p. 193). Hopefully, by engaging in an eco-spiritual practice, we will avert more deaths of living beings by making conscious the unconscious forces leading us to this abyss. Thus, Jung's self-inquiry is essential: 'What is the myth you are living?' Reflecting on this question can be the beginning of eco-spiritual practice, self-awareness, and eco-activism. Most importantly, self-awareness is the key to the individuation process: unless we differentiate from the crowd, unconscious forces will continue to drive us, leading to more environmental chaos. The eco-spiritual work begins with the individual and small acts of kindness towards all the *Pachamama*'s children.

Finally, accepting Jung's invitation to unlearn means to perceive the end in the beginning, as the prophet Isaiah revealed: 'I make known the end from the beginning, from ancient times, what is still to come.'[8] Eco-spirituality is about unlearning the centuries-old belief that humans are to tame, conquer and exploit the environment. It is about unlearning the word 'nature' as expressing separation between humans and the rest of creation. And finally, eco-spirituality is about returning to the initial project of creation manifested in creation myths from different ancient traditions: we are formed from the depths of the earth with a transcendent spirit. Our Earth-like body is just one more manifestation of creation, and our transcendent spirit is part of the mystery of being and interbeing.

Biographical note

Hannah Armbrust, PhD, LMHC, NCC is an adjunct faculty at Saybrook University, psychotherapist in private practice, a fellow faculty at the Jung Center of Houston, and a former professor at the Rondonia Federal Institute of Technology (IFRO), and at the Federal University of Rondonia (UNIR). Dr Armbrust has presented at various conferences in the US, South America, and Europe. She also has international clinical experience working with historically marginalized populations and advocates the use of decolonial options to psychotherapy, and Jungian studies. Dr Armbrust's research is focused on postcolonial and decolonial studies and epistemic practices, Jungian studies, archetypal intersubjectivity, Brazilian Amazonian mythologies, Ecospirituality, and ecopsychology.

Notes

1. The *Huni Kuin*, also known as *Kaxinawa*, inhabit a region located geographically within the Brazilian and Peruvian territories in the Amazon Rain Forest.
2. *Yusha Kuru* is a Huni Kuin healing goddess who became a vigorous Amazonian tree upon her death.
3. Bereshit (Genesis) 2:7-17.
4. Kohelet (Eclesiastes) 12-7.
5. What is the Anthropocene and why does it matter? Natural History Musuem, www.nhm.ac.uk/discover/what-is-the-anthropocene.html.
6. The Ecozoic Era – Schumacher Center for a New Economics, https://centerforneweconomics.org/publications/the-ecozoic-era/.
7. Jung's use of the word 'nature' is not congruent with his thoughts on this subject because it denotes separation. I use the word 'environment', which is inclusive of all beings.
8. Isaiah 46:10, New International Version (NIV).

Bibliography

Armbrust, H. 2023. Archetypal Feminine in *Kaxinawa*'s Stories: A Decolonizing Option to Jungian Approach. In: Segal, R., Blocian, I. and Kuzmicki, A., eds. *Collective Structures of Imagination in Jungian Interpretation*. Leiden: Brill, pp. 162–176.

Boff, L. 2009. *A Ética Da Vida: A Nova Centralidade*. Rio De Janeiro: Record.

Boff, L. 2016. *A Terra Na Palma Da Mão: Uma Nova Visão Do Planeta e Da Humanidade*. Petropolis: Vozes.

Coffey, Y., Bhullar, N., Durkin, J., Islam, Md.S., and Usher, K. 2021. Understanding Eco-anxiety: A Systematic Scoping Review of Current Literature and Identified Knowledge Gaps. *The Journal of Climate Change and Health*, 3, 100047.

Egerton, F.N. 2013. History of Ecological Sciences, Part 47: Ernst Haeckel's Ecology. *The Bulletin of the Ecological Society of America*, 94, 3, 222–224.

Eliade, M. 1959. *The Sacred and the Profane: The Nature of Religion*. New York: Harcourt.

Franz, M.-L. von. 1995. *Creation Myths*. Boston: Shambhala.

Jung, C.G. 1954. *The Collected Works of C.G. Jung, Volume 17: The Development of Personality, Paper on Child Psychology, Education, and Related Subjects*. Princeton, NJ: Princeton University Press.

Jung, C.G. 1955. *The Collected Works of C.G. Jung, Volume 18: The Symbolic Life, Miscellaneous Writings*. Princeton, NJ: Princeton University Press.

Jung, C.G. 1956. *The Collected Works of C.G. Jung, Volume 5: Symbols of Transformation*. 2nd ed. Princeton, NJ: Princeton University Press.

Jung, C.G. 1969a. *The Collected Works of C.G. Jung, Volume 9, Part 1: The Archetypes and the Collective Unconscious*. 2nd ed. Princeton, NJ: Princeton University Press.

Jung, C.G. 1969b. *The Collected Works of C.G. Jung, Volume 11: Psychology and Religion: West and East*. 2nd ed. Princeton, NJ: Princeton University Press.

Jung, C.G. 2002. *C.G. Jung on Nature, Technology & Modern Life*. Edited by M. Sabini. Berkeley, CA: North Atlantic Books.

Jung, C.G. 2009. *The Red Book*. New York: Norton.

Kopenawa, D. and Albert, B. 2023. *The Falling Sky: Words of a Yanomami Shaman*. Cambridge, MA: Belknap Press.

Panksepp, J. and Biven, L. 2012. *The Archeology of Mind*. New York: Norton.

Shamdasani, S. 2003. *Jung and the Making of Modern Psychology: The Dream of a Science*. Cambridge: Cambridge University Press.

Plum Village. 2021. To Be Is to Interbe – Thich Nhat Hanh. June 26. Available at: https://youtu.be/esyQnwz_yJ0?si=clfysrqloo-mdoU7.

Wittgenstein, L. 2009. *Major Works*. New York: HarperCollins.

9 Wellbeing is the feeling of being 'one with the world and my surroundings': Reflection about the environmental dimension of wellbeing in Brazil

Bettina E. Schmidt

Introduction

In 2010, I accompanied a group of students from the University of São Paulo and their professor, Vagner Gonçalves da Silva, to the *Sanctuario Nacional de Umbanda* outside São Paulo City. It is described as an ecological sanctuary in the Serra do Mar, founded and administered by the Umbanda Federation. A road sign near the entrance to the building has this quotation from *pai* [priest] Ronaldo Linares, one of the leaders of the federation: 'O umbandista não precisa de uma catedral como só o gênio humano é capaz de fazer, ele só precisa de um pouco de natureza come só deus foi capaz de criar.' ['The *umbandistas* do not need a cathedral that is created by humans, we only need nature which only god can create.'] The whole site covers a vast area at the edge of a forest, with several meeting houses that can be rented, outdoor places for sacrifices and other ceremonies, shrines for personal worship and impressive statues of various Orixas, the African deities at the core of the Umbanda pantheon, together with other spirits. The sanctuary offers a place to meet and worship close to nature. Many Umbanda communities in São Paulo do not have sufficient space for larger ceremonies due to the restricted space in such a huge mega-city. Worse still, however, is the lack of natural space which, while not required is desired, and indeed is integral to ceremonies.

Already during my earlier research in New York City, I often heard a complaint about lack of space or lack of the 'right' space. One of the temples of the Haitian religion Vodou I visited was in the basement of a residential house in Brooklyn. It had taken out the concrete floor in the ceremonial room and exposed natural ground. However, it became a health hazard: due to frequent noise complaints from neighbours the windows had to be shut, which had led to increasingly dusty air. When the musicians complained that they could not perform under these conditions, the *mambo* [Vodou priestess] gave in and covered the floor again with cement. However, one small area was left without the concrete cover: a small area around the *poteau-mitan*, a pole in the middle of the room decorated with drums that symbolised the link between the different levels of the cosmology and links the human earth with the space of the *lwa* [African spirits] and the space of the ancestors. The pole enables spirits to move to the human level to that they can manifest themselves during a ceremony. And the earth around it allows sacrificial blood to enter the ground and reach the spirits. Dianne Stewart describes it as spiritual grounding that reflects that there is life underground (2022, p. 219, referring to Walter Rodney's text *Groundings*, 1975).

Another problem for communities in urban settings is what to do with the sacrificial animals after the sacrifice. While parts of larger animals are used to cook a communal meal, the rest, as well as the smaller animals, cannot just be discarded as they have become sacred during the sacrifice and ritual order dictates that they are given to the spirits. This needs to be done by putting them close to water or buried under ground in fresh earth which is quite a problem in mega cities. I heard that some communities in New York take the remains to public parks or the ocean, usually in the night as it is against the law to leave animal remains in a public space though animal sacrifice has become legalised in the USA under certain conditions. This is not just a problem for Vodou temples but also for other communities of African-derived religions and came up in several conversations in New York. In addition to the complex issue of animal sacrifice (Schmidt, 2013a), the African deities are associated with natural places such as water (thus, rivers, lakes and the oceans), forest or mountains. The female deities, for instance, are linked to salty or fresh water and a preferred place for ceremonies to honour Yemaja, the mother goddess, is the Atlantic Ocean, or at least the beach in Coney Island in New York.

In São Paulo, where animal sacrifice is allowed, wealthy communities buy property for ceremonies outside the city, preferably close to water and trees, while smaller communities can hire space in the Umbanda sanctuary that offers both. Consequently, the sanctuary is not just a space for ceremonies and meetings, it also offers a place for people to come close to the spirits within their natural environment. During my visit, while we walked around the sanctuary and admired the statues and observed some offerings, we came across a small waterfall, where I noticed a young woman supported by someone else in the pool of the waterfall. I was told later that she was embodying a caboclo (a spirit associated with the Amazon) which is often around this place. While I attended other ceremonies of African-derived religions in and around São Paulo, the memory of this caboclo stayed in my mind. I realised that nature is not just important as a ceremonial place but also as an experiential place that allows experiences to occur. This little story sets the scene for the following discussion.

Focusing on the latter point – nature as experiential place – I will reflect first on the ways scholars discuss the importance of nature for spiritual experience before moving to reflect on the impact of the natural environment on wellbeing. I will use this section to criticise the One Health policy of the WHO which overlooks the spiritual dimension of wellbeing. This will lead to a discussion of wellbeing within the Brazilian context. I will illustrate that the environment is more than a place but is perceived as a living entity with which we develop relationships. Enriched by excerpts from interviews and surveys conducted in Brazil, the chapter illustrates the interconnectedness that is at the core of the expanding understanding of wellbeing.

Nature as experiential place

The natural environment is one of the core features within the study of religious experience as it inspires a feeling of awe and can trigger a non-ordinary experience, whether that experience is called religious, spiritual or 'just' unusual. This feature shines through in William James' description of his own experience. James who is one of the founding fathers of a non-theological approach to the study of religious experiences described his own experience when walking alone in the Adirondack Mountains:

> The streaming moonlight lit up things in a magical checkered play, and it seemed as if the God of all the nature mythologies were holding an indescribable meeting in my breast with the moral Gods of the inner life...the intense significance of some sort, of the whole scene, if one could only *tell* the significance; the intense inhuman remoteness of its inner life, and yet the intense *appeal* of it;... In point of fact, I can't find a single word for all that significance, and don't know what it was significant of, so there it remains, and mere boulder of *impression* (James and James 2008, pp. 76–77).

In a similar way, Alister Hardy, the founder of the Religious Experience Research Centre (RERC), recalled in his unpublished autobiographical notes his personal experiences during his walks along the banks of the river in Oundle,

Nottinghamshire that impacted on his life and might even have inspired him towards his later career in marine biology.

> There is no doubt that as a boy I was becoming what might be described as a nature mystic. Somehow, I felt the presence of something which was beyond and yet in a way part of all the things that thrilled me – the wildflowers, and indeed the insects too. I will now record something [that] I have never told anyone before, but now that I am in my 88th year I think I can admit it. Just occasionally when I was sure that no one could see me, I became so overcome with the glory of the natural scene, that for a moment or two I fell on my knees in prayer – not prayer asking for anything, but thanking God, who felt very real to me, for the glories of his Kingdom and for allowing me to feel them. It was always by the running waterside that I did this, perhaps in front of a great foam of meadowsweet or purple loosestrife. (Hardy, cited in Hay, 2013, p. 2)

These encounters in nature – some of them even ecstatic experiences – had a transformative impact on Hardy and inspired him after his retirement in 1969 to collect personal accounts of spiritual and religious experiences that became the foundation of the RERC archive. Hardy's as well as James' experience can be categorised in Walter Stace's model as extrovertive mystical experience, as they were triggered by the external physical landscape and environment, inducing 'a sense of the underlying unity of the natural world' (Hunter, 2021, p. 4, referring to Stace, 1960, p. 15). We see therefore two features regarding nature and spiritual and religious experience. The natural environment is often the place for such an experience, and it can also call from an individual a spiritual connection to nature.

Both aspects are also reflected in the accounts collected by Hardy and his successors in the RERC. One of the first accounts, for instance, describes eloquently the natural setting where the experience took place:

> As I sat on a low wall opposite a beautiful tree covered with pink blossom, thrown into relief by the high hill behind it, I was suddenly made aware of my surroundings in a manner difficult to describe in words. The tree became vibrant, 'real' (in the sense that the 'burning bush' did to Moses in the O.T.) and I was transported into what I can only term 'reality', and was filled with a great surge of joy (i.e. like C.S. Lewis's 'Surprised by Joy'). This was fundamental and I was 'caught up into it' and was a part of it. I felt a great sense of awe and reverence, permeated by the presence of a power which was completely real and in which I

had my part to play. I knew that all was well and that all things were working together for good. (RERC #000011)

Based on the prevalence of the natural world as the setting for an experience in the initial accounts he collected, Hardy identified in his book *The Spiritual Nature of Man* (1979), 'natural beauty' as one of the triggers of religious experience (1979, p. 81) – and was even more common in this regard than religious worship. Paul Marshall (2005) in his study on mystical experiences and the natural world echoes Hardy's characterisation which points to the second feature regarding experience and nature that I mentioned earlier, that nature can initiate a spiritual connection to nature. Marshall applies the label 'extrovertive' to mystical experiences to distinguish them 'from other mystical experiences by their orientation towards the natural world. In extrovertive experiences, the mystical features – unity, knowledge, reality, love, luminosity, and so forth – characterise experience of the natural world, not experience of something completely beyond the natural world, such as a transcendent god, self, soul, or realm' (2005, p. 3). Interestingly, the mystical experience of becoming one with the world can also take place in urban settings as this narrative shows:

> I was out walking one night in busy streets of Glasgow when, with slow majesty, at a corner where the pedestrians were hurrying by and the city traffic was hurtling on its way, the air was filled with heavenly music; and an all-encompassing light, that moved in waves of luminous colour, outshone the brightness of the lighted streets. I stood still, filled with a strange peace and joy, the music beat on in its majesty and the traffic and the pedestrians moved through the light. They passed on their way, but the music and light remained, pulsating, harmonious, more real than the traffic of the streets. I too moved on…till I found myself in the everyday world again with a strange access of gladness and of love. [RERC #000208]

Similar to the experience cited above, this mystical or, in Stace's term, 'extrovertive experience' was triggered by the location. Unfortunately, the relationship to the natural world is often overlooked by early scholars who focused on understanding the relationship between humans and the divine. But this is changing, as the interest in eco-spirituality and its impact on wellbeing shows. As we know today, 'a relationship with the natural world directly affects people's physical, mental, and overall wellbeing due to benefits gained by increased exposure to nature and positive experiences in the natural world' (Restall and Conrad 2015, p. 1). The increased awareness of the beneficial impact of nature has inspired new research on the way people experience nature and / or have experiences in nature. For instance, Thurfjell and Remmel recently highlighted in an article called 'The Forest Is My Church' that this trope captures the widespread notion among secular urban middle-class population in Northern Europe and illustrate that 'that they today experience in nature what people previously experienced in the church. In other words, that it is in nature – and not in traditional religion – that they find a sense of sacredness, authenticity, purpose, and stillness, – qualities that they imagine that religious people get out of their religion' (2023, p. 1). This shift to nature is not therefore new, although it is getting more attention recently. Beringer who already discussed ecospirituality over twenty years ago, gives her definition of 'true ecospirituality' as an extension to ecospirituality used simply as 'connection to nature'. Instead, she characterises 'true ecospirituality' using four ideas: nature (in the sense of the natural world) is seen as a source of meaning in one's life; 'God' is in nature with an 'otherwordly' dimension; commitment to the Earth reflected in moral conduct; and finally, that the universe is believed to be or experienced as a living cosmos and planet Earth a living sentient being 'Gaia' or 'Mother Earth' (Beringer, 1999/2000, p. 17). She argues that in 'authentic ecospirituality', land is 'considered to be a vessel of the sacred […] possible source of spiritual inspiration' (1999/2020, p. 17). Similarly, Valerie Lincoln defines ecospirituality as 'manifestation of the spiritual connection between human beings and the environment' (2000, p. 228). Beringer's 'spiritual inspiration' echoes the experiences of James, Hardy and others described above. However, there is a problem with the concept of ecospirituality and how it is discussed in the literature. The debate around ecospirituality usually focuses on Western movements and reflects on ideas of middle-class urban population in Western societies, despite acknowledging – often in passing – its roots in indigenous beliefs. It expresses warnings against environmental destruction in our postmodern world and even links, as Jane Bennett writes, 'environmental pollution to moral decline, or the desouling of ourselves, and seeks to recover a sense of the sacred' (2001, p. 91).

However, there is a shift as for instance in the article 'An 'Ecospiritual' Perspective: Finally, a Place for Indigenous Approaches' by John Coates, Mel Gray and Tiani Hetherington (2006). The authors highlight that the emergence of literature on spirituality and the environment has created 'a space where indigenous voices are being heard. […] Spirituality and ecology emphasise, respectively, a search for meaning and sustainability, and acknowledge the need to accept and value alternative perspectives' (2006, p. 389). For the authors, ecospirituality counters ethnocentric tendencies and points towards the knowledge of non-Western cultures from which we can learn, not just about the spiritual sense of interconnectedness but also about the need to integrate ecological harmony and social responsibility (2006, p. 392). There are also, of course, voices that show the Western roots of ecospirituality. Bennett, for instance, points out that Henry Thoreau could be read as an ecospiritualist who treats 'nature as a kind of spiritual tonic' (2001, p. 92). She cites for instance the following lines from 'Walking': 'I wish to speak a word for Nature, for absolute freedom and wildness, as contrasted with a freedom and culture merely civil, – to regard man as an inhabitant, or a part and parcel of nature, rather than a member of society. I wish to make an extreme statement, if so I may make an emphatic one' (Thoreau, 1851, cited by Bennett, 2001, p. 93). This love of nature is also reflected in Thurfjell and Remmel's research data from Sweden and Estonia. Citing from their interviews they point out that their participants – all of them urban, secular, middle-class – perceive the forest as authentic; they cherish its peace, silence and solitude; and regard the forest 'like a different world', connected to an experience of allure and enchantment (2023, pp. 4–5). Some even expressed a kind of 'animistic view of trees, speaking of them as persons with caring and energetic qualities' (2023, p. 5). They argue that their data transcends the dualistic religion-secular divide. Their participants' love of nature 'is neither religious nor secular and we hence conclude that it would be more fruitful to interpret their nature experiences in "both/and" rather than "either/or" terms' (2023, p. 15). Building on Lois Lee (2015) and her notion of 'existential cultures' that avoids the dichotomy of religion and secularity, they put forward the notion of 'existential field' and describe it as a category to:

> identify the domain in which our participants' love of nature takes place. Within this field, nature experiences co-exist with religious, spiritual, and secular matters. It contains (or cluster together) a variety of seemingly disparate phenomena, including frequenting the forest, sharing time with friends, doing yoga, visiting a psychotherapist, listening to classical music, attending a church service and so on – all framed within the context of caring for one's physical and spiritual (or, more widely, existential) health, pointing to the fact that the pervasive orientation of the existential field is that of wellbeing. (Thurfjell/Remmel 2023, p. 16)

Lincoln also highlights the link to wellbeing when she writes about 'a reciprocal relationship between the health and wholeness of humanity and the health and wholeness of the environment' (2000, p. 228). In this sense, the concept of ecospirituality when applied to healthcare practice contributes to the healing of self, other and planet (2000, p. 242).

However, as already mentioned at the start of this section, experiences that take place in natural settings have a spiritual dimension. Stace in his classification of them as extrovertive mystical experiences points out that people experiencing them associated what they experience with a sense of unity and oneness in nature, something that the participants in Thurfjell and Remmel's study echoed, and my research also confirmed. It is important therefore to acknowledge the plurality of ways in which people connect to nature as Irine Becci and Alexandre Grandjean (2022) point out:

> If the category of nature is a cultural construct, it is also an experiential and relational approach to biotopes, which humans learn to pay attention to and integrate into their local cosmologies. [...] these cosmologies are made of secular and religious cultures that interlace. Therefore, there is not one eco-spirituality but a multitude of ways to understand and practice the link between what is considered spirituality and what is considered ecology. (2022, p. 4)

The environmental dimension of wellbeing

Despite many attempts to define wellbeing as a universal term, wellbeing is a cultural defined concept. In English, 'well' relates etymologically to 'wealth', which according to Richard Woods meant 'happiness' (2008). This link to wealth is absent in Latin America where wellbeing has a less materialistic and more spiritual dimension. In the two dominant languages of Latin America, wellbeing is translated as *bem estar* (Portuguese) or *buen vivir* (Spanish), which means literally being or living well but implies the meaning of 'living well together'. In this sense, it is 'a holistic concept rooted on principles and values such as harmony, equilibrium and complementarity, which from an indigenous perspective must guide the relationship of human beings with each other and with nature (or Mother Earth) and the cosmos' (Rodríguez, 2016, p. 279, endnote 1). Wellbeing becomes perceived consequently as relational, 'as socially and culturally constructed, rooted in a particular time and place' (White, 2016b, p. 29).

However, Rodríguez's definition points to a wider concept; wellbeing does not depend only on living well together with other human beings but also with nature and other than human beings. The reply of one of the participants of my study on spirituality and wellbeing echoes this perspective when he describes wellbeing as 'the feeling of belonging to the whole and that everything is connected. When we understand and practice it, we feel that we are part of something bigger. By knowing this, daily problems become small' (#75, Brazil, 54 years old, male). This interconnectedness is at the core of the perception of wellbeing in Brazil, even today, in a neoliberal era in which wellbeing is increasingly seen as leading a good life (Schmidt, 2022).

However, in the academic debate, the environmental aspect within the notion of wellbeing was long neglected, despite the notion of One Health promoted by the WHO. This initiative is an improvement from its original definition of global health promoted by the WHO in 1948 that simply stated that 'health is a state of complete physical, mental and social wellbeing and not merely the absence of disease or infirmity' (WHO, 1948, p. 2). Influenced by this definition, wellbeing was long linked to measurable aspects of quality of life, hence ignoring immaterial aspects such as the spiritual dimension and the relationship with other than human agencies. This approach has been slightly adjusted in the One Health concept that the WHO currently advocates. The WHO characterises One health as 'an integrated, unifying approach that aims to sustainably balance and optimise the health of people, animals, and ecosystems. It uses the close, interdependent links among these fields to create new surveillance and disease control methods' (WHO, 2022).

The term One Health, first adopted in 2003 but further promoted in the wake of the global spread of viruses such as SARS and in particular the Covid 19 pandemic (Braverman, 2023, p. 1). It represents a political agenda to increase global collaborations and sharing knowledge in the light of the threat of transmission of infections from animal to human (Wood, 2023, p. 27). Irus Braverman in the edited volume *More-Than-One Health: Humans, Animals, and the Environment Post-COVID* critically discusses the ideology behind the One Health agenda that limits our engagement with diverse worldviews. While she acknowledges that One Health reflects the widely accepted idea that diseases cannot be controlled in relation to human health alone and that all living organisms are at stake, it is still based on an anthropocentric, Western and even neoliberal ideology, 'illuminating the structural biases and power dynamics that are still at play in this context' (2023, p. 2). Instead, she urges us to decolonise One Health. Her edited volume includes in consequence various local examples, from the Arctic, Israel and South Africa to Taiwan and India, to name just a few. In this way it echoes what Keller and Kearns highlight in their introduction of *Ecospirit: Religions and Philosophies for the Earth* – the need for a new ecodifference that reflects biodiversity and transnational pluralism (2007, p. 11).

However, though Braverman acknowledges the need to acknowledge differences, her critique is still mainly a critique against the anthropocentric focus 'on zoonotic and vector-borne diseases and on health services that integrate only human and animal health, without considering their environment' (2023, p. 7). I miss the reflection of the spiritual dimension of environment that can impact on health and wellbeing. Nevertheless, her critique that indigenous voices are neglected in the debate on One Health is important. Without understanding how people engage with their natural environment, we can't challenge the power hierarchy still embedded in One Health. And as I pointed out above, people relate to nature in a spiritual way, even if they are secular and even anti-religious. Ignoring spirituality in any discussion of health and wellbeing is therefore negligent of emic viewpoints. Tim Ingold refers to it as 'sentient ecology' (2000, p. 24). Referring to David Anderson's study of reindeer herders and hunters in Siberia, Ingold writes that the term 'captures the kind of knowledge people have of their environments […]. It is knowledge not of a formal, authorised kind, transmissible in contexts outside those of its practical application. On the contrary, it is based in feeling, consisting in the skills, sensitivities and orientations that have developed through long experience of conducting one's life in a particular environment' (2000, p. 25).

Another point that is important to make before I return to my research in Brazil is experiences in the realm of nature are not 'necessarily self-centred', as Becci points out, but include 'a strong emphasis on community. Indeed, a certain official ecological discourse has long referred to spirituality when pointing to values encountered in distant, non-western, indigenous, or native people, e.g., societies that attribute a spiritual value to all species in nature' (2021, p. 107). Based on her study in Switzerland, she and her collaborators put forward the notion of 'Subtle Green Spirituality' that 'comprises cultural ideas, beliefs, rituals, and practices that make reference to nature pragmatically and in relation to everyday life, as opposed to making reference to nature in a manner related to mysticism or transcendence' (Becci and Grandjean, 2022, pp. 18–19). In this way they regard 'Subtle Green Spirituality' as oriented towards solidarity and politically commitment, a notion that echoes one of my interviews with a Candomblé priest in Brazil.

Before I was able to interview him, I had met him in various situations in which he always campaigned for the acceptance of African-derived culture and religions in Brazil. He was indeed a strong advocate of Black Brazil, which caused his African heritage to become noted. However, in a time when Candomblé communities pushed towards cleansing their practices of all non-African features, he continued to celebrate annually a ceremony in honour of the *caboclo* [spirit] White Feather (Pena Branca) which is seen as a representation of the indigenous heritage. His position was in clear opposition to some of the leading priests of Candomblé. Take Mãe Stella, for instance, a celebrated national figure in Brazil who dismissed the inclusion of non-African elements as 'a disguise, a false construction, a façade under which real, authentic African cultural and religious traditions were preserved' (Sansi, 2007: 20). She fought against all non-African elements such as Catholic iconography or indigenous spirits such as the caboclo as part of her wider anti-racist campaign (Gebara, 1999: 410). While the position is not uncontested, it spread through the Candomblé communities across Brazil so widely that Gonçalves da Silva considered Candomblé as the 'reinvention of Africa in Brazil' (1994, p. 43). Why did this Candomblé priest differ so openly despite his strong political activism to promote his African heritage? The answer lies in the connection between the caboclo with the environment.

> Although I have been initiated into an African cult, I am Brazilian, and I have a Brazilian spirit, that is, White Feather.... He is an Indian who was born in the interior of *Goiás*, inside the bush. According to him [=the spirit], he belonged to another father of the saint [=initiated priest of Candomblé] who did not take care of him correctly. In the end, he [the spirit] gave up and caught me, still a young man. Really, before I made [=became initiated into the cult of] *Oxum* [=name of his *orixá*], this *caboclo* revealed himself in me. (interview on 21 May 2010)

Later in the interview, he went even further and demanded that everyone should pass a *caboclo* ceremony before becoming initiated into Candomblé because *caboclos* represent the indigenous identity of Brazil, they are 'men of the interior who had been abandoned, had been in the bush without civilization, without culture;....[however, they].... had contact with *Oxalá* because of its pureness, its stubbornness of living inside there without talking with the civilization.' For him the caboclos are his Brazilian motherland, his home, as he sees himself as 'a native Brazilian, with African heritage, but I am not a native African' (see Schmidt, 2013b for more information). While in some Candomblé communities the *caboclos* have been replaced by the *orixá* Oxóssi who is part of the (African) pantheon of *orixás* and linked to hunting, caboclos are often described as *Dono da Terra*, the master of the land, representing therefore the first owners of Brazilian land (Ferretti, 1998, p. 39). The inclusion of the *caboclos* in the Candomblé pantheon was seen as a way to celebrate the indigenous people as 'Brazilian hero and national symbol post-Independence' (Ferretti, 1998, p. 39).

But the inclusion of caboclos is not only a political statement, it also highlights the importance of the environment for wellbeing with its spiritual dimension. While I didn't discuss wellbeing with this priest, I realised much later that it was about wellbeing – or well-becoming as the two editors of this volume write – all along. He showed the importance of the place for his spirituality, and consequently for his wellbeing that is centred around his spirituality. As the editors point out in the introduction of this volume, the term 'well-becoming' includes a notion of past and present, that embraces a subjective and emotional mode of awareness. Fernando sees himself as Brazilian, linked by his Brazilian place of birth, and as African, linked by his ancestors, and both, present and past, are connected through Candomblé.

Wellbeing in Brazil and its environmental dimension

At this point I will return to my research on spirituality and wellbeing. During the initial stage of this project, I asked participants to describe wellbeing. While the replies are not representative for the Brazilian public, they illustrate some interesting features such as that physical health is not enough to achieve a sense of wellbeing. The participants mentioned mental features but also spiritual ones such as the divine. Living in harmony was also a common feature as well as the need for connectedness, whether to other human people or in a wider, all-inclusive sense (see Schmidt, 2022). While only a few referred to the word for nature in their replies, several pointed at the connection to the surroundings, to the feeling of being not alone, to being connected to a whole. However, the participants of the study lived all in an urban setting, most but not all in São Paulo, one of the global mega cities. Despite having some public gardens and being relatively close to the Atlantic coastline (relative for Brazilians at least), access to the natural environment is limited. It is therefore interesting to see that even in a study that did not focus on the environment, several replies point to the importance of their surroundings for wellbeing as the following sample shows.

1. Wellbeing is something that gets us in Peace with ourselves…with nature…with others and with God, at last it is happiness and joy different from the one we usually feel because it lasts. (#7, Brazil, 50 years old, female)
2. It means to feel well with oneself, tuned with world and nature, with no stress. (#16, Brazil, 19 years old, female)
3. To feel well with oneself and with the world surrounding you. (#19, Brazil. 18 years old, female)
4. Wellbeing is to feel well with oneself and at the same time to know that one is not alone. It is to feel supported although we don't see those who take care of us. (#31, Brazil, 45 years old, female)
5. To feel well with myself, with other and with the whole (#36, Brazil, 51 years old, female)

6. It is to feel good about yourself and with the one's surroundings. Which is very difficult nowadays with so many interests and bad influences around. (#49, Brazil, 63 years old, female)
7. Wellbeing is to feel well in the whole, to be sure of and how to be humble, seeking to be better everyday. (#51, Brazil, 27 years old, female)
8. Wellbeing is the feeling of belonging to the whole and that everything is connected. When we understand and practice it, we feel that we are part of something bigger. By knowing this, daily problems become small. (#75, Brazil, 54 years old, male)

Interestingly all but one of the participants of the survey that mention nature in various ways were female. While women were indeed the majority, there were 33 male participants out of the 97 in total.

In some follow-up interviews I discussed in more detail their understanding of spirituality and what it means to achieve a sense of wellbeing. Several interviewees told me detailed life stories how they overcame illnesses, addiction, psychological problems and more by exploring spirituality. Ultimately spirituality helped them to connect to people (family, friends or people in general), to other than human beings such as spirits, deities or ancestors, and to the world at large. This connection is at the core of wellbeing. In African-derived traditions, this spiritual connection is enabled via a spiritual energy called *axé* (see Schmidt, 2009, 2012). *Axé* is the spiritual force that links all living being with the divine. It is needed to live and exists in every living being, humans, animals and plants. Consequently, it is in the natural world, the forests, oceans and air that are all filled with living beings. According to Candomblé teaching, *axé* is given by Oludumaré, the supreme deity whose breath gives life to the physical form. During our lifetime, we lose *axé* which causes illnesses and other problems. If we live in an unbalanced way, *axé* can diminish dangerously and even lead to death. Central to this understanding is the definition of health as living in balance with *axé* (Gomberg, 2011, p. 144). The physical body can be treated by biomedicine and following nutritional rules. However, these rules do not cure the cause of illness, the spiritual imbalance. Without restoring this imbalance, people cannot achieve a sense of wellbeing which is, however, not the same as health. As one of the participants highlighted, one can have a sense of wellbeing even when critically ill (see Schmidt, 2020 for further discussion).

We can gain *axé* by observing rituals, performing sacrifices and following obligations towards the *orixás* (Schmidt, 2021). Among the participants were several members of a centre in São Paulo that offers training courses in various spiritual healing therapies in addition to healing sessions. The healing sessions and ceremonies are based mainly on Candomblé ideas. But it also offers workshops to explore different aspects of healing and therapy as a way of self-improvement which is becoming increasingly popular, not just in this centre (see Schmidt, 2023). The core thinking behind them is that healing starts in you. the first step towards healing is understanding why one is sick. As soon as people understand the cause for the disease or the addiction, and work on improving oneself, for instance change their habits, healing begins. In this way the overarching philosophy of the centre differs from other spiritual healers as the co-director outlined in an interview.

> We do not say that it was a spirit that brought you and healed you. Instead it was you who became aware of yourself, who transformed you. [...] we also have people that seek advice, we have the mediums in trance who receive guidance from above and give advice, certain teas, energy etc. [...] healing is in you. [...] healing is in oneself, and that is my understanding of spirituality. (interview on 20 August 2016)

In addition to my visits to the centre in São Paulo and my conversations and interviews with some of the members, I was also able to attend a core healing ceremony that takes place outside São Paulo, closer to the natural environment. It focuses on Olubajé, the *orixá* of healing, and is performed in a specific place, bought and developed by the centre. Like the other healing sessions that are regularly conducted in São Paulo, the ceremony is led by various mediums who can be consulted by members of the public. However, participation at the ceremony itself is important as it helps to restore the energy within. Gomberg describes it as a complex ritual whose central objective is to restore the health of everyone present, members as well as guests (Gomberg, 2011, p. 170).

This ceremony and its natural setting highlight an aspect of *axé* that is often overlooked in the literature – the connection to nature. *Axé* is not only in human beings and animals, but is in every tree, every flower and even every weed. The natural world shares *axé* with us because we are part of it. Feeling connected does not refer only to being connected to other humans and the *orixás*, but also to the trees, to the mountains and to nature in its glory. We see here therefore a perfect example of the connection between spirituality, nature and wellbeing. All is seen as interrelated by *axé*, the divine energy that keeps us and the world alive.

It complements Stewart's aspect of spiritual grounding which I mentioned in passing in the introduction. Working in Trinidad on the Yoruba-Orisa tradition, Stewart explains that Yoruba-Orisa mothers 'have a long tradition of *grounding*, of claiming spots of ground for spiritual fixation' (2022, p.

219). For Stewart these practices of grounding and honouring Mother Earth in Trinidad reflect the preoccupation with land that she sees as legacy from slavery. Black landlessness, which she describes as 'a haunted *place* of non-belonging', is 'the most fertile province of African religious imagination and invention in the Caribbean and the Americas' (2022, p. 219). Stewart points here in particular to women and their leadership roles in Yoruba-Orisa tradition, which is also relevant for Brazil, at least to some degree (Matory, 2005).

As I already have pointed out in the introduction, by emphasising the place of the *poteau-mitan* in a Haitian Vodou temple with its base in the earth, the ground has importance as it enables the connection to ancestors, spirits and deities. The need to belong is also an important feature for all diasporic communities. However, when we consider wellbeing, the concept of grounding needs to be extended. Instead of perceiving it (literally) as ground, I suggest using it in a wider sense as connection to nature. Hence it is not only the ground below but also the sky, the sun and the air above and around. *Axé* connects everything and everyone, what is below and above the ground and in the air. It embraces fire, water, air and the earth, and in this way, we are grounded in more than one way, not just to the ground below but also the atmosphere above. It even links us with the past and the future, with our ancestors and our descendants. It supersedes a lineal, two-dimensional concept of living and wellbeing with spiritual connection at its core.

Conclusion

Sharon Betcher points to an interesting link between ideas of health and environmental activism because health 'serves to personalise the concern': 'Given the loosing of cesium from nuclear malfunctions, like endocrine disrupters escaping from plastics, each leading to genetic, even epigenetic mutations, there appears every good reason to conjoin environmental discourse with our culture's health obsession' (2015, p. 10). However, she warns that in the name of health, we are too easily manipulated, and give over to a neoliberal agenda related to the narcissistic optimisation of self. While I agree with her concern, my chapter has shown a different link between health and environment. Looking initially at nature as the location of spiritual and religious experiences and afterwards at the environmental dimension of wellbeing, I presented my research insights from Candomblé as a way both can be seen as interrelated.

I will conclude the chapter as I started, with my visit to the *Sanctuario Nacional de Umbanda*. As I outlined in the introduction, the Sanctuary offers a place for ceremonies close to nature. It has places that trigger experiences and can even initiate the embodying of a spirit in a human body during trance. But it is more than a place to explore spiritual experience. It is also a place to be close to the divine. As the sign at the entrance announces, nature is seen as the cathedral, not made by humans but by the divine.

Biographical note

Bettina E. Schmidt, DPhil (habil.), PhD, MA in cultural anthropology (Marburg University, Germany), professor in the study of religions and anthropology of religion at the University of Wales Trinity Saint David, UK and the director of the Alister Hardy Religious Experience Research Centre, UK. Previously she has worked at the universities of Marburg, Oxford and Bangor. She has been visiting professor at the City University of New York and visiting scholar at the Pontifícia Universidade Católica de São Paulo. She served as President of the British Association for the Study of Religions (2018–2021). She has published extensively on Caribbean and Latin American religions. Her academic interests include anthropology of religion, diaspora identity, religious experience, spirituality and wellbeing, and gender. Her main fieldworks to date have been conducted in Mexico, Puerto Rico, Ecuador, New York City and in São Paulo, Brazil. She is the author of *Spirit and Trance in Brazil: An Anthropology of Religious Experiences* (2016, Bloomsbury) and other monographs as well as co-editor of the *Handbook of Contemporary Brazilian Religions* (2016, Brill) and *Spirituality and Wellbeing: Interdisciplinary Approaches to the Study of Religious Experience and Health* (2020, Equinox), among others.

Bibliography

Becci, I. 2021. Grounding Eco-Spiritualities: Insights Drawing on Research in Switzerland. *AЯGOS 1 Special issue Religion and Ecology*, 103–125.

Becci, I., Monnot, C. and Wernli, B. 2021. 'Sensing "Subtle Spirituality" among Environmentalists: A Swiss Study', *Journal for the Study of Religion, Nature and Culture*, 15, 3, 344–367.

Becci, I. and Grandjean, A. 2022. Is Sacred Nature Gendered or Queer? Insights from a Study on Eco-Spiritual Activism in Switzerland. *Religions*, 13, 23.

Bennett, J. 2001. *The Enchantment of Modern Life: Attachments, Crossings, and Ethics*. Princeton, NJ: Princeton University Press.

Beringer, A. 1999/2000. On Ecospirituality: True, Indigenous, Western. *Australian Journal of Environmental Education*, 15/16, 17–22.

Betcher, S. 2015. The Picture of Health: 'Nature' at the Intersection of Disability, Religion and Ecology. *Worldviews*, 19, 9–33.

Braverman, I. 2023. Introduction: More-Than-One-Heath, More-Than-One-Governance. In: Braverman, I., ed. *More Than One Health: Humans, Animals, and the Environment Post-COVID*. London: Routledge, pp. 1–23.
Coates, J., Gray, M. and Hetherington, T. 2006. An 'Ecospiritual' Perspective: Finally, a Place for Indigenous Approaches. *The British Journal of Social Work*, 36, 3, 381–399.
Fatheuer, T. 2011. *Buen Vivir. Eine kurze Einführung in Lateinamerikas neue Konzepte zum guten Leben und zu den Rechten der Natur*. Schriften zur Ökologie, 17. Berlin: Heinrich-Böll-Stiftung.
Ferretti, M. 1998. Non-African Spiritual Entities in Afro-Brazilian Religion and African Amerindian Syncretism. In: Clarke, P.D., ed. *New Trends and Developments in African Religions*. Westport: Greenwood Press, pp. 37–44.
Gebara, I. 1999. A Recusa do Sincretismo Como Afirmação da Liberdade. In: Martins, C. and Lody, R., eds. *Faraimará – O Caçador traz Alegria: Mãe Stella, 60 Anos de Iniciação*. Rio de Janeiro: Pallas, pp. 404–412.
Gomberg, E. 2011. *Hospital de Orixás: Encontros terapêuticos em um terreiro de Candomblé*, Salvador: Edufba.
Hardy, A. 1979. *The Spiritual Nature of Man: A Study of Contemporary Religious Experience*. Oxford: Clarendon Press; New York: Oxford University Press.
Hay, D. 2013. Zoology and Religion. Available at: https://metanexus.net/zoology-and-religion-work-alister-hardy/ (accessed 10 August 2023).
Hunter, J. 2021. Editorial: Religious Experience and Ecology. *Journal for the Study of Religious Experience*, 7, 2, 3–16.
Ingold, T. 2000. *The Perception of the Environment: Essays on Livelihood, Dwelling and Skill*. London and New York: Routledge.
James, W. and James, H. 2008. *The Letters of William James*. Two Volumes Combined (Reprint of the 1920 edition). New York: Cosimo.
Keller, C. and L. Kearns, eds. 2007. *Ecospirit: Religions and Philosophies for the Earth*. Chicago, IL: Fordham University Press.
Lee, L. 2015. *Recognizing the Non-Religious: Reimagining the Secular*. Oxford: Oxford University Press.
Lincoln, V. 2000. Ecospirituality: A Pattern That Connects. *Journal of Holistic Nursing*, 18, 3, 227–244.
Marshall, P. 2005. *Mystical Encounters with the Natural World: Experiences and Explanations*. Oxford: Oxford University Press
Matory, J.L. 2005. *Black Atlantic Religion: Tradition, Transnationalism, and Matriarchy in the Afro-Brazilian Candomblé*. Princeton, NJ: Princeton University Press.
Restall, B. and E. Conrad. 2015. A Literature Review of Connectedness to Nature and its Potential for Environmental Management. *Journal of Environmental Management*, 15, 1–15.
Rodríguez, I. 2016. Historical Reconstruction and Cultural Identity Building as a Local Pathway to 'Living Well' among the Pemon of Venezuela. In: White, S.C. and Blackmore, C., eds. *Cultures of Wellbeing: Method, Place, Policy*. Basingstoke: Palgrave Macmillan, pp. 260–280.
Sansi, R. 2007. *Fetishes and Monuments: Afro-Brazilian Art and Culture in the 20th Century*. London: Berghahn Books.

Schmidt, B.E. 2009. 'Meeting the Spirits: Espiritismo as Source for Identity, Healing and Creativity'. *Fieldwork in Religion* Vol. 3.2: 178–195.

Schmidt, B.E. 2012. 'When the Gods Give Us the Power of Ashé' – Afro-Caribbean Religions as Source for Creative Energy. In: Cusack, C.M. and Norman, A., eds. *Handbook of New Religions and Cultural Production* (Brill Handbooks on Contemporary Religion series). DenHague: Brill, pp. 445–461.

Schmidt, B.E. 2013a Animal Sacrifice as Symbol of the Paradigmatic Other in the 21st Century: Ebó, the Offerings to African Gods, in the Americas. In: Zachhuber, J. and Meszaros, J., eds. *Sacrifice and Modern Thought*. Oxford: Oxford University Press, pp. 197–213.

Schmidt, B.E. 2013b The Spirit White Feather in São Paulo: The Resilience of Indigenous Spirits in Brazil. In: Cox, J., ed. *Critical Reflections on Indigenous Religions* (Vitality of Indigenous Religions series). London: Ashgate, pp. 123–141.

Schmidt, B E. 2020. Narratives of Spirituality and Wellbeing: Cultural Differences and Similarities between Brazil and the UK. In: Schmidt, B.E. and Leonardi, J., eds. *Spirituality and Wellbeing: Interdisciplinary Approaches to the Study of Religious Experience and Health*. Sheffield: Equinox, pp. 137–157.

Schmidt, B E. 2021. Spiritual Healing in Latin America. In: Lüddeckens, D., Klassen, P., Stein, J. and Hetmanczyk, P., eds. *Handbook of Religion, Medicine and Health*. London: Routledge, pp. 113–125.

Schmidt, B.E. 2022. The Entanglement of Spirituality, Wellbeing and 'Spiritual Economy' in Brazil: The Shift from 'Living Well Together' to 'Leading a Good Life'. In: Mossiere, G., ed. *New Spiritualities and the Culture of Well-being* (Religion, Spirituality and Health: A Social Scientific Approach, Vol. 6). Frankfurt/New York: Springer, pp. 117–133.

Schmidt, B.E. 2023. Living with Spirits: Spirituality and Health in São Paulo, Brazil. In: Pierini, E., Groisman, A. and Espírito Santo, D., eds. *Other Worlds, Other Bodies: Embodied Epistemologies and Ethnographies of Healing*. Oxford: Berghahn, pp. 73–91.

Silva, V.G. Da. 1994. *Candomblé e Umbanda: Caminhos da devoção brasileira*. São Paulo: Ed. Ática.

Stace, W.T. 1960. *The Teachings of the Mystics*. New York: The New American Library.

Stewart, D.M. 2022. *Africana Nations and the Power of Black Sacred Imagination*. (Vol. 2 of Obeah, Orisa & Religious Identity in Trinidad, by T.E. Hucks and D. M Stewart). Durham and London: Duke University Press.

Thurfjell D. and A. Remmel (2023): 'The Forest is My Church': Christianity, Secularisation and Love of Nature in a Northern European Existential Field. *Religion*, 2023, 1–21.

White, S.C. 2016. Introduction: The Many Faces of Wellbeing. In: White, S.C. and Blackmore, C., eds. *Cultures of Wellbeing: Method, Place, Policy*. Basingstoke: Palgrave Macmillan, 1–44.

Woods, R. 2008. *Wellness: Life, Health and Spirituality*. Dublin: Veritas Publications.

Woods, A. 2023. One Health: A More-Than-Human History. In: Braverman, I., ed. *More Than One Health: Humans, Animals, and the Environment Post-COVID*. London: Routledge, pp. 47–62.

World Health Organization. 1948. *Constitution of the World Health Organization*. Available at: www.who.int/about/governance/constitution.
World Health Organization. 2022. *One Health*. Available at: www.who.int/newsroom/fact-sheets/detail/one-health 27/07/2023.

10 Biosynergy and person-centered psychology of ecospiritual well-becoming: Creative Biosynergy of persons, species, societies and ecosystems sanctifies earth's biosphere

Anthony L. Rose

Life in Earth's biosphere and across the Universe flourishes in processes that are sublime, not simple. Inspiring, transcendent, exalted, heavenly, wonderful, mystical…not mundane.

The interplay of organisms, earthscapes, waterways and weather patterns is indescribable by the divisive sciences of cause and effect… 'all forms of glory on this planet blend in mysterious ballets & symphonies, all minds & voices contribute, all eyes & ears are tuned to the numinous interplay of life. Tortoises, monkeys and men – we are all strands of blood & bone, spirit & feeling, informing the dance of many, calling out in the voice of all. The biota of earth is interwoven in ever-changing *Biosynergy*, like threads on a multi-dimensional loom, the tapestry of nirvana' (Rose, 2006, p. 31).

As a citizen of the biosphere I've devoted my life to exploring, describing and enhancing the synergy of earthlife; its threads, looms and tapestries. While earning my PhD in comparative experimental psychology at UCLA, I became compassionately bonded to the monkeys in my research lab. In 1967 after hearing my story, psychologist Carl Rogers invited me to apply for a postdoctoral fellowship at WBSI. With a large cadre of Humanists, we founded the Center for Studies of the Person and I devoted two decades to creating new theories and applications of person-centered psychosocial processes in diverse human communities and organizations. On sabbatical in 1982 I found myself being welcomed into the sacred *synergy of life* in a Sumatran rainforest by kindly orangutans and caring leeches! Four more decades of profound interspecies and ecospiritual epiphanies have convinced me that Creative Biosynergy is the key driving force in the Ecospiritual Well-becoming of EarthLife!

I'll begin this epistle by sharing some profound personal experiences I've had while searching Earth for 'Wisdom found & Truth told'. As a person-centered explorer unveiling the wonders of Life, I'm obliged to reveal my main source of evidence: my self!

As a scientist and consultant I warn you that *writing is storytelling and science writing is science fiction!*

As a poet and biosynergist I assure you that *you're about to read my honest heartfelt story of hope.*

As a human person I beg you to *forgive my pride and pedantry and feel my passion and prayer.*

Personal prologue: All truth is born and raised in the person who tells it

Five personal epiphanies that turned the author's still small spark into an eternal bonfire.

- Have you been hugged by an orphan ape or monkey and felt deep kinship make you cry?
- Has your life evolved into a quest for profound revelations of the Synergy of all Life?
- Are you Called to foster ecospiritual well-becoming for all Souls who seek Eternal Bliss?

Yes – I have… It has…I am! Below are brief descriptions of five of my early 'personal epiphanies': they're about bonding, seeking, mortality, transcendence and biosynergy. Perhaps you've had similarly profound experiences!

Bonding

Being held by apes and monkeys isn't something I seek. When other primates seek my physical company, it's on their terms. My first such embrace was an 'Interspecies Epiphany' (Rose, 1994a, 1996a) that occurred in 1963 in my addiction research lab at UCLA Brain Research Institute, while collecting data for my doctoral dissertation. I was 24.

> …a janitor tracked me down to tell me that a monkey had escaped his cage and was ransacking my lab. This had never happened before.

> Handling a docile macaque in its home cage or experimental chamber was one thing. Catching an escapee was another. I became extremely nervous walking through the long shadowed corridors. As I entered the room and peered through the haze and clutter, a familiar smacking sound drew my eyes to the far wall. Snicky, a four-year-old male macaque, glared down from atop a bookcase, hair on end, muscles bulging, eyes wide, teeth bared.
>
> Alarmed by his hostile posture, unsure what to do, I mechanically smacked my lips & cooed: our usual morning greeting. He shuddered through a monkey tension melt-down and jumped from the shelf to my desk, leapt into my arms and held tight. First time ever! In the distance he had seemed so large, daunting, wild. Now in my arms he was small, vulnerable, helpless. I sat on the linoleum floor with this trembling macaque in my lap – cleaned the scab that edged his skullcap, checked to be sure his brain implants weren't loose, & examined his dilated eyes. I remember thinking 'after all I've done to him, he wants my friendship more than his freedom.' Then I cried. (Rose, 2006, p. 24)

This experience turned me away from medical science. I had become bonded to kindred animals! How could I continue to experiment on my friends, my surrogate children, my primate family? I completed my research, wrote my dissertation, took my doctorate and moved into a field working with people in creative endeavors – far from laboratory lives of trial, torture and tragedy.

Seeking

After my epiphanies with monkeys, I joined Carl Rogers and a cadre of humanists, founded and built the Center for Studies of the Person and facilitated collaborative community among nurses, nuns, teachers, preachers, doctors, developers, military units, indigenous leaders, forest rangers, urban planners, tax collectors, bankers and a score of other persons at work (1967 to 1987). I wrote a book called *Growing Up Human* (Rose and Auw, 1974) that was filled with prophetic theory, empathic example, and introspective exercise to help persons enhance the quality of their lives, their relationships with others and their collaboration in communities and cultures. My friend Andre Auw added pastoral examples, while I focused on visionary theory, self-discovery exercises and poetics. I named the first chapter 'Seeking' and began with this poem, which threads through the book to end on the final page:

Seeking is the process
ever-changing day to day to day
in endless freeform interplay
of fate and dreams, accomplishment and schemes.

What's in a life beyond the strife of seeking?
Something special, something very special, waits for us.
Keep your senses open, keep your heart open, keep your being open
and you shall find it, you shall know it, you shall cherish it
in an unlikely place, in an unpredictable way, at an unfathomable depth.

Something special, something very special, waits for us:
sometimes in a dark alleyway, sometimes in an open field,
sometimes by a mountain stream.

It grows slowly, it explodes suddenly, it moves through us
touching our centers, reaching stars, manifesting Gods…

It waits for us and one day we shall find it.
   We shall know it, we shall cherish it, *we shall become it*
      for a moment, for a lifetime, forever.

The promise of that poem, written in my 34th year, has stirred my soul and steadied my faith to this very day. Subconsciously, my lifelong quest for *ecospiritual pathways to transcendent becoming* is impetus for the theory, science and application of *Creative Biosynergy* – key to this treatise. 'Seeking' is my homage to ecospiritual, global and universal wellbecoming.

Mortality and Transcendence

Truth be told – revelation of Paths to Eternity had come to me two decades earlier at age 15 in a life-transforming *Near-Death-Experience* (NDE: Kübler-Ross, 1969; Moody, 1975) during an auto accident while a passenger in a friend's new sports car.

> Lying face down on Mulholland Drive, spine and back crushed beneath my friend's rolled-over Porsche Speedster, I awoke in a dream-state and found myself floating through a Dark Tunnel towards a brilliant Golden Light. All fear was replaced by bliss as I reached the Light and glided through to an endless sacred forest topped by blue skies streaked with mystic meteors. Seated on pearl & marble benches in a clearing

just below me were my beloved grandparents and a dozen unknown yet familiar ancestors from generations past, all smiling and murmuring exalted welcomes. My astral body relaxed, and gratitude filled me as I floated towards my kindred spirits, ready to join the heavenly host.

Suddenly, the car was lifted off my back and I sensed my body being pulled out from under. *I returned from Eternity to the road!* Aromas of asphalt, engine oil & exhaust were quickly flooded by horrid pain. A voice said, 'call an ambulance.' Another said, 'I think we need a Priest.' Shock returned me to silent empty Darkness. Oblivion was interrupted by flashes of pain and anguish as the ambulance lurched to a start, and again when my stretcher bounced past the entrance to Cedars of Lebanon Hospital. (Rose, 2024a)

Suffice to say, the next 30 days spent alone in the hospital were punctuated by enigmatic illusions. Absent discussion with others and with minimal religious experience, I managed to make my own sense of these realizations. Foremost, having surrendered to *the dusk where imminent death abides,* my wounded heart accepted the truth of my personal Mortality. I then began to see the *dawn of a pathway to spiritual synergy* on which my awakened Soul may find caring Spirits during Lifetime and reunite with them in Eternity. I returned to high school a changed person. With counsel solely from my loving heart and hopeful mind, I made two silent promises that became my lifelong lodestars:

1. As Mortal Human, I will leave ill-fitting roles and false pursuits behind to find and follow the Incentives of My Sacred *Calling*.
2. As Eternal Soul, I will wander Earth seeking and building community among Kindred Spirits with whom I may share Eternity.

Those promises have manifest in my subsequent seven decades through diverse actions, experiences and innovations. 'Try something new!' is my standard response to obstacles like alienation, anger, malaise, ennui, misunderstanding and incompatibility. That can mean a new approach to a person or problem; a new line of questioning or answering; a new friendship, consultancy, job, field of study, subjective science or synergy theory, etc. With this chapter, I invite you to try a new Biosynergistic outlook and approach to life at home and work, throughout Earth's biosphere, and across the Cosmos. *If the view fits, and fulfills, wear it!*

Biosynergy

In 1982 I took a break from a decade working with urban humans in hospitals to trek across Indonesia with my wife, searching for wildlife and wise cultures. In a Sumatran rainforest, once homeland to my late lab monkey, I had a new interspecies epiphany – this time with a family of wild orangutans. They appeared on my third day slogging along narrow muddy paths through thick undergrowth shaded by a lush 100-foot-high canopy of hardwoods. By chance I stopped to rest, looked up, saw splashes of red orange in the trees. Three Orangutans had viewed my innocent approach.

As my escaped monkey had done, the apes perched above me. They looked down from a huge fruit tree. Having never been captured, caged or tortured by humans, they showed neither hostility nor fear. Mama with babe in arms and her youngster on a nearby branch stared at me with more than curiosity. I sensed a mutual longing to connect, and I cooed as I had done when greeting monkey friends 20 years earlier in the lab. Orangutan faces softened; bodies shifted, leaned closer, into open airspace. Mama orangutan twisted a fig from a vine and gently tossed it down towards me. Her offer to share fruit sent my mind whirling, my heart beating, my tears falling. I realized why people across the Indonesian archipelago called these great ape cousins 'Orang Hutan – Person of the Forest'. We are kindred spirits! Approach wild primates softly with love in your heart, and our kinship will be affirmed (Rose, 2001a)!

> That profound event confirmed a life changing epiphany I'd had hours earlier as I stood at a bend in the trail. A group of leeches, attracted by my heat, climbed on my shoe for a meal. Curious, I bent down, offered my forefinger to the leader of the pack, watched him crawl on board and attach his jaws to my skin. In a minute or two his size had doubled, filled with my blood. I removed him and saw the small red dot on my finger. In thanks for my fluid offering, he had injected his decoagulant. I pondered 'Tit for tat' – I give you my blood: you clean my wound. *Biosynergy!!*
>
> A new Truth whirled through me! I was part of a living ecosystem that thrives in a state of synergy, with all life forms engaged in mutual service. More than service, in mutual attraction, fascination, interdependence, synergy. I had entered to explore and the biosynergy of the place had transformed me from observer to participant, from interloper to inhabitant, from utilizer to synergizer. My personal epiphany of *biosynergy with a leech*, confirmed later by mama orangutan's gift, transformed me from person-centered explorer to global biosynergist. (Rose, 2007, pp. 123–4)

After two more months of spirit-bracing discovery across the Indonesian archipelago, I returned home and told my staff at Kaiser-Permanente headquarters I'd be leaving.

Two years later I was out of the corporate world, tracking mountain gorillas in Rwanda, seeking signs and sensations of biosynergy across Earth's biosphere.

Now, starting my fifth decade of worldwide exploration, thousands of profound epiphanies with wildlife, wilderness, indigenous people and global wonders have catalyzed new visions of a Biosynergy-enriched Person-Centered Psychology (Be-PCP). In this seminal chapter we will identify factors that can anchor, inform, construct and animate a Comparative Be-PCP that includes all living organisms and life-enhancing icons in its purview. This is a crucial place to start, if Biosynergy enrichment is to be globally applied. *Biosynergy* pertains to the mutual collaborative interaction of all earthlife in the quest to create optimal futures for individuals, families, communities, habitats, ecosystems, biomes and all Life in Earth's biosphere.

> *Biosynergy is a Sacred Creative Force! Life's Mission is to Foster Infinite Love.*

Seek Love in Alien Eyes

Let humans not glory simply in this:
that we love our country and our kind,
for to thrive we must love All Creation.

And be not bound to thy homeland,
nor celebrate solely the wondrous Synergy of Earth,
though thy province is bounteous and thy planet magnificent.

It's the Universe in its endless expanse
where great miracles converge in Cosmic Synergy,
and Eternity is ample timeframe for Thy Seeking.

Know that each organism in every biosphere is called to Pilgrimage,
and archetypal lifeforms in all Worlds are revered as Saints.

And so, as Thou carry out Thy Journey, O Wayfarer, remember this:

Divine Love twinkles in an infinity of Alien Eyes.
Humanity Must Honor Godliness in All Earthlings
and Revere the Sacred Global Community.

We have placed the name 'God' in human chains and have broken our holy Commandments!

Tragically, wide-reaching human religions stripped other earthlings of holy personhood, making God in Man's image. The selfish penchant to denigrate other organisms as mindless, uncouth, insensitive and godless creatures spread many millennia ago as people built agricultural clearings where 'natural life' was unwelcome. Thus began human dismissal of biosynergy, and Man's abuse of earthlife and nature as the Lord's reward for the *Sapiens* Master Race.

The false pretence that humans are not 'animals' feeds the elitist argument that only superior humans can become 'autonomous self-aware persons'. Setting aside the false idea that any organism can be autonomous, this claim that 'Only my People are endowed by God with sacred Personhood' has produced deadly human supremacy beliefs and battlegrounds.

The deceit of selective human omnipotence imbues 'super-men' with God-egos causing them to construct worlds solely for themselves that enslave and exclude 'inferior' people and beasts. Civilization through biodominance isn't viable, and no misled self-worshiping person or species can make it so. We need to restore the all-inclusive Biosynergistic core of global community.

Millennia of agriculture and urbanization led Man to enact a patriarchal industrial revolution that bestowed ranchers and farmers, landlords and businessmen, political bosses, oligarchs and kings with 'Hands of the Creator' and reduced common humans to 'Cogs in the Wheel'. Before long, covetous Man invented murder weapons to speed his takeover of the life space of 'alien' earthlings. He converted natural wonders, flora and fauna, and most indigenous human tribes and cultures into 'resources' for his avarice and pride. Human demagogues stripped *Personhood* from all but the wealthiest and most powerful people and classified others as 'consumables' (Rose et al., 2003).

Now in 2025 most elite-wealthy-powerful people consider 95% of humans and all other species as expendable targets for bullets of bigotry, swords of supremacy and bludgeons of business. Today sadistic oligarchs on most continents send militias and missiles to slaughter neighbors, steal promised lands, crush personhood and replace synergy with slavery to serve their cruel supremacy. It is these atrocities that motivate my quest to recover sacred Personhood for All Earthlings. This mission was launched in 1994 at an International Primatological Congress in Bali, Indonesia. I began my Ethics Symposium for an audience of 130+ professionals with a keynote speech entitled – 'New Paradigms for Personhood in the Age of Atonement':

> Out of this Age of Atonement emerge new paradigms for personhood. Paradigms that take us beyond legal, moral, economic or political projections of human self-interest onto other organisms. Paradigms that recognize that all boundaries are permeable, no hierarchies are valid, all life forms are sentient and intelligent, no individuals are without culture, each earthling is a godforce, and every organism is a numinous intersection in the web of life. Personhood is imbued, then, in every ant and every ape. We can rule out no one. We can ignore no one. We must atone to all persons in accord with their definitions of our sins. (Rose, p.1, 1994b)

To optimise Synergy of All Life we must treat every individual organism and earthly icon as a unique and sacred wholistic entity. Persons of all species may join into positive Partnerships. Cohesive communities can merge as synergised societies. In home and habitat, ocean and continent, planet and galaxy, dark space and deep mystery – bonds, linkages, mergers or amalgams are protected from reductionist dissection and empiricist objectification.

Adherence to holistic personal principles and processes is crucial to Biosynergy. Honour each animated and iconic entity as a whole sacred 'Person' who seeks and shares mutual goodwill and compassion with other 'Persons' at home, around the Earth…and beyond.

> *We Dance in Synergy through Infinite Space to Eternal Well-Becoming in a Loving Universe.*

As *poet-scientist*, I envision the Eternal Universe as an ever-growing Synergistic Ballet of interacting galaxies, stars, planets, comets, asteroids, meteors and infinite organisms, atmospheres and spirits in endless Space. The *driving forces* in universal systems are a creative synchrony of affirmative, inclusive, collaborative and progressively optimized *well-becomings*. As *psychosocial consultant* I see all marriages and mergers among elements and ecosystems, cells and cultures, persons and populations, species and spirits becoming bonded on *trajectories of allied actualization*. As a *biosynergist* I know the Universe and Earth's biosphere have expanded ardently and optimally through too much time and space to accept less than 'eternal & infinite progressive positive biosynergy-enriched personal & iconic eco-spiritual well-becoming.'

Within the all-inclusive endless progress of earthlife-in-synergy we have discovered a Golden Rule for the Biosphere (Rose, 2024b). This rule reaches beyond extant wellbeing. *Biosynergy optimizes Well-Becoming that arises forever on the advancing horizon of infinite tomorrows.*

Earth's Golden Rule: 'Live and Love Together in Global Creative Biosynergy to Assure the Eternal Well-Becoming of All Life in Earth's Sacred Biosphere.'

Since the origins of EarthLife, progressive Well-Becoming has prevailed throughout the Biosphere. Biosynergy's profound role – witnessed through endless Earthlings' eyes – is pre-eminent in every far-flung biome and ecosystem, affirmed in myriad wise and mystic minds, and seen as essential to cultivating community among all the tough and tender persons of Earth. Synergy of globally shared love, beauty, health, harmony, spirit, mystery, wisdom, wonder and worth is essential to Earth-Biosphere's pursuit of *All-Inclusive Ever-growing Well-Becoming*. Species from dragonfly to dinosaur, landscapes from low desert to high forest, landmarks from lakes to volcanoes, tall mountains to deep seas, and all the planet's auroras and atmospheres affirm and insist that Earth's wonderful biosphere corresponds to, connects with, and emulates the synergistic majesty of the Universe.

The Universe and its Spheres, Species, Spirits and Space Thrive in Safe & Sacred Synergy!

From within the minutely monitored, monstrously unmeasurable, and mostly mysterious Universe that surrounds our tiny solar system, we postulate that the eternal spread of emergent material and spiritual phenomena into ever-expanding space governs itself in fealty to a process of 'Cosmic Synergy'.

What I, as earthbound optimist, conjure for the Universe is a great and endless span of open yet orderly Cosmos, populated by widespread interwoven worlds endowed with eco-spiritual devotion to eternal enlightenment, elegant integrity and habitual harmlessness (ahimsa) in their ballets of infinite well-becoming. My cosmic ideal is in line with a rising consensus of global visions amalgamated from the discoveries of multidisciplinary earthlife scientists and all-life theorists.

Symbiotic/synergistic collaboration of organisms from mycorrhizal networks among plants to facultative mutualism of mammals and birds have been verified in many hundreds of research studies in diverse biomes for decades. In the 30 years since Jan Sapp's *Evolution by Association* (1994) revealed *mutual symbiosis as the prevailing process in development of Earth's synergistic biosphere,* co-evolution has been validated as norm, and selfish genes as anomaly.

In the very first ticks of Earth's life-clock, biologic, behavioral, social and ecological symbioses among and within coexistent organisms and species burgeoned, eventually escalating into Biosynergy – the eco-dynamic 'Synergy of All Life'. Cells, microbes, organisms, species and ecosystems that worked and merged together for the common good survived and ultimately thrived. Selfish life forms were overwhelmed by hordes of collaborators, while contrarians ended their lineages by turning too aggressively on one another. When hairless human apes emerged, late in the global game, we adhered to the common cooperative plan.

Benevolent Biosynergy par excellence is the secret to our species' early success, migrating all around the planet (see Rose in Caporale, 2024, p 153). *Synergistic Well-Becoming* may be a new concept in the separate schools of traditional linear causative-science, but evidence for progressive biosynergy's pre-eminent importance is documented thoroughly in Peter Corning's books and articles, spanning research from coevolutionary genetics to global economics. Based on decades of scholarly research and theory-building with many multidisciplinary colleagues (Corning, 2018), Corning declares *synergy drives the evolution of life & the fate of humankind*:

> Synergy is a great governing principle of the natural world. It has been a wellspring of creativity in the evolution of the universe and has greatly influenced the overall trajectory of life on Earth. It has played a decisive role in the emergence of humankind. It is vital to the working of every modern society…it's no exaggeration to say that our ultimate fate depends on it! (Corning, 2003, p. 1)

Amidst eons of collaboration on Earth, these synergistic ideations, inspirations and animations have ranged from *communal cohesion* of related Persons and *symbiotic coevolution* of connected species to the mutually advantageous *co-management of environments* in ways that foster Creative Biosynergy of Life and the ever-hopeful Quest for Future Paradise.

Imagine alien observers in outer space had seen and sensed the joy of earthlife's progressive evolution from the sublime early cells and seeds through the careful pre-agricultural migrations of humans across Earth's biosphere! Witnessed from North Star, the conclusion would likely be unanimous: 'Earth once hosted a harmonic, harmless, mutually helpful and blissfully hopeful expanding ballet of well-becoming Synergistic Souls.'

How much have careless, caustic, competitive people damaged that dance! We who see the destructive, despotic, deadly conduct of modern Man agree with singer-songwriter Joni Mitchell's (1970) view of the human condition:

> We are stardust – billion-year-old carbon
> We are golden – caught in the devil's bargain
> And we've got to get ourselves back to the Garden.

Building a Biosynergy-enriched person-centered psychology of ecospiritual wellbecoming: Seeking cosmic aligned and globally actualized keys to the synergy of earthlife

Biosynergy – the Synergy of Life (Rose, 2007, 2009, 2017) – is an interwoven ever-adapting array of monitored and mysterious processes that motivate individuals and assemblages to commingle, connect and collaborate in ways that catalyze progressive improvement and optimization of the all-inclusive whole. Whole persons and whole partners, whole species and whole eco-systems, whole biomes and Earth's whole biosphere will learn, act, adapt, evolve and grow through ideal modes of Biosynergy in places where they emerge, migrate, settle, commune and become. As individual and alliance – each intact and in-touch living organism is subject to holistic arousal of its biosynergy propensities.

As Persons, all entities may be perceived, projected and synergized as Whole Becomings. As Earthlings, all kindred spirits seek shared salvation. Despite hierarchies of human healers proudly fixing others' hurt, only in loving reciprocal synergy and mutual altruism will we truly *heal and rise*.

Person-centered psychology

Since the 1960s when client-centered therapy became the 'person-centered approach' (PCA), the robust ethos and innovative application of self-directed, personally emergent and positively facilitated actualization processes have been abundant. In the Center for Studies of the Person's first decades we built positive PCA programmes to facilitate educational innovation, religious community, indigenous leadership, drug abuse prevention, cross-cultural and race relations, organization design and development, management training, workforce team building, urban planning, military deployment and diplomacy, health care quality and much more. By year six I was helping design and develop innovative person-centered 'social change systems' in the largest Health Maintenance Organization in the United States.

It's a huge leap from counsellor in one-hour therapy sessions and co-facilitator in weekend encounter groups to co-director of a cadre of 20 person-centered consultants enabling 2,000 physicians, 3,000 nurses, 1,100 administrative staff, and 2 million health care clients to develop long-term action research (LTAR) programmes that create, monitor, maintain and enhance compassionate and collaborative patient-provider and healthcare-team relationships and inspire a caring corporate climate for decades (Stebbins, Hawley & Rose, 1982)! Still, we stayed person-centered!

To co-create and enhance scores of person-centered programmes that encourage and instill individual, workgroup and organizational kindness and empathy was life-changing. Embedded in my mind/heart/soul is 15 years of authentic interaction, mutual caring and co-creative innovation that prepared me for exploring and restoring ecospiritual biosynergy worldwide. It is memories, emotions and deep fulfillment born in the synergistic enrichment of countless lives & communities that compels me to *encourage facilitation of eco-spiritual well-becoming through creation of a Biosynergy-Enriched Person-Centered Psychology (Be-PCP)*.

> *'Person' is the primary all-inclusive category for each and every holistic self-animated entity. Well-becoming is the incentive motivation experienced uniquely by individuals and collectively by communities.*

Be-PCP science and theory use 'Person' to encapsulate each individual organism – ant and ape, bacteria and blue whale, red fox and redwood tree. We amalgamate *Convergent Subjective Perceptions (CSPs)* from significant others, with confirmation from the perceived persons, to validate depiction of individual personhood and personality, interpersonal synergy, and the person-centered processes and outcomes of ecospiritual well-becoming. *United in biosynergy, all persons are dressed for shared subjective success!*

Only qualitative interactive experience can produce sufficiently robust, lucid and inclusive perceptual and experiential data to inform description and analysis of diverse organisms engaged in novel behaviors intended to establish complex collaborations progressing towards mutual ecologic and spiritual well-becoming in dynamic integrated ecosystems. Numbers don't count! Crucial to person-centered processes and phenomena is the diverse perceptions all involved persons share of themselves and one another. In a chapter on 'Science and Collective Reality' (Rose, 1996b, p. 31) I proposed a 'CSP' process of perceiving orangutan as 'Person of the Forest':

> As Henri Walton asserted: 'the unique image is not the point of departure. Perception begins by multiplying the points of view for the needs of practical action…' (Clay, 1978, p. 127). Failure to act has come from the insistence of individual observers that their unique images of their orangutans must be the singular points of departure. Defining the metaphor of orangutan to serve oneself, rarely serves the orangutan.
>
> The optimal reality with regard to any species is the collection of *Convergent Subjective Perceptions (CSP)* of all those who define, describe, and relate to that species. To craft such a reality requires movement through metaphor to metonymy, through relationship of

similarity to relationship of contiguity (Jakobson, 1962). We must place the orangutan metaphors of disparate human observers, as well as the self-portrayals of orangutans and the 'red-ape fables' of their allied fauna & flora, into contiguity to form a collective reality that imparts robust validity and motivates the dominant (human) public to protect orangutans & enrich (the synergy of) their rain forest habitat.

The above quote is from a chapter focused on amalgamating CSPs that are *personally valid authentic depictions (PVADs)* of orangutans that inspire and instruct humans to support the conservation of endangered great apes and their habitats. The first criterion – PVAD – is required in all descriptive amalgams. The ultimate affirmation for validity of a CSP is 'review & approval by the subject organisms (studied persons)'. We must find and invent face-valid ways for the depicted organisms to confirm that an amalgam is complete, cogent, correct, and likely to support their pursuits of personal and global well-becoming. Biosynergy researchers need to develop a comparative psychology of positive, empathic perception that enables congruent and authentic expression from diverse observers and verification from organisms-of-interest.

We biosynergists recognize that what maintains and improves life on earth is how well the organisms of all species sharing a habitat embrace communal biosynergy that improves life and landscape, self and society. To optimize life for all Life, we must go way beyond monitoring 'biodiversity' and protecting 'endangered species' (Rose and Mittermeier, 2007). We empathize with all organisms in conflict, confusion and synergy; honor the anguish, ennui and elation, needs and satisfactions, drives and incentives that they experience in pursuit of well-becoming. To know other organisms as persons allows us to discover how they thrive in caring community and suffer in servitude. Profound encounters with countless life-forms have shown the absolute necessity of mutual empathic *personal* compassion to foster multi-species biosynergy.

- When you hold an orphan monkey and weep with it, you'll experience its fear and anguish.
- You will only recognize the leeches' care and gratitude when you share your blood with them.
- If you try to sneak up on an orangutan, you'll learn no more than the impact of your mistrust.

After five decades observing collective caring among organisms of myriad species around the globe, I'm certain that a *Comparative* Biosynergy-enriched

Person-Centered Psychology – if fully developed and executed by sensitive, creative, competent and life-loving persons – will find and activate cosmically aligned and globally actualized keys to the biosynergy, salvation and ceaseless well-becoming of life in wild, rural and urban habitat on Earth. When 'Personally Valid Collective Reality' (PVCR) *points to aspects of Global Creative Biosynergy that can enable wellbecoming in a struggling ecosystem, Synergy Keys conceived and optimized by collaborative inhabitants will be used to revitalize the needy ecosystem so it may thrive.*

Global Creative Biosynergy: Key force for effective application of personal synergy

We must synergize PCA's 3 Core Conditions and add a 4th Key Driving Force.

Global Creative Biosynergy (GCB) signifies the positive, inclusive, compassionate and authentic forces of interpersonal-synergy and community-cohesion that optimize conception and actualization of new and greatly improved persons, partners, icons, organizations, societies, cultures, ecosystems and biospheres. GCB comes to play when crisis and/or opportunity call.

GCB steps up when conflict, tragedy, chaos and calamity threaten the viability of essential life support, the extinction of crucial organisms, the demise of vital ecosystems and the breakdown of biomes and biosphere. GCB rallies to capitalize on opportunities emerging from communal mergers, societal peacemaking, ecosystem enrichment and global good fortune. Whether it's severe crisis or sudden opportunity, GCB rumbles bellies, warms hearts and lifts spirits so loving persons procreate, sane societies integrate, weary realms rejuvenate. Global Creative Biosynergy incentivizes key persons in failing and flourishing biospheres with synergistic visions that will coalesce diverse inhabitants' personal and communal quests for future well-becoming.

When applying person-centered principles in human *social change systems* (Rose & Auw, 1974, p. 109) and in *shifting natural ecosystems* (Rose, 1994a; 2001a), the three original conditions for Person-Centered Applications (PCA) remain cogent but must be 'synergized' to become useful. Carl R. Rogers (1966) observed and postulated that *therapists and counselors provide necessary and sufficient conditions for positive personal change to occur in their clients by establishing psychological atmospheres of 1) unconditional positive regard, 2) accurate empathic understanding and 3) personally congruent authenticity.*

My half century of experience developing person-centered innovations in diverse sociocultural and ecospiritual contexts has expanded Carl's assertion. *Synergistic revisions* of Rogers' Three Core Conditions plus a profound 4th Key Condition *are necessary* for full personal functioning, let alone to enable enduring well-becoming in Earth's everchanging communities, ecosystems and biosphere. Below are synopses of the three Synergized Core Conditions and the crucial new 4th Key Condition – Global Creative Biosynergy (see Rose in Caporale, 2024).

Condition #1 All-Inclusive-Positivity (AIP): We must actively expand our positive regard to all earthlings and help make it mutual. For Creative Biosynergy to emerge, all organisms in every ecosystem must exchange caring kinship with one another. This interactive prizing of all life is the foundation for psychosocial harmony and ecospiritual fulfillment.

Condition #2 Mutually Empathic Compassion (MEC): A foundation of all-inclusive-positivity supports growth of global interspecies compassion. This enables all organisms to co-facilitate *reciprocal altruistic functioning and mutual flourishing* in collaboration within the vast panoply of correlated 'becomings' in diverse species, cohort groups, ecosystems and biomes.

Condition #3 Ecologically Adaptive Authenticity (EAA): To become well-integrated members of a multi-species ecosystem requires all immigrants and inhabitants to appreciate and accept one another as prized community members. This calls for valid self-awareness to shape congruent and complementary personal expression and interaction. The extended family of earthlings needs to share and synergize the ecologically adaptive signals and symbols of our authentic selves.

The 4th Key Condition – 'Global Creative Biosynergy' (GCB) is a transformative process that manifests 'Creative Powers' in eco-spiritual collaborators across all life-forms. By integrating the three synergized core conditions, GCB enables persons and communities to become conjoint *Creators of Eternal Well-Becoming.* All Earthlings will clean wounds, touch wings, pollinate plants, share food, give blood, fight fires, divert flood – to save and sanctify the synergy of life on Earth. GCB inspires communal creativity among individuals, partners and multi-species cohort – often in sacred iconic settings – thus enabling divine ecospiritual well-becoming worldwide.

This 4th Key Condition arises from the inherent personal biosynergistic drive to create communities and ecosystems that flourish through mutual enrichment shared among collaborating lifeforms in fertile habitat. GCB accelerates co-creation of new ways to thrive together. Despite modern humanity's destructive global domination, people are born with proclivity for positive, authentic, compassionate support of biosynergy that enables all-inclusive ecospiritual well-becoming.

Yes, all organisms and icons have the potential to co-actualize creatively, but not isolated or in conflict. Each species evolved with a capacity to synergize psycho-socially and eco-spiritually in biodiverse ecosystems. The 4th Key Condition can encourage and enable us all to become globally collaborative, caring and genuine earthlings again! I've experienced and been told profound tales of Creative Human/Nature Biosynergy in beautiful thriving habitats around the globe: All Are Sacred Communions. Here's one!

> My wife & I have returned dozens of times to cherish the streams & spirals of ecospiritual magic that fly through California's *Anza Borrego Desert* in the annual spring migration of Swainson's hawks. Tens of thousands of migrants fly from Argentina to breed as far north as Alaska. They float in like an afternoon cloud, kettle-down like a tornado, and roost in droves in the groves of lush trees tended by local farmers for the predators' comfort and safety. We've returned in the morning to watch huge flocks of 300 to 700 hawks eat & then take their exit, circling upward & streaming north toward the Arctic. Beyond the devotion of awestruck hawk-watchers, the epiphany of seeing thousands of winged predators flying through each Spring has inspired generations of local farmers and families to set aside trees for overnight roosting and to nurture insect rich habitat for daytime feasting of these rare & remarkable nomads. In sanctuaries throughout the Americas, reverent naturalists enrich their sacred homelands for migrating hawks to rest and eat. They've created a stopover for wayfarers that serves the well-becoming of the Continents – an altruistic act of Global Creative Biosynergy.

Eternal Quests for Global Creative Biosynergy have three EcoSpiritual Well-Becoming Goals:

1. to optimize the creative capacity of Biosynergy so that persons of all types may unite to accelerate well-becoming of ecospiritual life throughout Earth's biosphere
2. to enable holy persons of all species to inspire ecospiritual Biosynergy that uplifts promised lands from thriving habitats to Spiritually Endowed Environments (SEEs)
3. to enrich each SEE into a Holy Eden from which generations of virtuous earthlings may rise as sacred spirits into the synergy of eternal and infinite cosmic space.

GCB fosters Earth's return to Eden with divine personal, communal, & eternal well-becoming.

Participants in these Eternal Quests seek beyond earthly well-becoming. Entry to Eternity is enabled when individuals and communities are immersed in sublime psychosocial and eco-spiritual synergy with kindred souls of diverse species in shared ecosystems.

From that love-point on the horizon of eco-spiritual wellbecoming, individual and communal actualization can expand and rise to its ultimate state of eternal and infinite bliss. When my teenage soul rose from crushed incarnation to golden invitation and I felt my loving spirit-family welcome me into eternity, I knew that heaven awaits me. When a scared monkey, kindly ape and grateful leech introduced me to the Biosynergy of Mutual Well-Becoming, I began the long quest to integrate Comparative Person-Centered Psychology, Eco-spiritual Phenomenology, and Global Creative Biosynergy, as the foundation for description of an *All-Loving Theology*.

Persons in Paradise: the Path to Eternal Love Begins in Eden

My long-evolving vision of the *Path to Salvation of Earthlife* has grown while writing this epistle thanks to inspiration and wisdom of my dear friend and co-mentor Jeff Leonardi. Jeff's expansion of Rogers' client-centered *12th quality of the Person of the Future* ('a yearning for the spiritual') suggests that 'self-giving love is the defining characteristic of the fully-functioning person in both person-centered and religious terms' (Leonardi, 2010, p. 63).

We agree when personhood abides in all life. My ecospiritual frame appears in an excerpt on biosynergy and paradise (Rose, 2011, p. 245). It's my starting point for this spirited conclusion!

> The belief in a harmonic unitary reality inclusive of all living beings has been expressed in the paradise myths of societies throughout human history (Jacoby, 2006). The characteristics of the state of paradise almost universally include human friendship with other animals and knowledge of their languages (Eliade, 1960). In Africa, where human and nonhuman primates first evolved, most indigenous cultures have long believed a panoply of paradise myths asserting that people once understood the languages of the animals and lived with other creatures in peace, but through careless acts humans broke interspecies bonds and lost their place in paradise (Baumann, 1936).
>
> Whether local forest dwellers or expatriate primatologists, people often see tropical rain forests as the last remnants of Eden & mourn their destruction as examples of 'paradise lost' [e.g. Galdikas, 1998; Goodall & Berman, 2000]. It's been suggested that the drive to explore pristine wilderness & to bond with wild animals reflects our desire to

experience paradise as our human ancestors knew it, before they 'fell from grace' [Lorenz, 1952].

During decades in native villages and verdant wilderness I focused on helping change local personal values and eco-social practices from colonial dominance back to indigenous synergy (Rose, 2001b). In return I found Paradise among family, flora and fauna in the Rainforest, thus embedding Eden in my Soul (Rose, 1998). Today an *Enigma* taunts me. Will I surrender to my Soul's inner Eden and arise from my own family home – or will I return to my sacred Eden in the wilderness to transcend!

How shall I approach this Mystery? Where, after all, does the Soul abide? Does not my Spirit's love-of-life already over-flow? Or do I need to succor Eden one more time? Can we stop the Search in sublime surrender, or must we wander the Earth for all lifetime seeking more?

> 'Something special, something very special, waits for us:
>   sometimes in a dark alleyway, sometimes in an open field,
>   sometimes by a mountain stream'…
>
> It waits for us and one day we shall find it.
>   We shall know it, we shall cherish it, *we shall become it*
>   for a moment, for a lifetime, forever.

Will we rise in spiritual serenity? Will we stand or slumber in silence, feel complete in body and soul, and transcend from live becoming to spiritual being? Or must we leave this Earth bereft of biosynergy, and rise still seeking nirvana, alone?

Spirits Rising: My father passed on a spring evening in 1993, his 86th year. As he stood at the bedside, his weary heart stopped. He sunk to his knees and fell forward. His oldest child, my sister Gail, heard him fall and ran down the hall, found him collapsed across his bed, and called our mother, his lifelong partner, to help turn him over and tuck him into bed. As she sat by our father's side holding his cooling hand, Gail's artistic eye saw an ephemeral form float above his head. She sensed its good will, and smiled as more friendly spirits came to watch over our beloved father.

'Familiar spirits,' she told me, 'who hovered together above his body; they knew him and were waiting for Dad to join them.' And he did. That night our father joined the holy spirits; the same ones who had welcomed me four decades earlier as I lay near death on a country road.

At the start of this essay, I described the spirit ancestors who hailed me as I floated through golden light into the Forest of Eternity. My sister knew nothing of my *near-death experience* and recalled very little about my auto accident. To see her oil painting on canvass of our father's spirit escorts shivers my Soul. Having held secret my flight into our family afterworld for nearly forty years, the revelation's repetition to my unknowing sister at our father's passing shifted my Cosmic Faith from tentative to secure.

It also elevated my Calling. A year later I was discussing 'Interspecies Epiphanies' with primatologists in Bali and tracking orangutans and forest spirits in Borneo with dear Birute Galdikas and her Dayak community. Another thirty years of ecospiritual explorations, revelations, encounters, interventions and professional talks and publications has applied nuanced and numinous paints to my own elaborate canvass of pathways to ecospiritual wellbecoming. My conclusion has become strong, and yet not so startling:

> If I love, live, work, & explore in positive, compassionate, authentic Creative Biosynergy within a panoply of organic and iconic wellbecoming persons, then the journey of my Spirit will flow through enough Edens on Earth to assure that at death my Loving Soul will transcend, prepared to share Eternal Bliss in the Cosmic Synergy of the Universe!

I learned to honor and assert the attributes of inclusive positivity, mutual compassion, and adaptive authenticity when I was a child during two decades with our large and loving extended family. It was with dear friends in the Person-Centered movement that I recognized the well becoming impact of the three core conditions. During the next half century my immersion in far-flung communities, cultures and ecosystems evoked ecospiritual expansion of the core conditions that enabled Global Creative Biosynergy. This elevated my experience beyond personal actualization and encounter and allowed my Soul's immersion in the sacred synergies of Eden. Did that prepare me for spiritual transcendence! I feel ready to rise! But have I done enough?

When I get to Eden, how can I assure my transcendence into Eternity?

Each and every Earthling is a 'Sacred Soul Seeking Eternity!' That is who we are, and – *if we work to recreate Eco-spiritual Eden on Earth and reach for Eternal Love in the Universe* – that is where we are headed. Keep your eyes wide open. Hush all thoughts and listen to wind in leaves. See the scat of coyote and buzzard and pray for the rising souls of their scavenged supper. And when you lay down to sleep after all is silent in your world, hear your heart beating soft percussion to punctuate the sweet sublime symphony of your loving Soul.

Those kinds of small epiphanies nourish earthly Eden, maintain ecospiritual well-becoming, fuel our impetus to transform from living entity to everlasting spirit and prepare us to transcend into the Eternal Cosmic Synergy of our Infinite Loving Universe.

No matter the physical size or social significance in Eden of persons and icons in your uplifting epiphanies, your transformation from earthly enabler to ecospiritual synergizer to divine eternal Spirit in Cosmic Synergy is driven by your own personal holistic engagement in the exalted Global Creative Biosynergy that enriches Loving EcoSpirituality of Eden. *The more 'all-in Eden' you are, the more smooth, soft and swift your flight to 'all-out Eternity' will become.*

May Each Person Find Bliss in the All-Loving Universe!

May we all flourish in Creative Biosynergy
with myriad beloved fellow earthlings
in sacred iconic life-space worldwide!

May we wander in Earth's holy Wilderness
gathering magnificent Revelations in Nature
and experiencing profound Epiphanies of Eden!

May our Revelations & Epiphanies inform and
enable our positive, inclusive, compassionate,
biosynergy-empowered, psychosocially united,
and ecospiritually integrated Quests for lasting
Personal, Societal, & Global Well-becoming!

May all Quests for Well-becoming illuminate
effective Personal Pathways, Social Synergies,
& Global Guides to peace & prosperity on Earth
& Eternal Bliss in the Infinite All-Loving Universe.

Biographical note

Anthony L. Rose, PhD is a poet, scientist, consultant and biosynergist with over six decades of professional involvement in the innovation and revelation of positive pathways to psychosocial synergy and ecospiritual wellbecoming worldwide. After completing his NIH- and USPHS-funded research at UCLA Brain Research Institute on etiology of addiction in humans and other animals, Rose took a NIMH postdoctoral fellowship and co-founded Center for Studies of the Person (CSP) with Carl Rogers and colleagues in 1967–9. The next two decades Rose and his CSP friends designed and conducted scores of person-centered interventions in educational innovation, drug abuse prevention, and community and organization development. The importance and application of *social synergy* in education, religion, military, government, business and healthcare became clear to him. In 1982 Dr Rose began his search for *biosynergy* in rainforests, savannahs, mountains and deserts around the world. After four decades of in situ biosynergy research & development in over 25 countries on six continents, Rose has returned to build a Biosynergy Revelations Center where his writings, films and video, games and collaborative artistry will be available around the world.

Bibliography

Baumann H. 1936. *Creation and the Primal Era of Mankind in the Mythology of African Peoples*. Berlin: Reimer.

Caporale, A.B. (with Rose, A.L. and Cirincione, D.L.). 2024. *Shaping the Counselor's Identity: Perspectives on a Transformative Profession*. CSP Books: La Jolla, California.

Clay, J. 1978. *Modern Art*. Secaucus, NJ: Chartwell Books,

Corning, P.A. 2018. *Synergistic Selection: How Cooperation Has Shaped Evolution and the Rise of Humankind*. Singapore: World Scientific.

Corning, P.A. 2003. *Nature's Magic: Synergy in Evolution and the Fate of Humankind*. Cambridge: Cambridge University Press.

Eliade M. 1960. *Myths, Dreams and Mysteries*. New York: Harper Torchbooks, Harper & Bros.

Galdikas, B.M.F. 1998. *Reflections of Eden: My Years with Orangutans of Borneo*. New York: Little, Brown & Co.

Goodall J. and Berman, P. 2000. *Reason for Hope: A Spiritual Journey*. New York: WarnerBooks.

Jacoby, M. 2006. *Longing for Paradise: Psychological Perspectives on an Archetype*. Toronto: Inner City Books.

Jakobson, R. 1962. *Selected Writings I*. The Hague: Mouton Press.

Kübler-Ross, E. 1969. *On Death & Dying*. New York: Simon & Schuster/Touchstone.

Leonardi, J. 2010. What We are Meant To Be: Evolution as the Transformation of Consciousness. In: Leonardi, J., ed. *The Human Being Fully Alive: Writings in Celebration of Brian Thorne.* Ross-on-Wye: PCCS Books, pp. 58–75.

Lorenz K. 1952. *King Solomon's Ring.* New York: Crowell Co.

Mitchell, J. 1970. Woodstock. In: *Ladies of the Canyon.* Album. Los Angeles: Reprise Records.

Moody, R. 1975. *Life After Life.* New York: Bantam Books.

Rogers, C.R. 1966. *Client Centered Therapy. In:* Arieti, S., ed. *American Handbook of Psychiatry, Vol. 3, Part 2.* New York: Basic Books, pp. 183–200.

Rose, A.L. 1968. The Experimental Control of Alcohol Drinking Behavior. Paper presented at annual meeting of the Western Psychological Association, San Diego, California. (Doctoral Dissertation: UCLA Dept. of Psychology; Ph.D. awarded – December 1967.)

Rose, A.L. 1994a. Description & Analysis of Profound Interspecies Events. *Proceedings of XVth Congress of International Primatological Society,* Bali, Indonesia, August.

Rose, A.L. 1994b Paradigms for Personhood in the Age of Atonement. Keynote address at Symposium on Ethics in Primatology, presented at XVth Congress of International Primatological Society, Bali, Indonesia, August.

Rose, A.L. 1996a. Epiphanies with Animals & Nature Transform the Human Weltbildapparatur. Paper for Symposium on Human-Animal Interaction, International Society of Comparative Psychology, Montreal.

Rose, A.L. 1996b. Orangutan, Science, and Collective Reality. In: Nadler, R.D. et al., eds. *The Neglected Ape.* New York: Plenum Press, pp. 29–40.

Rose, A.L. 1998. Finding Paradise in a Hunting Camp: Turning Poachers to Protectors. *Journal of the Southwestern Anthropological Association,* 38, 3, 104–115.

Rose, A.L. 2001a. Bushmeat, Primate Kinship, and the Global Conservation Movement. In: Galdikas, B. et al., eds., *All Apes Great and Small Volume 1: Chimpanzees, Bonobos, and Gorillas.* New York: Kluwer Press, pp. 241–258.

Rose, A.L. 2001b. Social Change and Social Values in Mitigating Bushmeat Commerce. In: Bakarr, M.I et al., eds., *Hunting & Bushmeat Utilization in the African Rain Forest.* Washington, DC: Conservation International, pp. 59–74.

Rose, A.L. 2006. On Tortoises, Monkeys, and Men. In: Solisti, K. and Tobias, M., eds. *Kinship with the Animals: Expanded Edition,* San Francisco, CA: Council Oak Books, pp. 15–32 .

Rose, A.L. 2007. Biosynergy: The Synergy of Life. In: Beckoff, M., ed. *Encyclopedia of Human-Animal Relationships, Volume 1.* Westport, CT: Greenwood Publishing Group, pp. 123–129.

Rose, A.L. 2009. Biosynergy: The Synergy of Life. In: Farson, R., ed. *Making the Invisible Visible: Essays by the International Leadership Forum, Western Behavioral Sciences Institute.* Norcross, GA: Greenway Communications, pp. 109–117.

Rose, A.L. 2011. Bonding, Biophilia, Biosynergy and the Future of Primates in the Wild. *American Journal of Primatology,* 73, 245–252.

Rose, A.L. 2017. Biosynergy. In: Fuentes, A. and Riley, P., eds. *International Encyclopedia of Primatology.* New York: John Wiley, pp. 111–116.

Rose, A.L. 2024a. *Facing Death: Finding Eternity. Tales of an Accidental Life*. Los Angeles, CA: Altisima Press.

Rose, A.L. 2024b. *Biosynergy: Earth's Golden Rule*. (in press). Los Angeles, CA: Altisima Press.

Rose, A.L. and Mittermeier, R.A. 2007. Global Diversity and Bushmeat. In: Beckoff, M., ed. *Encyclopedia of Human-Animal Relationships, Volume 1*. Westport, CT: Greenwood Publishing Group, pp. 41–45.

Rose, A.L., Mittermeier, R.A., Langrand, O., Ampadu-Agyei, O. and Butynski, T.M. 2003. *Consuming Nature: A Photo Essay on African Rainforest Exploitation*. Los Angeles, CA: Altisima Press.

Rose, A.L. and Auw, A. 1974. *Growing Up Human*. New York: Harper & Row Publishers.

Stebbins, M.W., Hawley, J.A. and Rose, A.L. 1982. *Long-Term Action Research: The Most Effective Way to Improve Health Care Organizations*. In: Margulies, N. and Adams, J., eds. *Organization Development in Health Care Organizations*. Reading, MA: Addison-Wesley, pp. 105–136.

Sapp, J.A. 1994. *Evolution by Association: A History of Symbiosis*. New York: Oxford University Press.

Index

Note: Page numbers followed by '*n*' refer to the endnotes; those by '*f*' to figures.

A Rocha UK, Eco Church 54
acceptance 78–9, 85, 109
Actualising and Formative Tendencies (Rogers) 29, 100–1, 102
addiction (cravings) 104, 105
African traditions 12, 165–7, 174–6, 177–9, 201
after-death communications (ADCs) 67, 186, 202–3
    see also near-death experiences (NDEs)
Age of Reason (Enlightenment) 22–3, 46
agriculture, regenerative 40–2
AIP (All-Inclusive Positivity) 199
Albert, B. *see* Kopenawa, D.
Alfeyev, Bishop Hilarion 27
alienation, spiritual 1–2, 5
Alister Hardy Religious Experience Research Centre (RERC) 6, 59–60, 62–7, 68–73, 168–9
Alister Hardy Trust 5
All-Inclusive Positivity (AIP) 199
altruism, after RSEs 72–3
Amazon Rainforest 131–2, 136, 146, 157, 163*n*, 202
Amerindian myths 135
ancestral wisdom 161, 179
Andean myths, *La Pachamama* 10, 11, 152, 158, 159, 161–2
animals
    biosynergy 185–6, 189–94, 196–201
    consciousness in 31
    decline in birds 4, 43–4
    epiphanies with (Rose) 12, 31, 184–5, 203, 204
    nature apps 36–7
    personhood of 191–2
    sacrifice of 166, 177
    see also nature
animism 134, 171
Anthropocene era 97, 159–60, 161, 173
anthropocentrism 141–2, 144, 147
apophatic tradition 28, 53
apps, nature 43–4

archetypal intersubjectivity 152–3, 155, 159
archetypes 29, 153, 154–5, 157–8
Armbrust, Hannah
    about 163
    chapter by 10, 151
Armstrong, K. 103, 124
Assagioli, R. 122
Athanasius, St 27
attention, focus of 51–4, 105
awakening, four stages 122–3
awareness, developing 17, 18, 19–20, 39, 40
axé (spiritual energy) 3, 12, 177, 178, 179

Baimel, A. 141, 142
Barfield, O. 20, 22
Batchelor, S. 104
Be-PCP (Biosynergy-enriched Person-Centred Psychology) 190, 196, 197–8, 201
Beauregard, Mario 26–7
Becci, I. 172, 174
Bendell, J. 106, 108
Bennett, J. 170, 171
Bereshit, book of 158
Beringer, M. 170
Berry, T. 160
Betcher, Sharon 179
Bible 23, 158
bifurcation of nature 46, 51
biodiversity 41, 53
biomedicine 143, 177
biosynergy
    animals 184–6, 189–94, 196–201
    Creative Biosynergy 186–7, 198–204
    and early history 193–4
    Earth 156–7
    eco-spirituality 196, 200–1
    Person-Centred Approach and 190, 195–8, 199–200
Biosynergy-enriched Person-Centred Psychology (Be-PCP) 190, 196, 197–8, 201
birds 4, 36–7, 43–4, 200
blame, eco-crisis 98–9, 107, 108–9, 110
body–nature dualisms 44–5
Boff, L. 133, 159, 160
Braverman, I. 173–4

Brazier, D. 103
Brazil
  Amazon Rainforest 131–2, 136, 146, 163*n*, 165, 202
  Candomblé community 174–6, 177–8
  colonialism 132, 133, 134
  environmental psychology study 141–2
  indigenous culture and health 9, 132–4, 142–6
  Santuário Nacional da Umbanda 165, 166–7, 179–80
  socioeconomic conditions 162
  Wellbeing in 175–9
  Yanomami people 135–6, 142–3, 146
breath 61, 137, 146, 151, 158
Bregman, R. 105, 106, 108
buddhata (buddha nature) 8, 28, 103, 105
Buddhism
  noble truths 102–4
  and Person-Centred Approach 98–9, 100–1
  suffering 105
  Thich Nhat Hanh 103, 105, 107, 108–9, 110, 111
  on unitive consciousness 28
  Zen *koan* 8, 98
butterfly effect 61

caboclos (spirits) 24, 166–7, 174, 175
Candomblé community, Brazil 174–6, 177–8
capitalism 22, 39
carbon 41, 54, 131
Care (*Cura*) myth 136–7
Cartesian dualism 23, 45, 158
Casablanca (film) 36, 52, 53
Center for Studies of the Person (CSP), USA 185, 186, 195, 204
Cézanne, Paul 143
Chauí, Marilena 142
children and young people
  commercialisation of 107
  eco-anxiety in 109
  holistic education 31, 41–3
Christ, Jesus 81, 82–3, 84, 85, 86–8
Christianity
  apophatic tradition 28, 53
  Bible 23, 158
  in Britain 115–16
  creation myth 25, 158
  and RSEs 69–73
  Trinity, the 84–5
  unitive consciousness 27–8
  see also God
church attendance 66, 69–70, 71, 115

La chute du ciel: paroles d'un chaman Yanomami (Kopenawa and Albert) 135, 142–3, 146, 151
climate change 41, 53–4, 102, 124–5, 158–60, 162
Climate Psychology Alliance 99
collective unconscious 29, 154–5
colonialism, Brazil 132, 133, 134
Columbus, Christopher 134
compassion 108, 109, 110, 199
congruence theory 30, 33, 101, 102
connectedness
  axé (spiritual energy) 3, 177, 178, 179
  Buddhism 8, 28, 99, 103–4, 105
  collective unconscious 29, 154–5
  and eco-crisis 105, 106
  as interbeing 155–6, 158–9, 161–2
  myths 157–8
  nature 31–2, 39, 111, 119, 156–7, 159, 168–70
  religion 152
  therapy 30, 33, 117, 118, 198–204
  and Wellbeing 176
  see also disconnectedness; interconnectedness
consciousness
  at death 6, 67–8
  evolution of 9, 20, 21–2, 23, 124, 162
  spectrum of (Wilber) 122
  unitive 18, 26–7, 29, 31, 61–2
consumerism 4, 93–4, 104, 107, 152
contemplative spirituality 1, 25, 28
Convergent Subjective Perceptions (CSPs) 196–7
Cooper, M. 118
Core Conditions (Rogers) 30–1, 33, 198–204
Corning, Peter 194
Cosmic Synergy 193, 204
cosmos 133–4, 143–4, 160, 161
counselling and psychotherapy
  acceptance 85–6
  connectedness 30, 33, 117, 118, 198–204
  Core Conditions 30–1, 33, 198–204
  and eco-crisis 109
  felt sense 118
  Person-Centred Approach 7, 18, 29–30, 33, 78, 100–1
  rituals 151–2
  RSEs 117, 121–2
  selfishness 103–4
  spiritual development 2, 3–4, 9, 120–4
Countryfile (TV) 43
Covid-19 pandemic 146, 173

Index   211

cravings (addiction) 104, 105
creation myths 25, 157–8, 162
Creative Biosynergy 186–7, 198–204
CSPs (Convergent Subjective Perceptions)
     196–7
Curtis, M. 124

death, experiences of 6, 67–9, 187–8, 202–3
Deleuze, G. 52, 134
depopulation, Brazil 134
depression, and RSEs 66, 74
Descartes, René 23, 45, 158
detachment (non-participation) 22, 24–5
digital devices, and nature 4, 40, 43–4, 46–7
disconnectedness 101, 105–7, 110
diseases 37, 144, 173–8
Dogen 104
dogs, humans and 31
Donovan, Peter 72
Doomsday Clock 146
Douglass, B.G. 99
dreams 67–8, 154
dualisms 23, 24, 26, 44–5, 51
Duncan, R. 106

EAA (Ecologically Adaptive Authenticity) 199
Earth
   early history 193–4
   geological eras 159–60, 161
   grounding to 179
   marriage with Heaven 9, 133, 142–6, 147
   see also Mother Earth
eco-anxiety 98, 109, 160–1
Eco Church, A Rocha UK 54
eco-spirituality 154–7, 159, 161, 162, 170–1, 200
ecological crisis (eco-crisis)
   Be-PCP 190, 196, 197–8, 201
   Buddhist views 8, 97, 98, 103–5
   and future 12–13
   geological eras and 159–60
   individualism 9, 124, 136, 159
   Julian of Norwich and 79, 93–4
   person-centred views 100–2, 105–9
   psychological roots 2, 98–9
   spiritual experiences and 124–5
Ecologically Adaptive Authenticity (EAA) 199
ecology, defined 152, 156
Ecozoic era 159, 160
Eden, return to 200–4
education, holistic 31, 41–3
ego, the 11, 23, 26, 106, 161
EHEs see religious and spiritual experiences
   (RSEs)

Eliade, M. 151–2, 153
Elvey A. 45
emergence, spiritual 122–4, 125
emotional intelligence 22–3
emotions, and climate change 97, 98
empathy 18, 30–3, 73, 84–6, 101, 102
empirical evidence 17, 18, 19, 20, 154
end-of-life experiences (ELEs) 60, 67
   see also near-death experiences (NDEs)
energy, spiritual (axé) 3, 177, 178, 179
Enlightenment (Age of Reason) 22–3, 46
environment
   awareness of 23–4, 38
   care of 106, 136–7, 156–7
   climate change 41, 53–4, 102, 124–5,
      158–60, 162
   consumerism 153
   defined 2, 163n
   and health 146–7, 167, 173, 174, 179
   interconnectedness 74
   and religion 139–41
   technology and 43–4, 47–8
   Wellbeing in Brazil 175–9
epicurean spirituality 79, 93
equality 32, 107, 158, 195
Etherington, K. 99, 110
evil 72, 101–2, 103
experiencing, dimension of 3, 38, 139
extrovertive spiritual experiences 61, 167–72,
   174

farming 40–2
fear 68, 111
Figueres, C. 107
folds, language of 51–3
forest bathing 37–8
forest schools 42–3
Formative and Actualising Tendencies (Rogers)
   29, 100–1, 102
Francis of Assisi, St 28
Francis, Pope 99, 131–2, 159
Franciscans 17
Frankenstein myth 48
Franz, Marie-Louise von 10–11, 157
Freire, B. 100, 101
Freitas, Marta Helena de
   about 148
   chapter by 9, 131
Freud, Sigmund 23, 154
Fruehwirth, Robert
   about 95
   chapter by 6–7, 77
future visions, eco-crisis 12–13

gaming 43
Gendlin, E.T. 118
Genesis, book of 23, 158
geological eras 97, 159–60, 161
Global Creative Biosynergy (GCB) 186–7, 198–204
global health agendas 173, 174
God
    apophatic approach 28
    creation myth 25, 158, 191
    existence of 17
    and Frankenstein myth 48
    Julian of Norwich and 81–2, 84–5, 88
    Jung on 20–1
    in nature 170
    in RSEs 66
    spirituality and 93–4
Gomberg, E. 178
Grandjean, Alexandre 172
Grof, S. and Grof, C. 122–3, 125
grounding to Earth 178–9

Haeckel, Ernest 156
Haiti, Vodou religion 179
happiness, Wellbeing and 1, 12, 176
Happold, F.C. 61–2, 65
Hardy, Sir Alister
    RERC 6, 59–60, 62–7, 68–73, 168–9
    spiritual experiences 5–6, 62–3, 167–8, 169
Hari, J. 105
Harth, N. 97
hawks 200
Hay, David 61, 62, 68
health 146–7, 171, 173, 174, 177, 179, 195
health professionals, Brazil 132–3, 144, 145–6
Heart of England Forest 37–8
Heaven and Earth, marriage of 9, 133, 142–6, 147
Hebrews, Letter to the 18, 25
heuristic inquiry 99
Hick, J. 61
Hillesum, E. 94
Hippocrates 146
holistic approaches 31, 41–4, 177–8
Holy Spirit 17
humanistic philosophy 100, 108
humans
    and eco-crisis 98, 99, 109, 141–2, 160–1
    as good 107, 108, 199, 111
    negative characteristics 101–2, 104, 106–8, 191
    personality types (Jung) 20–3
    self-acceptance 78–9, 85, 109

separation from nature 159, 160, 161
Huni Kuin myth 157, 163*n*
Husserlian notion of intentionality 138
Hyginus, Gaius Julius, *Cura* myth 136–7

incongruence, theory of 30, 33, 101, 102
indigenous people
    Amerindian people 134, 135
    Brazil 9–10, 132–4, 135–6, 142–3, 146, 174–6
    colonialism and 202
    eco-spirituality 170–1
    medicine 142–4, 145, 147
    myths 157–8, 159
    and natural world 24
    One Health agenda 173
    Sami people, Sweden 133
    Yanomami people 135–6, 142–3, 146
individualism, and eco-crisis 9, 124, 136, 159
Individuation (Jung) 30
Indonesia 189–90, 191–2
Industrial Revolution .24, 191
inequality *see* equality
Ingold, T. 174
integration, psychology of 18, 29
interbeing 155–6, 158–9, 161–2
interconnectedness
    and eco-crisis 124–5
    and eco-spirituality 170, 176–9, 193
    Hippocrates on 146
    individualism 124, 125
    myths 157
    oneness 71, 72, 74
    in RSEs 63, 64, 70
    self-absorption 6
    spirituality and 3
    and Wellbeing 167, 172–6
    see also connectedness
International Primatological Congress, Indonesia 191–2
intersubjectivity, archetypal 152–3, 155
intuition 21
Isaiah, prophet 162

James, William 61, 167
Jenkins, Chris 123–4
Jesus Christ 81, 82–3, 84, 85, 86–8
Judaism 25, 158
Julian of Norwich
    background 80–1
    and eco-crisis 93–4
    relational intimacy 78–9, 85
    self-acceptance 77–9, 82–4

showings 79–80, 84–93
Jung, Carl Gustav
  archetypes and myths 153, 154
  collective unconscious 29, 154–5
  Individuation 29, 30
  on natural world 161, 163*n*
  personality types 20–3
  psyche 10, 153, 156, 161
  psychology of integration 18
  shadow side 29, 102
  tension of opposites 162

Kearns, L. 173
Keller, Catherine 52, 173
Key Conditions (Rose) 199–200
knowing, ways of
  apophatic approach 28
  connectedness 25–8
  and God 20–1
  non-participation 23–5
  participation 29–33
  rationality 12, 18, 22–3
  un-knowing 7, 8, 17–18
  see also Person-Centred Approach
koan (Zen) 8, 98
Kopenawa, D. and Albert, B., *La chute du ciel: paroles d'un chaman Yanomami* 135, 142–3, 146, 151
135, 142–3, 146, 151

Langdon, E.J. 143, 144
Latour, Bruno 4, 42, 43, 45, 47–9, 52
Lee, Lois 171
leeches, synergy with 185–6, 189, 197
Lent, Jeremy 45–6
Leonardi, Jeff
  about 1, 34
  chapter by 12, 17
  on relational spirituality 3, 5, 8, 38
  on self-love 201
LeShan, L. 61
Lesson of Love, A (Swanson) 80, 95*n*
Letter to the Hebrews (Hebrews) 18, 25
Lévi-Strauss, C. 135–6, 142
LGBT+ rights 117
libido 154
Linares, Ronaldo 165
Lincoln, Valerie 170
long-term action research (LTAR) programmes 195
Loy, D. 103
Lucas, C.G. 119, 123, 125
Lukoff, D. 123

macaques, synergy and 185
Macdonald B. 37
Macy, J. 109
Mãe Stella 174–5
Marshall, Paul 169
Marvelous Clouds, The (Peters) 46–7
materialism 68, 93–4, 104, 107
McLeod, J. 125
Mearns, D. 106, 118
MEC (Mutually Empathic Compassion) 199
medicine 142–6
medieval period 80–1, 95*n*
mental health 107, 115, 119, 121, 123
Merleau-Ponty, M. 143, 145, 146
mindfulness 50, 123
Mitchell, Joni, 'Woodstock' 194
monkeys 184, 185–6, 189, 196–7
Moody, Raymond 68
Mother Earth
  creation myths 25, 157–8, 162
  Cura myth 136–7
  La Pachamama 10, 11, 152, 158, 159, 161–2
  relationship with 10, 152, 156–7, 159–61, 170, 172
  see also Earth
Moustakas, C. 99
Mutually Empathic Compassion (MEC) 199
Myers–Briggs theory 21–2
mystical experiences, nature 61–2, 73, 119–20, 167–72, 174
myths
  creation myths 25, 157–8, 162
  Cura myth 136–7
  Jung on 153, 154
  La Pachamama 10, 11, 152, 158, 159, 161–2
  paradise myths 201
  Yanomami people 135–6, 142–3, 146

native cultures *see* indigenous people
nature
  bifurcation of 46, 51
  and body dualisms 44–5
  reconnecting with 36, 39–40, 46–7, 50, 51–2, 53, 110
  religion and 139–41
  RSEs in 61–2, 73, 119–20, 167–72, 174
  separation from 48–9, 106, 159, 160
  synergy with 193
  terminology 45, 159, 163*n*
  trees and forests 37–8, 41–2, 157, 171
  Wellbeing and 103, 169
  see also animals; connectedness
near-death experiences (NDEs) 6, 67–9, 187–8

see also after-death communications (ADCs)
Net Zero Carbon 2030 54
Neville, B. 105
Nhat Hanh, Thich 103, 105, 107, 108–9, 110, 111
noble truths, Buddhism 102–4
non-participation (detachment) 22, 24
  see also participation
nonsense, living in 89–93
Northcott, M. 54
Norwich school of person-centred counselling 78

One Health agenda (WHO) 173, 174
oneness 61–2, 68, 71, 72, 73, 89, 172
  see also unitive consciousness
orangutans, synergy with 185, 189, 196–7, 203
organismic self (Rogers) 29–30
out-of-body experiences (OBEs) 60
  see also near-death experiences (NDEs)

Pachamama, La 10, 11, 152, 158, 159, 161–2
Pahnke, Walter 27
pain *see* suffering
pandemic, Covid-19 146, 173
paradise myths 47, 201–2
participation 2, 4, 20, 22, 24, 25, 30–1
PCA *see* Person-Centred Approach
peace with self 77, 79
Peacock, Arthur 61
perfection 79, 82, 93
Person-Centred Approach (PCA)
  acceptance 85–6
  Biosynergy 190, 195–8, 199–200, 201
  and Buddhism 98–9, 100–1
  Core Conditions 30–1, 33, 198–204
  in counselling 7, 18, 29–30, 33, 78, 100–1
  and human nature 100–2, 103, 107, 108
  individualism 105–6
personality, typology of 11, 20–3, 78
personally valid authentic depictions (PVAD) 197
personally valid collective reality (PVCR) 198
personhood of beings 191–2, 201
Peters, John Durham, *The Marvelous Clouds* 46–7
phenomenology 140f, 201
physis and techne 43–6, 47–9
Pihkala, P. 98, 108
Pinker, S. 106
planet *see* Earth; Mother Earth
plastic pollution 159–60

Plato 45
poetry, ecospiritual (Rose) 186–7, 190, 202
policies
  conservation 141, 142
  health 146–7, 173, 174, 175
Polkinghorne, John 61
pollution 159–60, 179
Portuguese colonialism, Brazil 132, 133, 172
positive regard, unconditional 30
Postlethwaite, Martha 111
postmodernism 32, 99
poteau-mitan (Haiti) 179
Preston, J.L. 141, 142
primates 184, 185–6, 189, 196–7
psyche 151, 153, 154, 156, 158, 161
psychoanalysis 21, 23, 100, 154
psychology of integration 18
psychology of religion and spirituality 137
psychospiritual development 2, 3–4, 9, 117–19, 120–4
psychosynthesis (Assagioli) 122
psychotherapy *see* counselling and psychotherapy
PVAD (personally valid authentic depictions) 197
PVCR (personally valid collective reality) 198

Quakers 118, 120, 124–5
quantum entanglement 61

Rankin, Marianne
  about 74–5
  chapter by 5–6, 59
rationality 12, 18, 19–20, 23
Reader, John
  about 55
  chapter by 4, 36
realism 21, 22
regenerative agriculture 40–2
relational depth (Mearns and Cooper) 118
relational intimacy (Julian of Norwich) 78–9, 85
relational spirituality (Leonardi) 3, 5, 8, 38
religions
  African religions 166, 201
  Candomblé communities, Brazil 174–6, 177–8
  and environment 141–2
  as community builder 152
  equality in 117
  Judaism 25, 158
  and RSEs 69–73, 139–41, 140f
  silence in 118, 120, 124–5

Vodou 165–6
  see also Buddhism; Christianity; God
religious and spiritual experiences (RSEs)
  childhood and 69
  in counselling 116, 121–2
  of death 67–9, 187–8, 202–3
  emergence 122–4
  and interconnectedness 60
  in nature (extrovertive) 61, 167–72, 174
  negative 3, 63, 66, 72
  positive 69–71
  religions and 69–73
  RERC archives 5, 6, 59–60, 62–7, 68–73, 168–9
  taboos around 60
  as transformative 66–7, 72–3
religious places 54, 66, 69–70, 71, 115
Remmel, A. 171
RERC (Religious Experience Research Centre) 6, 59–60, 62–7, 68–73, 168–9
Revelations of Divine Love (Julian of Norwich) 77, 79–80, 81, 82, 84–84, 86–91, 95n
rituals 151–2, 153, 177, 178
Rodríguez, I. 12, 172
Rogers, Carl
  Actualising and Formative Tendencies 29, 100–1, 102
  Center for Studies of the Person 184, 186, 204
  Core Conditions of therapy 30–1, 33, 198–204
  organismic self and Fully Functioning Person theory 29–30, 78, 83, 86–91
  presence concept 117
  see also Person-Centred Approach
Rohr, Richard 24–5
Rose, Anthony L.
  about 185–6, 204
  chapter by 12–13, 184
  epiphanies with animals 12, 31, 184–5, 203, 204
Royal Society for the Protection of Birds (RSPB) 4, 36–7, 40

sacrifices, animal 166, 177
Sami people, Sweden 133
Sapp, Jan, *Evolution by Association* 193
SBNR (spiritual but not religious) people 116
Schmidt, Bettina E.
  about 180
  chapter by 11–12, 165
Schofield, Lee (RSPB) 40
Schor, J. 107

science
  empirical evidence 12, 17–18, 19, 33
  ethics 39
  and indigenous cosmology 9, 132, 142–6
  and nature 40, 46–8, 51–2
  postmodernism and 99
  and spirituality 60–2, 74, 155–7
  technology 2, 24, 46–9, 51–3, 94
Seale, Becky
  about 97–8, 111
  chapter by 8, 97
SEEs (Spiritually Endowed Environments) 200
self-absorption 6
self-acceptance 78–9, 82–6, 87–8, 101–2, 104, 109
self-alienation 77
self-awareness 162, 178
self-perfection 79, 82, 93
self-pity 64–5
self-rejection 77
Self, the 29–30, 65, 82, 83, 99
self-transcendent experiences (STEs) 67
selfishness
  awareness of 65, 67
  in counselling 103–4
  and health policies 179
  from individualism 106
  and nature 109, 193–4
  as not intrinsic 102, 105, 108
  and RSEs 174
separation from nature 110–11, 156, 158, 159, 160, 161
sexual energy 3, 154
shadow side (Jung) 29, 102
shamanism 135–6, 142–4, 145, 146
Sheldrake, R. 31, 46
shifting baseline syndrome (SBS) 55
Shohet, R. 111
showings (Julian of Norwich) 79–80, 84–93
sickness, and soul 5, 18, 40
silence, and spiritual intimacy in therapy 118
Silva, Gonçalves da 175
sin 90–1, 108
'slow' movement 39–40
smartphones 43, 105
social media 105
societies, organisation of 97, 106–7, 109, 192, 198
socioeconomic status 162
soil health 40–1
solastalgia 98
  see also eco-anxiety
Solnit, R. 110

soul, the 18, 77, 82, 93, 151, 161
South American myths 10, 11, 151, 152, 153, 158, 159, 161–2
spaces, sacred 151–2, 165–6, 167–72
spirits (*caboclos*) 166–7, 174, 175
spiritual but not religious (SBNR) people 70, 116
spiritual emergence 122–3, 125
spiritual formation 94
Spiritual Nature of Man, The (Hardy) 169
spiritual practices 50
spirituality
  defined 1, 2–3, 137–8, 151
  epicurean 79
  four stages of awakening 122–3
  Hardy on 63
  and health 173–4, 177
  meaning of 38
  relational depth 8
  rituals in 151–2
  stepping stones to 4, 36, 50, 54–5
  subjective awareness 17, 18, 19–20, 32
  and technology 49, 52
  see also religious and spiritual experiences
Spiritually Endowed Environments (SEEs) 200
Stace, Walter 27, 168, 172
Stengers, Isabelle 4, 39–40, 51, 55
Stewart, Dianne 166, 178–9
Stockholm Resilience Centre 53
stories *see* myths
subjective awareness 17, 18, 19–20, 32
Subtle Green Spirituality (Becci) 174
suffering
  in Buddhism 102–3, 105
  of Christ 84, 86–7
  collective 107, 119
  Julian of Norwich on 79, 81, 84, 86–9, 90–2
  and nature 11, 120
  positive experiences in 72
Sufism, silence in 118
Swanson, John-Julian, *A Lesson of Love* 80, 95n
symbolism 29, 139, 153
synergy *see* Biosynergy
Systematic Comprehension 79

taboos around RSEs 60
technology (techne) 2, 24, 46–9, 51–3, 94
Templeton Prize for progress in religion (Hardy) 63
temptation 87–8, 89
tenderness, notion of (Thorne) 117–18
therapy *see* counselling and psychotherapy
Thich Nhat Hanh 103, 105, 107, 108, 110, 111
Thomas, R.S. 25

Thoreau, Henry, 'Walking' 171
Thorne, Brian 78, 102, 106, 117–18
Thurfjell, D. 171
Totton, N. 109
transcendence
  after NDEs 67–9, 187–8
  Buddhism 8, 28, 103, 105
  false 79, 86–9
  shamanism 145
transcendental spirituality 87, 138
transformation, after RSEs 66–70, 102
trauma experiences 106
trees and forests 37–38, 42–43, 157, 171
Trinidad, Yoruba-Orisa tradition 178–9
Trinity, the 84–5
Tudor, K. 100

Umbanda Federation, Brazil 165, 166–7, 179–80
unconscious, the 21, 23, 29, 151, 154–5, 157, 162
Unitarians 120
United States of America (USA) 141, 142
unitive consciousness 18, 26–7, 29, 31, 61–2
  see also oneness
urban settings, spirituality in 166, 169
USA (United States of America) 141, 142

Vainfas, R. 134, 135
violence, human 106
virtual reality 43
Viveiros de Castro, E. 134, 144–5
Vodou religion, Haiti 165–6, 179
von Franz, Marie-Louise 10–11, 157

war 94, 146, 162
Weintrobe, S. 99, 100
Well-becoming
  Creative Biosynergy 192–3
  defined 1
  and eco-spirituality 185, 193–4, 196–201, 203–4
Wellbeing
  in Brazil 172, 176, 179
  defined 172
  and eco-crisis 98–9
  grounding to Earth 179
  happiness and 1, 12, 176
  mental health 169–70
  and nature 103, 169
  and spirituality 1
  wholeness and 171
Welwood, J. 103–4, 106, 108, 109

West, William
  about 125
  chapter by 8–9, 115
Western medicine 144
Whitehead, A.N. 46, 51, 52, 55
WHO (World Health Organization) 167, 173, 174
wholeness, human 2, 106, 109, 171, 172–3, 195
Wilber, K. 122
Williams, Rowan, *The Wound of Knowledge* 25
Wittgenstein, Ludwig 155
women, Yoruba-Orisa 179
Woods, Richard 172
World Health Organization (WHO) 167, 173, 174
Worrall, M. 100
worship, places of 66, 69–70, 71, 115
Worsley, R. 109
Wound of Knowledge, The (Williams) 25
Wyatt, Jonathan 121

Yaden, David 67
Yanomami people 135–6, 142–3, 146
Yoruba-Orisa tradition 178–9
young people *see* children and young people
Yusha Kuru creation myth 157, 163*n*

Zen 8, 98, 103, 104
zoonotic diseases 37

www.ingramcontent.com/pod-product-compliance
Lightning Source LLC
Chambersburg PA
CBHW062026220426
43662CB00010B/1492